The Craft of Inquiry
Theories, Methods, Evidence

Robert R. Alford

New York   Oxford
OXFORD UNIVERSITY PRESS
1998

Oxford University Press

Oxford   New York
Athens Auckland Bangkok Bogota Bombay Buenos Aires
Calcutta Cape Town Dar es Salaam Delhi Florence Hong Kong
Istanbul Karachi Kuala Lumpur Madras Madrid Melbourne
Mexico City Nairobi Paris Singapore Taipei Tokyo Toronto Warsaw

and associated companies in
Berlin   Ibadan

Copyright © 1998 by Robert R. Alford

Published by Oxford University Press, Inc.
198 Madison Avenue, New York, New York 10016

Oxford is a registered trademark of Oxford University Press

Library of Congress Cataloging-in-Publication Data
Alford, Robert R.
The craft of inquiry : theories, methods, evidence / Robert R.
Alford.
p.   cm.
Includes bibliographical references and index.
ISBN-13 978-0-19-511902-2; 978-0-19-511903-9 (pbk.)
ISBN 0-19-511902-9 (cloth).—ISBN 0-19-511903-7 (paper)
1. Sociology—Research—Methodology.   I. Title.
HM48.A5 1998   97-13588
301'.07—dc21   CIP

7 9 8 6
Printed in the United States of America
on acid-free paper

To Thorstein Veblen and to Jacques Barzun
Teachers in American Higher Learning

I draw lessons for my teaching of the craft of inquiry from the following quotes: (1) Pick Critical and Challenging Research Questions, and (2) Be Kind to Yourself while Thinking about your Research Question.

> ... the social sciences are occupied with inquiry into the institutions of society—customs, usages, traditions, canons of conduct, of morality, law and order. No faithful inquiry into these matters can avoid skepticism as to the stability or finality of the received articles of institutional furniture. An inquiry into the nature and causes of this institutional apparatus will disturb the habitual preconceptions on which they rest.
> —Thorstein Veblen, *The Higher Learning in America* (Originally published by B.W. Huebsch in 1918, although written in the early 1900s, pp. 131–2. Edited slightly.)

> The least suspected fact of the intellectual life ... is that thinking is a haphazard, fitful, incoherent activity. If you peer in and see thinking going on, it would not look like that trimmed and barbered result, A THOUGHT. Thinking is messy, repetitive, silly, obtuse, subject to explosions that shatter the crucible and leave darkness behind. Then comes another flash, a new path is seen, trod, lost, broken off, and blazed anew. It leaves the thinker dizzy as well as doubtful; he does not know what he thinks until he has thought it, or better, until he has written and riddled it with a persistence akin to obsession.
>
> Young scholars should believe this in order to overcome their too frequent discouragement at the sight of their first thoughts or their first drafts. Too much has been talked about "cold reason" and "orderly processes of mind." The momentary glimpse of a relation, a truth, or a method of proof does not come at will. It is watched for like big game, and only when captured and tamed with others like it can it be shown off in orderly sequence.
> —Jacques Barzun, *Teacher in America* (Doubleday Anchor Books, 1955, p. 267)

Contents

Acknowledgments   *vii*

Introduction   *1*

The Audience   *1*
Paradigms of Inquiry   *2*
Personal History   *4*
Works Illustrating the Working Vocabulary   *7*

Chapter 1: The Craft of Inquiry   *11*

Theory vs. Method vs. Research   *11*
Theory, Methods, and Evidence in the Classic Canon   *13*
Solidarity, Rationality, and Production   *15*
Conclusions   *18*

Chapter 2: Designing a Research Project   *21*

Cognitive and Emotional Sources of Anxiety   *22*
Selecting a Problem   *24*
Research Questions as Entry Points   *25*
Theoretical and Empirical Tracks of Analysis   *28*
Conclusions   *30*

Chapter 3: The Construction of Arguments   *32*

Evidence and Theory   *34*
Human Agency   *37*
Foreground Multivariate Arguments   *38*
Foreground Interpretive Arguments   *42*
Foreground Historical Arguments   *45*
The Divorce of Theory from Evidence   *49*
Conclusions   *50*

Chapter 4: Foreground Multivariate Arguments   *54*

How Does the Social Integration of Groups Explain Suicide?   *55*
Multivariate Relations   *55*
Symbolic Meanings   *56*

Historical Processes   *57*

What Is the Importance of "Class" vs. "Race" for American Blacks?   *58*
   Multivariate Relations   *59*
   Historical Processes   *61*
   Symbolic Meanings   *63*
   Conclusion   *63*

What Are the Causes and Consequences of Racial Segregation?   *63*
   Multivariate Relations   *64*
   Historical Processes   *65*
   Symbolic Meanings   *66*
   A Dialectical Explanation   *67*
   An Action Agenda?   *67*
Conclusions   *70*

Chapter 5:   Foreground Interpretive Arguments   *72*

What Symbolic Meanings Construct the Protestant Ethic and
the Spirit of Capitalism?   *73*
   Symbolic Meanings   *73*
   Historical Processes   *74*
   Multivariate Relations   *74*

How Are Individual Identities Undermined in Total Institutions?   *76*
   Symbolic Meanings   *78*
   Multivariate Relations   *80*
   Evidence and Theory   *80*
   Historical Processes   *81*
   Conclusion   *82*

How Do Men and Women Negotiate Housework?   *82*
   Symbolic Meanings   *82*
   Historical Processes   *83*
   Multivariate Relations   *84*
Conclusions   *85*

Chapter 6:   Foreground Historical Arguments   *86*

What Historical Processes Explain the Coup d'État in France by Louis Bonaparte
on December 2, 1851?   *87*
   Historical Processes   *88*
   Symbolic Meanings   *89*
   Multivariate Relations   *90*

Why Did Japan Become Fascist, China Become Communist, and Britain Remain
Democratic?   *93*
   Historical Processes   *95*
   Multivariate Relations   *96*
   Symbolic Meanings   *97*

How Did the Language of Labor Lead to Revolutionary Action in
France Before and After the Old Regime?   *98*
   Historical Processes   *98*

Multivariate Relations   *99*
Symbolic Meanings   *100*
Conclusions   *102*

Chapter 7:   The Theoretical Power of Multiple Paradigms   *103*

Multiple Paradigms of Inquiry About the Welfare State   *103*
The Unit of Analysis   *105*
The Dependent Variable   *105*
The Independent Variables   *108*
The Analysis   *112*
A Historical Argument   *113*

Multiple Paradigms of Inquiry About Revolution   *115*
Tracks of Analysis   *116*
A Historical Argument   *119*
Conclusions   *120*

**Chapter 8:   Dialectical Explanations and the
                Sociological Imagination**   *121*
Multiple Paradigms of Inquiry   *121*
Dialectical Explanations   *123*
Institutional Constraints on the Production of Social Knowledge   *125*
Sources of the Sociological Imagination   *129*
The Promise of Sociology   *131*
Conclusions   *133*

Notes   *135*

Selected Readings   *147*

Index   *160*

Acknowledgments

In the years this book has been in the making, I have accumulated personal and intellectual debts that it will be impossible to repay. First and foremost, I am indebted to Paul Lubeck, with whom the project was first conceived as we taught a course together on the logics of inquiry at the University of California at Santa Cruz. Paul and I spent innumerable hours arguing about the vocabulary and the strategy of social inquiry. Because of changes in my geographical location and in our differing priorities and obligations, it proved impossible for him to remain a coauthor. Paul has my deepest thanks and gratitude.

Others have challenged particular points or—in a few cases—critiqued the entire manuscript. Entire draft chapters have been saved for my next book because of the incisive comments they elicited. I shall not specify the difficulties that each of the following family members, friends, and colleagues (highly correlated variables) created. I have already thanked each of you in appropriate ways: David Alford, Paul Attewell, Richard Berk, Lynn Chancer, Randall Collins, Mustafa Emirbayer, Cynthia Epstein, E. P. Faithorn, David Freedman, Roger Friedland, Elwin Hatch, Rosanna Hertz, Lily Hoffman, Al Imershein, Larry Isaac, Jim Jasper, Paul Johnston, Albyn Jones, Gary Kamiya, Joe Kamiya, Charles Kadushin, Viviane Brachet Marquez, Mark Mizruchi, Neil McLaughlin, John Myles, David Nasatir, Frances Fox Piven, Francesca Polletta, Jill Quadagno, Alice Robbin, Guenther Roth, Dean Savage, Mark Schneider, Mildred Schwartz, Samuel Sieber, Allan Silver, Alan Sokal, Peggy Somers, Andras Szántó, Stephen Steinberg, Susan Steiner, Nancy diTomaso, and Will Wright. Several anonymous reviewers for the *American Sociological Review* convinced me that a book was the right format for my argument.

Students in several contexts—years of "Logics of Inquiry" seminars; theses or dissertations; workshops at Florida State University, the University of Michigan, the University of British Columbia, and elsewhere—have contributed greatly, by letting me try out the "working vocabulary" on their own projects. I cannot name you all, but thank you.

I thank all the persons at Oxford University Press who accepted, edited, designed, and produced this book.

I would appreciate receiving any comments or questions which readers of the book have, addressed to: ralford@email.gc.cuny.edu.

Introduction

꧁꧂

Sociology is a challenging discipline. Its multiple theoretical and methodological traditions offer a range of choices of important questions and ways to answer them. Using examples selected from classic and contemporary studies, this book presents several ways that research questions can be framed. A major purpose is to "unfreeze" the traditional associations between certain kinds of theories, methods, and evidence. I argue that neither qualitative nor quantitative data should be privileged, likewise historical or ethnographic method, micro or macro levels of analysis, theory or data.

We all start a project with vague ideas that come from different places in our own history—personal experiences and issues, some readings in theory that puzzle us, a moral or political or policy concern. Understanding how to translate your own history into the formulation of research questions is the process of learning the craft of inquiry. Techniques for *answering* the research question—statistics, interviews field work, archives—should flow from the research question, not vice versa.

THE AUDIENCE

The audience for this book is primarily advanced undergraduates or graduate students early in their careers. Students ideally will be familiar with some core sociological ideas and will have been exposed to some research techniques. Judging from my own experience giving research design workshops, the book will also be useful to graduate students working on a research paper, an M.A. thesis, or a dissertation proposal. The "working vocabulary" of the craft of inquiry will help those struggling to frame a coherent argument from a tangled mess of field notes, interviews, statistical tables, and summaries of documents, while also trying to locate their argument within "the literature on the topic." The book can be used in both theory and methods courses as auxiliary reading or could be the principal text for courses called Sociological Explanation, Sociological Analysis, or ProSeminar in Research Design, a course like the one I have taught for many years.

The book does not take an extreme position on either theoretical or methodological issues. Instructors (and students) who have widely varying theoretical stances and methodological preferences should find the book useful if they are open to different views about the relations among theory, method, and evidence. Regarding different paradigms of inquiry as legitimate is seen as a polemical stance by some, particularly staunch positivists and ardent postmodernists. I advocate a broad range of theoretical and methodological choices but also believe that integrating multiple paradigms in a dialectical manner produces the richest results of inquiry.

PARADIGMS OF INQUIRY

"Paradigms" are the operating rules about the appropriate relationship among theories, methods, and evidence that constitute the actual practices of the members of a particular scientific community, research program, or tradition. Paradigms are the combination of theoretical assumptions, methodological procedures, and standards of evidence that are taken for granted in particular works, are "in the foreground," to use one of the vocabulary of the craft of inquiry.

The term "paradigm" may treat the craft of inquiry too much as a *cognitive* enterprise, as if rules and procedures exist apart from the emotional, economic, and political context within which problems are defined, theories defined, and data gathered. A working craft vocabulary always runs the risk of becoming reified, of being mistaken for real things rather than seen as a useful abstraction.

Within sociology there are three major paradigms of inquiry, which I label "multivariate," "interpretive," and "historical." My core claim is that every good work combines elements of all three paradigms in various ways, either as a foreground argument or as background assumptions. The typology of paradigms gives you a set of analytic distinctions to use in thinking through your research choices.

Insights from both *positivism* and *postmodernism* are used to construct the working vocabulary for the craft of inquiry. Postmodernism and positivism are usually seen as sharply opposed alternatives, and they are—if debated as competing philosophical positions. I approach these issues not as philosophical ones but as part of a pragmatic strategy to help develop effective research practices.

I start from the postmodern standpoint: Human beings are both emotional and intellectual selves, constantly constructing the world around us. The categories we use in that complex process of self-construction are embedded in standpoints derived from our social memberships and identities. The world is thus socially constructed by language, and language is constituted by cultural meanings negotiated by persons with identities shaped by their historical experiences and social location. Knowledge is historically contingent and shaped by human interests and social values, rather than external to us, completely objective, and eternal, as the extreme positivist view would have it.

The postmodern critique of the orthodox conception of scientific method offers us few clues about how to do our work. The extreme postmodern position rejects any possibility of moving beyond the linguistic constructions of discourse. But the postmodern critique is an indispensable starting point for the critical evaluation of assumptions about how to produce knowledge (epistemology) about reality (ontology).

The usefulness of a positivist epistemology lies in the pragmatic assumption that there is a real world out there, whose characteristics can be observed, sometimes measured, and then generalized about in a way that comes close to truth. Empirical correlations between behavior and events can be discovered and inferences made about their significance. Assessment of the relative importance of different factors that explain a social phenomenon can be made with some degree of reliability and validity. There is a strong drive within the field toward developing something that approximates "scientific method," an attempt to realize the positivist vision of theories existing independent of evidence, evidence independent of theories, and methodologies autonomous from both.

Nothing to my knowledge has been written on the relationship between the emotional and the cognitive issues that arise as you try to decide on a research problem. Instead, the culture of research takes for granted that research interests are clearly defined, by the constraints of getting funded, by your thesis adviser, by your theoretical preferences, or by your political and policy commitments. This private lore is communicated from teachers to students, as research proposals are drafted and dissertation prospectuses reviewed. If I am right, this is an example of the tribal culture of social research that emphasizes objectivity and impersonality—the virtues of "science." The result is secret panic and unacknowledged anxiety, communicated only to a few friends and trusted colleagues. Each of us faces this predicament anew with each new project. I deal with "first- and second-level panic" as endemic aspects of the research process in Chapter 2.

This book attempts three related tasks. In order of importance, it first offers strategies to help you formulate research questions, by presenting a working vocabulary for the craft of inquiry. Second, it illustrates the working vocabulary by critically examining several classic and contemporary texts. Theories, methods, and evidence are connected via paradigmatic arguments. Third, it is a critical sociology of sociology. Current instruction arbitrarily severs sociological theory from research methods. The discipline has failed to be self-conscious about the ways choices of theory, method, and evidence reflect deeply embedded, even "cultural" presuppositions about how social knowledge is produced.

The tensions between these goals cannot all be resolved. Current configurations of power within the discipline make it difficult to combine different paradigms of inquiry. Good historical and institutional reasons explain why the multivariate paradigm of inquiry is dominant. Excellent practical reasons might lead you to make a strategic choice of one paradigm of inquiry, if only because a research project can be completed more easily and rapidly if you follow established and legitimate research practices. Because of the dominance of the multivariate paradigm, I use it as a point of reference in my examples throughout the book. However, the emphasis on the multivariate paradigm as the only "real" social science is impoverishing, a mark of the insecurity of the discipline, not a sign of its scientific maturity.

The field of sociology has exciting possibilities, if it can remain open to a wide range of theoretical and methodological options. Sociology should become more adventurous, less clannish, more open to other disciplines. It would also be better able to understand not only the limitations of each paradigm of inquiry, but also its potentialities.

PERSONAL HISTORY

My own intellectual history has exposed me to diverse theoretical traditions and methodologies at the institutions where I received my education, have taught, and have been involved in research. The craft vocabulary has been developed in the course of years of writing comments on student papers and theses at the University of Wisconsin at Madison, the University of California campuses at Santa Cruz, Berkeley, San Francisco, and Santa Barbara, Columbia University, New York University, the University of Essex in England, and—the last stop on my academic journey—the City University of New York.

My experiences as teacher and researcher have given me more than a superficial exposure to the major paradigms within modern sociology. Much of my scholarly work has been within the subfield of political sociology: voting and participation, the structures of local government, and public policy. The substantive topics varied considerably: voting in the English-speaking democracies, decision making in four Wisconsin cities, health care politics, comparative urban policymaking. I have also done work on theories of the state and on the social construction of pain among pianists. In the course of those projects I have analyzed many kinds of evidence: interviews with 2,000 leaders and voters in four Wisconsin cities, fifty-six public opinion surveys done over thirty years in the United States, Britain, Canada and Australia, archives of New York hospitals, field observations of piano teachers.[1]

I graduated from the University of California at Berkeley in 1950, after majoring in general curriculum (a combination of sociology, psychology, and anthropology). My first course in sociology, from Robert Nisbet, embodied many of the ideas later published in *The Sociological Tradition* (1966). Nisbet presented a historical perspective on the way human beings are shaped by social institutions, intellectual traditions, and human values. He saw social science as an essentially humanistic discipline (one of his best-known books is called *Sociology as an Art Form*).[2] Nisbet opened my mind to a new world: I could now explain my social origins and location in more than a purely personal way.

I started graduate work in 1951, during an escalating Cold War year in which a loyalty oath was instituted that required all university employees to swear that they were not members of any organization dedicated to overthrowing the government by force and violence. The period was one of general political repression: Many unions adopted similar loyalty oaths; the "Hollywood Ten" screenwriters were blacklisted after Senator Joseph McCarthy accused them of having Communist ties; Julius and Ethel Rosenberg were executed for allegedly stealing atomic secrets. For me, as for others, academic life seemed impossible because of the loyalty oaths, and also because it seemed far removed from "real" action for social change.

So, I went to work in auto plants for five years, becoming active in the United Auto Workers. With hindsight, I find that those experiences were invaluable for my sociological imagination, although those years were complicated and often painful because my cultural background differed from that of my Southern white and black coworkers. Both racism and class solidarity were intermixed in baffling ways.

I returned to graduate school in 1957 at Berkeley. No "modern" sociology department existed at Berkeley until Herbert Blumer came from the University of Chicago in 1952 to create one, and that occurred after I received my B.A. degree. Key faculty brought to Berkeley by Blumer included Reinhard Bendix and Erving Goffman from Chicago and Seymour Martin Lipset, Philip Selznick, Charles Glock, and Hanan Selvin from Columbia. Neil Smelser came from Harvard later.

Bendix was a refugee from Nazi Germany who had received his Ph.D. from the University of Chicago and who became known for his comparative historical studies *Work and Authority in Industry* and *Kings or People* and for his classic exegesis of Weber's work, *Max Weber: An Intellectual Portrait*.[3] Bendix became a model for me, as well as for many other scholars, embodying a passionate commitment to truth and reason.

The faculty members from Columbia were heirs to the grand tradition of sociology there of Robert K. Merton and Paul F. Lazarsfeld, on the one hand, and of C. Wright Mills and Robert S. Lynd, on the other. These pairings are significant. Merton and Lazarsfeld were teammates in the building of the Bureau of Applied Social Research, one of the great institutional innovations in modern sociology. The Bureau became the model for research institutions that tried to represent the academic interests (and fund-raising capacities!) of a community of scholars and graduate students.

Through the influence of the Columbia-trained faculty, I read Merton's *Social Theory and Social Structure*, an elegantly written analysis of the relationship between science and society, of functional analysis, and of the relationship between theory and empirical evidence.[4] Following Merton's "theories of the middle range," Bureau projects tended to analyze particular institutions (medical schools, science, universities) and behaviors (voting, consumer choices).

I also learned Lazarsfeld's "multivariate methodology." Bureau projects usually involved sample surveys of particular populations—medical students, voters, teachers, union members, scientists. A host of dissertations as well as reports and books flowed from the Bureau as generations of graduate students found employment on projects that could be used for dissertations. Merton and Lazarsfeld personally and intellectually (and the Bureau institutionally) were part of the process of professionalization of the discipline of sociology. They advanced a vision of middle-level research as a contributor to pragmatic institutional and social change. The Bureau developed a methodological culture that was transmitted to us, the graduate students, by the faculty members who had been trained at Columbia. The word "story" was always used, for example, to denote the sequence of statistical tables in a chapter or an article, rather than a traditional narrative of events and actions. The narrative was an *argument*, in which one point succeeded another as the inner meaning of the relationships in a complex body of data was revealed to the reader.[5]

The other pair at Columbia—Robert S. Lynd and C. Wright Mills—were both radical critics of American society. They had a quite different vision from that of Merton and Lazarsfeld of the role of sociology in society. Lynd was author (with his wife, Helen Merrell Lynd) of two classic studies of Muncie, Indiana, *Middletown* (1929) and *Middletown in Transition* (1937). Lynd never did any quantitative research and never developed any formal theoretical scheme or catchy concepts. With the possible exception of *Middletown*, used in courses on the history of American communities, his work is not read today. Just before the Second World War, Lynd published a challenging critique of both American society and sociology in *Knowledge for What?* (1939).[6] The argument of that book is perhaps even more relevant now than when it was written.

C. Wright Mills, despite his academic attainments, was another sociological maverick. His premature death in 1962 at the age of only forty-six was a tragic loss. It is impossible to know what intellectual trajectory he might have followed, because in his last book, on the Cuban revolution, he was moving toward polemical political statements. His best-known books, *The Power Elite* (1956) and *The Sociological Imagination* (1959), are still sometimes assigned in courses. The last book made an immediate impact on my graduate student cohort, partly because it was an "in-house" critique.[7]

Herbert Blumer was one of the founders of the symbolic interactionist school of contemporary sociology (and a disciple of the philosopher George Herbert Mead). The other faculty members at Berkeley within that tradition were Erving Goffman and Tamotsu Shibutani. Goffman had come to Berkeley in 1957. He had done field work in the Shetland Islands (off the coast of Scotland) that became the basis for his doctoral dissertation at Chicago, published as his classic *The Presentation of Self in Everyday Life*. Goffman's distinctive perspective on the rules that govern interaction was already clear. The interpretive paradigm is represented by his analysis of social life as a complex communication of meanings, expectations, and warnings among people via words, gestures, and body language. Goffman is probably the best known of those who have done empirical work within this sociological paradigm.

Goffman arrived at Berkeley after his field work in a mental hospital in Bethesda, which resulted in *Asylums* (see Chapter 5). I vividly remember waiting for him in his little office on the top floor of the Berkeley library, sneaking a look at his bookshelves crowded with the most amazing assortment of seemingly unrelated texts. Memoirs, cookbooks, fashion ads, gossip magazines, travel journals, advice manuals on manners were all jumbled together. I was mystified by what they might mean. Later, I realized that Goffman used a bricolage of empirical materials to construct an argument about how individual selves are constituted in interaction, presented to others for admiration, repaired when damaged, and denied when necessary.[8]

My graduate career at Berkeley thus sensitized me to the principal paradigms of inquiry in sociology: to historical processes through Nisbet and Bendix, to symbolic meanings through Blumer and Goffman from the Chicago school, and to multivariate relations via Lipset, Glock, and Selvin, trained in the Merton and Lazarsfeld tradition of survey analysis.

The point of this reconstruction of my own history is to demonstrate that different ways of gathering evidence and constructing theories correspond to the ways in which people do real research projects in real institutions.[9] My own intellectual biography may help clarify how research choices are and can be made. Sociology is created by people in specific times and places, with lives as well as careers.

WORKS ILLUSTRATING THE WORKING VOCABULARY

The working vocabulary will become clear as I show throughout the book what is powerful and useful in influential works that illustrate foreground and background arguments within different paradigms of inquiry.[10] The books I discuss have been chosen with several criteria in mind. First, they must exhibit a foreground argument that illustrates one of the paradigms. Second, they must be rich and complex studies that contain enough substance to show the background paradigms clearly. Third, they must be in some sense classics: old enough to be widely known, young enough to have had recent impact on the field. Fourth, they must be familiar enough so that a complete summary is not necessary.

In addition to these criteria, another important consideration enters. These books are not perfect; they have flaws of theoretical argument or of supporting evidence, of consistency and clarity of methodology. Those flaws are highlighted in my summary and discussion. But the flaws are not pointed out in order to establish my (or your) superiority to what after all are major contributions, or to show how much progress has been made. Rather, the flaws themselves illustrate the human character of any contribution to social science. In some sense, the contributions occurred not despite the flaws but because of

them. These books have not settled the questions they raised but have contributed to debates around central issues that have gone on now for more than
a century.[11]

What constitutes a "good" explanation of a social phenomenon is a highly
controversial issue. These works are used, read, assigned, and cited, despite their
flaws. They are defined as classics. The answer to this seeming paradox is not
that these works are evidence of the intrinsic difficulty of analyzing social phenomena or of the immaturity of sociology as a science, although these claims
may be true. Rather, diverse paradigms of inquiry contain contradictory criteria for a "good" explanation. Normative, theoretical, and empirical judgments
are difficult to separate, for good sociological reasons.

Chapter 1, "The Craft of Inquiry," critiques the division of intellectual labor between theory and method and shows how the classical canon of Marx,
Weber, and Durkheim provides examples of multiple paradigms in sociology.
The craft of social inquiry lies somewhere between art and science. It combines
the creativity and the spontaneity of art (although art can be hard work) and
the rigorous and systematic character of science (although science can be joy-
ful).

Chapter 2, "Designing a Research Project," deals with the concrete problems of actual research choices, given our always limited resources. The tools
of the craft of inquiry include a working vocabulary (in italics) to aid you in
making the strategic choices, first of a *problem* and then of an *entry point* into
a *theoretical* or *empirical research question*. The *argument* of a particular work
combines *theoretical* claims and *empirical* generalizations. Such arguments can
be classified into one or more *paradigms of inquiry: multivariate, interpretive,*
and *historical.* Paradigmatic assumptions can be in either the *foreground* or the
background of the argument of a particular work. Important but unresearch-
able questions must be *exorcised*. The boundaries of the phenomenon being
studied can be *mapped*. As you go back and forth between theoretical and empirical *tracks of analysis,* you engage in *rolling reformulations* of the research
question. The research process creates both *first-* and *second-level panic*, but
there are ways of coping.

A stylistic note: I have put a number of concepts within quotation marks,
more than would usually be done. The reason is to emphasize the implicit theoretical and empirical assumptions contained in the concept. Words are not
neutral and innocent descriptions.

Chapter 3, "The Construction of Arguments," deals with the ways in which
theoretical claims and empirical generalizations are constructed within multivariate, interpretive, and historical paradigms of inquiry. The ideal multivariate
argument within that paradigm defines a model of a chain of control, independent, intervening, and dependent variables within a social structure or system, measured by quantitative data and analyzed by statistical techniques. The
experiment is the ideal typical model for research. The typical argument within
the interpretive paradigm constructs a dense network of symbolic meanings
constituting a "culture" or "subculture," in the typical case supported by field

work, participant observation, or ethnography. The typical argument within the historical paradigm devises a narrative of events located in time and place, with specific actors, within a named totality or environment ("France in 1789," "Bosnia in 1997"), based on an analysis of documents or texts.

One paradigm is likely to be in the background and others in the foreground of a given work, but there is no *logical* necessity for the theories, methods and evidence conventionally associated with a paradigm to be used together in a given work. My own foreground claim is that the most satisfactory general explanations and insights are provided by dialectical explanations that integrate theories, methods, and evidence drawn from the assumptions of each paradigm.

Chapter 4, "Foreground Multivariate Arguments," illustrates the different ways in which a multivariate paradigm can be foregrounded and other paradigms backgrounded. Emile Durkheim's *Suicide* (1897) argues—from census data—that when our attachments to social groups are either too weak or too strong, certain individuals respond to this lack of normative "regulation" by killing themselves. William Julius Wilson's *The Declining Significance of Race* (1978) is a mixture of historical and multivariate arguments. Wilson, using economic and demographic data, argues that black Americans' life chances are shaped more by changes in the organization of work than they are by racial discrimination. Douglas Massey and Nancy Denton's *American Apartheid* (1993) shows the consequences of urban racial segregation for American democracy.

Chapter 5, "Foreground Interpretive Arguments," gives examples from classic and contemporary works of this paradigm. Weber's *The Protestant Ethic and the Spirit of Capitalism* (1904) shows—on the basis of Calvinist texts—how certain kinds of religious beliefs create motives to work hard and accumulate capital. Erving Goffman's *Asylums* (1961) is a powerful ethnographic account of how the destruction of the personal identity of patients occurs in mental hospitals, "total institutions" attempting to control every aspect of their inmates' behavior. Arlie Hochschild's *The Second Shift* (1990) combines interpretive and other paradigms but is based primarily on observations of who does the household tasks in families.

Chapter 6, "Foreground Historical Arguments," analyzes several classic and contemporary works within this paradigm. Karl Marx's *The Eighteenth Brumaire of Louis Bonaparte* (1852) tells the story, using newspaper articles and historical accounts, of how a "grotesque nonentity" managed to become emperor of France and carry out a coup d'état on December 2, 1851. Barrington Moore's *Social Origins of Dictatorship and Democracy* (1966) is a historical panorama of the path followed by five Western nations in the twentieth century, through convulsive transformation from and through communism, fascism, and/or democracy. Certain types of class alliances—particularly that of the landed classes with the bourgeoisie, rather than with the peasantry—were more likely to lead to democracy. In this respect Moore's argument is also multivariate. William H. Sewell Jr.'s *Work and Revolution in France* (1980) combines historical and interpretive paradigms to investigate the language of politics in prerevolutionary France.

Chapter 7, "The Power of Multiple Arguments," presents hypothetical examples of research on the welfare state and on revolution to illustrate the way that sensitivity to multiple possible combinations of theories, methods, and evidence can help you develop theoretical and empirical questions not limited by the assumptions of a particular paradigm.

Chapter 8, "Dialectical Explanations and the Sociological Imagination," considers the possibility of integrated or "dialectical" explanations and discusses the institutional constraints on the freedom to choose research questions. The book concludes with a call for the maintenance of the diverse sources of the sociological imagination.

CHAPTER

1

The Craft of Inquiry

From the origins of the discipline to the most recent scholarship, a gap has widened between theory and method in the discipline's self-understanding of what it means to "do" sociology. Much work in the discipline today consists of abstract theoretical speculations, methodological analyses of the properties of various statistics, or rigorous empirical analyses that lack theoretical substance.

The American sociologist C. Wright Mills in 1959 characterized this intellectual division of labor as "grand theory" versus "abstracted empiricism" in his classic work *The Sociological Imagination*. For Mills, "grand theorists" like Talcott Parsons were committed to theory without evidence while "abstracted empiricists" such as Paul Lazarsfeld practiced method without theory. Although Mills overstated his critique of both Parsons and Lazarsfeld for polemical purposes, he accurately focused on their all too frequent failure to integrate theories, methods, and evidence. (Mills failed to make the further distinction between method and research). Addressing this problem, institutional statesmen like Columbia University's Robert K. Merton advocated "middle-range theory" that could mediate between the camps of theory and method. While this formulation helped avoid a civil war between theorists and methodologists, Merton's strategy smooths over rather than confronts directly the intellectual issues raised by the specializations in theory, methodology, and empirical research in sociology.

THEORY VS. METHOD VS. RESEARCH

"Theory" has become a specialty in its own right, with examinations, courses, and journals. Critical consideration of the categories of discourse is thriving within sociology. The effect of the cognitive separation of theory from method, sanctioned by academic specialization, is that theorists do not deal with the relationship of theory to evidence. They ignore the empirical foundations that would support or negate their ideas or, when evidence is a central issue, deal with it primarily in philosophical terms. The resulting divorce of theory from evidence leads, on the one hand, to ever more complex conceptual elaborations and, on the other, to empirical research that is often insufficiently linked to theoretical claims. The arbitrary distinction between theorists and methodologists obscures the full range of available theoretical and empirical choices.

The specialization in theory is even enshrined in dictionaries. The Blackwell *Dictionary of Twentieth-Century Social Thought* (1993) pays no attention to problems of method or evidence, except as theoretical categories. There are no entries for "evidence," "data," and "quantification" and only a brief article on "method" (by the French sociologist Raymond Boudon) and on "statistics"; these are seen as theoretical issues.[1]

"Method," broadly viewed, is a series of strategies for finding a way to associate the abstractions of theory with the actual social relations being mapped, interpreted, or explained by the theory. Techniques for collecting, verifying, and evaluating the validity and reliability of specific kinds of evidence constitute the narrow meaning of "method" and comprise the skills usually taught in methods courses. How to assess the biases in a historical document, how to reduce error in coding, how to do a regression analysis, how to guard against "over-rapport" in a field study are indispensable *techniques* for gathering and evaluating evidence, but they are not my concern here.

Methodology has also become a subfield, with specialists offering courses, giving exams, and publishing in professional journals. The writings of methodologists are as one-sided as those of the theorists: Books on methodology typically pay little attention to the way that categories of analysis are theoretically constructed, and they ignore the assumptions that underlie particular ways of gathering, aggregating, and analyzing the data.[2] These issues are left to the theorists, who don't deal with them.

Methodologists who focus on statistical techniques, interviewing skills, coding procedures, rapport in field work, or archival search strategies also perpetuate this misleading distinction by not acknowledging the theoretical assumptions implicit in ways of gathering or creating evidence. Even some methodologists who complain that particular statistical techniques are used inappropriately sometimes neglect the theoretical sources of particular technical procedures.

Methodologists are usually divided into *quantitative* and *qualitative* specialists. Quantitative methodologists are further specialized into applied and theoretical statisticians. Qualitative methodologies divide into ethnomethodologists, symbolic interactionists, grounded theorists, historical methodologists, and ethnographers, each with a specialized vocabulary and set of techniques.

The intellectual division of labor within sociology is also represented by "researchers" who analyze substantive problems defined as part of the subfields of social stratification, political sociology, the family, education, the sociology of organizations—subfields that deal with one or another social institution. Researchers call on theoretical assumptions to frame and justify their research question and rely on established methodological tools to answer the question.

These established divisions of intellectual labor among "theorists," "methodologists," and "researchers" have a built-in inertia that stems from institutionalized powers to reward specialization and punish interdisciplinary work. Ironically, works that are honored with awards for the best scholarship are frequently those that combine multiple paradigms of inquiry. Practitioners in the field recognize excellent interdisciplinary scholarship, even while they themselves have powerful incentives to stay within their disciplinary specialization.

THEORY, METHODS, AND EVIDENCE IN THE CLASSIC CANON

I have chosen works by Emile Durkheim, Max Weber, and Karl Marx to exemplify the integration of theory and method as well as the creative use of multiple paradigms of inquiry. Each of them accepts as theoretical premises key elements of each paradigm, although foregrounding one of them in the particular work I analyze.

Durkheim, Weber, and Marx all assumed that there is a continuous interplay between theoretical assumptions and the objects of inquiry. "Theory" and "method" form moments, as it were, within the process of inquiry. To put the point another way, they assumed that theories do refer to a reality outside themselves and that the relationship between theoretical abstractions and that reality is eternally problematic.

The classic thinkers also realized the importance of understanding the conscious actions of human actors in historical situations in which actors are embedded in multiple social relations, whether defined as a community, a group, a complex organization, a class, a political party, a marriage, or a religious or ethnic group. The distinctive forms of social relations indicated by those categories are the meaningful context within which actors construct their own identities.

The three thinkers also took for granted that there are empirical regularities of human behavior, human perceptions, and human experience that it is the distinctive task of social inquiry to investigate and explain. Recurring patterns of human experience and their association with features of social structure and history can be known. If human experiences in history were totally chaotic, random, and arbitrary, there would be nothing to investigate.

Their theories were grounded in historical and empirical evidence and attempted to answer quite concrete questions. Their works, by implication, thus challenge current definitions of theorizing as an activity disconnected from empirical inquiry. It is striking how little of their work is, in the modern sense, self-consciously theoretical.[3]

Their works have inspired methodological discussions about how to connect evidence to our theories. Durkheim's concept of the "social fact" as an external force constraining individual behavior has, as he intended, helped define sociological method. Weber's concepts of the "ideal type" and "verstehen" assume that observers bring to any empirical analysis a set of abstract concepts and a subjective understanding that shape the meaning of the evidence. And Marx, always remaining outside academic constraints on tone, content, and range, defined in the "dialectic" (originally from Hegel) one of the most puzzling and challenging ways of looking at the production of social knowledge. Marx attempted to grasp both the internal contradictions in knowledge (the way that abstractions simultaneously conceal some essential qualities of the object of study and reveal others) and the external contradictions between the living, human producers of knowledge and the social conditions that alienate them from their own product.

I will show how three of their classic works foreground either a structure of multivariate relations, a texture of meanings, or a narrative of events. Each argument presupposes the others as background.[4] My craft vocabulary recognizes and attempts to integrate their differences.

If you read Durkheim, Weber, and Marx with the difference between theoretical and empirical questions in mind, what is striking is the tremendous gap between the theory and the evidence. Durkheim's theoretical concern in *Suicide* (1897) is with the consequences of different degrees of individual integration into social groups, but his empirical focus is on differences in suicide rates among (for example) Protestants and Catholics, single and married men, officers and enlisted men.[5] Weber's theoretical concern in *The Protestant Ethic and the Spirit of Capitalism* (1904) is with the consequences of a religious ethic for capitalist accumulation, but his empirical focus is on the interpretation of texts about economic action written by Calvinist theologians.[6] Marx's theoretical concern in *The Eighteenth Brumaire of Louis Bonaparte* (1852) is with class alliances and class struggles, but his empirical focus is on political factions and the actions of political leaders.[7] The integration of the answers to these theoretical and empirical questions is in each case a rhetorical tour de force; you cannot predict the theory from the evidence, or vice versa.

These works exemplify the interdisciplinary origins of sociology. Only Durkheim was a "sociologist," attempting to create a scholarly discipline. Weber was an economic and legal historian by training, Marx had a classical education. Both Weber and Marx ranged over the intellectual terrain, writing books that have become seminal for work in many fields. Together, Weber and Marx define the boundaries of what has come to be known as "comparative-historical sociology." That the three writers have become canonical "theorists" in sociology is a historical accident (albeit one with historical causes, of course!). Because of this complex and contradictory intellectual heritage, it is impossible to expect consensus within the field; the best that can be hoped for is a creative tension between different paradigms of inquiry.

These classic works make clear that "society" is the traditional and core unit of analysis, seen not as an aggregation of individuals, groups, communities, and organizations but as an emergent phenomenon that has its own reality independent of "lower" levels of social existence. Whether society is defined as "capitalism" and seen as polarized by class conflict or as "modern society" and seen as a differentiated congeries of groups with specialized functions ("organic solidarity") or as dominated by potentially rational bureaucratic organizations, the societal environment was always the theoretical context for the development of arguments.

Although mainstream sociological research rarely cites any of these thinkers anymore—a maturing science is supposed to forget its ancestors—the perspectives they brought to bear on society still inform our outlooks on how a society is organized and how it changes. These works are our common intellectual heritage. The paradigms of inquiry that sociologists use to construct theoretical claims and empirical generalizations were institutionalized within the discipline with the canonization of the classic nineteenth-century writings of Durkheim, Weber, and Marx. Their texts have shaped our sociological consciousness by shaping the definitions of important theoretical and empirical questions. Many of their concepts have disappeared into the assumptions that underlie contemporary work. Their impact is all the greater for having become implicit.[8]

What continues to attract scholars to the work of these classic thinkers is that each attempted in his own way to provide insight into the social totality and each made use of multiple paradigms of inquiry. While none of them had the advantage of contemporary theoretical and empirical tools, each still analyzed historical processes, patterns of structural relations, and cultural meanings to create explanations for the society being transformed around them.

SOLIDARITY, RATIONALITY, AND PRODUCTION

The classic theorists of sociology are also still relevant because—despite the profound social changes of the past century—we still live in a world that has some of the major characteristics they analyzed. Durkheim, Weber, and Marx each analyzed the simultaneously progressive and yet crisis-prone character of modern societies. Such societies exhibit enormous economic productivity, scientific progress, and technological innovation, as well as gradually expanding democratic institutions and ideals of justice and freedom. Nonetheless, racial and class inequality, injustice, lack of opportunity, political repression, and ethnic and racial violence and prejudice continue to exist. Modern societies are still subject to the crises of solidarity analyzed by Durkheim, the crises of rationality emphasized by Weber, and the crises of production that were central for Marx. And, most relevant for my argument, these crises are seen in the institutions of social science and the production of teachers, students, and knowledge. A brief sketch, focusing on how central theoretical assumptions lead to research questions, is in order.

Emile Durkheim saw modern societies as subject to crises of *solidarity:* a breakdown of the common values and sense of community needed to integrate societies faced with multiple social divisions. Racial and ethnic and religious conflict, the high incidence of divorce, the breakdown of family life, the disruption of stable jobs and careers—all these fit Durkheim's image of the pathological destruction of community and the pervasiveness of anomie: Life is no longer predictable.

Social science is one of the differentiated functions that helps integrate a complex division of labor into the "organic solidarity" envisioned by Durkheim by producing knowledge with social uses, as well as social roles (teachers, students, researchers) whose practitioners carry out the necessary functions. In normal times, students can make a series of decisions about courses and majors that will prepare them for stable careers and that enable them to count on finding a niche appropriate to their interests, talents, and skills.

But social science is not exempt from crises of solidarity, manifest in an anomic division of labor among departments, fields, and universities, as well as a forced division of labor as teaching loads increase for young scholars unable to work in their specialties. Occupational groups—such as the professoriate—are increasingly unable to provide the moral certainty of contributing to a valued social function. For students, anomie may occur if their major can no longer be counted on to prepare them for a good job.

Possible research questions might be: What are the consequences of the changing status and social role of different academic disciplines for the career choices of students? How much of a lag is there between the occurrence of changes in the labor market and a change in the self-conceptions of students? How much anomie is produced by the disruption of stable career paths?

Note that these questions are not yet empirical ones. That is, the kinds of evidence potentially available to answer them could vary tremendously. You could ask: How do private and public universities that differ in prestige compare with respect to changes in graduation rates and the proportion of students who choose particular majors? You could ask, of a sample of graduates: What was the salary of your first job? Was it in the field of your college major? You could do a historical study and ask: What have been the different sources of funding of universities (private donations, tax monies, research grants) since World War II? Has declining public funding led to pressures to reduce support for the humanities and social sciences and to increase it for work in technical fields and in the traditional professions?

These are only a few of the possible research implications of Durkheim's theory of the division of labor in modern societies and the impact of institutional crisis on academic life.

Max Weber saw industrialized societies, increasingly legitimated by bureaucratic principles of organization, as being in a crisis of rationality, and this foreboding remains relevant. Popular beliefs in public and political accountability have eroded. Opportunistic political leadership abounds. Bureaucratic organizations justify their power with ideologies of efficiency. Weber also saw the dangers of increasing militarism in a world of contending nation states mobilizing virulent ethnic loyalties for nationalist goals. Here I shall deal only with the implications of his theory of rationality for academia.

Social science is rationally organized into bureaucracies (departments, divisions, fields, public and private universities, research foundations) that produce knowledge. For students, this rational organization is manifest in sequences of required courses developed and enforced as a "major."

But social knowledge is also vulnerable to crises of rationality. "Major" requirements can inhibit a student's attempt to integrate fragmented knowledge by taking courses in many fields. Similarly, technically competent research is organized by bureaucratized "policy research" agencies that manage staffs of research assistants and generate research grants to keep the organizations going. Such research is likely to be "formally rational"—it conforms to internal criteria for "good" research. Yet, standards for theoretically coherent research on socially important problems ("substantive rationality") are all too frequently abandoned, sometimes if powerful funders object, sometimes simply because of the requirement to focus on narrow questions that can be answered by highly technical research procedures.

Some possible research questions that flow from this theoretical perspective might be: Does the rise of charismatic fundamentalist religions signify a decline in the legitimacy of science and rational bureaucratic organizations? Is being a "student" as central a personal identity for young people enrolled in college in the 1990s as it was in the 1950s? Empirically (and note the gap): Are sociology majors less religious than business majors? Has the conversation of students "hanging out" in "bull sessions" become focused more on career difficulties than on philosophical issues and politics over the past twenty years? What is the balance of perceptions among students doing research papers: Is the work only a course requirement? Is it a creative self-identified project to learn something interesting, or just a necessary part of the training for a possible social science career?

Again, these are only a few examples of ways in which Weber's theoretical perspective can be translated into research questions.

Karl Marx saw capitalist societies as in a constant crisis of *production*, resulting from a growing gap between rich and poor and an inability of many of those who produce the cornucopia of consumer goods to be able to purchase them. Marx saw market and exchange relationships based on calculation of advantage rather than on bonds of feeling as permeating more and more aspects of social life in capitalist societies. The glorification of the market, of efficient productivity, of competition (under such rubrics as "human capital") was seen as the ideology of a privileged class rather than as valid social theory. Marx's thesis that the glittering spectacle of capitalist productivity and commodity innovation masks increasing human inequalities is still relevant to an understanding of modern societies.

Social science is part of the accumulation of capital and the exploitation of labor in capitalist societies. In periods of growth and expansion, particular fields or research programs will grow, winning the competition for funds and labor power. Certain majors (law, business, computer science) will have their moment of optimistic expansion.

But, the production of social knowledge also exhibits what Marx saw as the fetishism of commodities and an anarchy of production. The contradiction between the new forces of production (computers, statistics, census data, archives) and the social relations of production (the proliferation of part-time adjunct teachers, the overproduction of Ph.D.s, the product differentiation of journals, the pressure to publish) will lead to social crises in which investment in education will shrink, academic unemployment grow, libraries lack the funds to buy books and journals. Certain majors may become almost unemployable.

Research questions flowing from Marx's theoretical perspective might include: To what extent does competition among university departments for positions, salaries, and grants mimic the model of capital accumulation and profitability in private industry? Is students' alienation from their work, from other students, from their own goals, analogous to the alienation of workers employed in factories? How necessary is the production of social science knowledge for the continuation of the core institutions of capitalist societies?

Specified empirically (again, remember the gap between theory and evidence), you might ask: What is the relationship between the status and income of a professor and the time he or she spends with students? Does this relationship vary by size of college, the college's prestige, the class background of the students? Or, to what extent are student research assistants treated as junior colleagues rather than hired labor? In conversations between professors and students, how much emphasis is placed on "training" for a career versus "liberal education" of the mind, versus simply fulfilling course and major requirements? How much change has there been in teaching loads in different types of universities, and is this change correlated with how much students have learned by graduation?

This quick attempt to show how one can restate some of Durkheim's, Weber's, and Marx's canonical theories into research questions relevant to possible contemporary trends in social science is only a background assumption for my argument here. I present this sketch only to suggest how their theories about modern society could be translated into research questions that are potentially testable with methods and evidence. Some of the questions I have posed would be answerable only with an enormous investment of time and resources, but it is important at the early stage of a research project to be playful and experimental. Push the boundaries of possible questions as far as possible before you must become concrete, realistic, and "responsible."

CONCLUSIONS

The craft of inquiry teaches you how to connect theory to evidence in order to construct valid explanations of the workings of society. Sociology needs to reunite theory, method, and evidence in a way that can be both legitimate and powerful. My core assumption is that how you define a research question and then analyze its *theoretical* context and its *empirical* implications significantly influences the trajectory and the quality of your research. Neither sophisticated theory nor high-technology statistics—not even a wealth of data—can create significance from a fuzzy research question.

This book is intended primarily to be a guide to the craft of inquiry, by presenting and illustrating a "working vocabulary" that is useful as a tool for the craft. Its goal is to broaden awareness of the wide range of theoretical and empirical choices available to answer different kinds of research questions. My purpose is not to challenge sociology's multiple traditions; quite the opposite. Research questions are currently defined in overspecialized ways. Showing the relationships of each paradigm to the others will reveal their full intellectual potential.

Not every possible kind of evidence is necessary to answer a particular research question, nor can you always obtain the resources of time and energy to answer all potentially interesting theoretical and empirical questions. No one can simultaneously survey hundreds of persons (or companies, families, or communities), conduct depth interviews with key informants, search the relevant government archives, and engage in years of participant observation. The author of every published work has selected painfully among many possible lines of inquiry.

There is no one "best" way to combine different kinds of evidence or theory. Sometimes a research question requires a combination of approaches in a single work. Depending on the state of knowledge in the particular field, a dialogue between individuals defending particular research traditions may open up debates about both evidence and theory. At some point, final choices have to be made in order to finish the paper, thesis, or other work. Chapter 2 deals with the practical issues of using the working vocabulary of the craft of inquiry.

Developing coherent arguments that recognize historical processes, symbolic meanings, and multivariate relations is the best way to construct an adequate explanation of a complex social phenomenon. Pushing historical and intersubjective aspects of social processes into the background in order to construct models based only on quantitatively measured variables may actually prevent an adequate explanation of the processes under study, as I argue in Chapter 7. The process of abstracting from history and from intersubjective meanings into quantitatively measured variables guts the analysis of substantive significance. Theory becomes an abstract statement of correlations between variables. Paradoxically, perhaps the very process of attempting to abstract in order to generalize may prevent an understanding of cause. But just as concepts and theoretical arguments should not be reduced to data, neither should evidence be regarded as merely subjective interpretations and social constructions without empirical substance.

Sociological inquiry cannot be converted to a set of formulas that instruct you in "research methods" in the same way that you can write down rules for baking a cake or the formula for mixing hydrogen and oxygen to produce water. Combining theory, method, and evidence in sociology is a craft that must be learned in practice. The working vocabulary I present brings theory and method together again as a way of learning the craft of inquiry.

With C. Wright Mills, my concern is to advance a theoretically informed, empirically grounded, and historically oriented social science that matters for the society outside the academy. This book is an introductory guide for the perplexed and a warning of things to avoid, designed for young social science students embarking on research projects. The craft of social inquiry can be learned only through a theoretically informed analysis of actual research practices.

This book is thus centrally concerned with the complex conditions, internal dynamics and consequences of research *choices*. Although based on the particular research traditions of sociology, my argument applies to all the social sciences. The main focus is on the research *process*: the grounds on which theoretical claims and empirical generalizations are constructed from research questions framed within the major paradigms of inquiry available in the social sciences.[9]

Much conceptual work without empirical content helps to clarify the theoretical bases of the field. Specialists in "theory"are making legitimate and important contributions to the field. Similarly, some sociologists must specialize in the mathematics underlying particular statistical techniques. And the sheer technical problems of defining and measuring "poverty" or "ethnic identity" or "gendered behavior," for example, and then analyzing the complexities of the data deserve and require specialized training. I am not challenging these divisions of intellectual labor *after* one makes a decision to specialize in a particular aspect of the profession and the discipline. But they should not be built into the implicit culture of the field—in courses, textbooks, examinations—in a way that precludes exposure to the full range of theoretical and methodological traditions—that is, the different "paradigms of inquiry." Students must somehow pick their way through the complicated decisions that have to be made in specific research projects, taking into account both available resources and institutional constraints.

CHAPTER

2

Designing a Research Project

ॐॐ

No work springs out of thin air; it is a historical product, grounded in the intellectual traditions you have absorbed, in the theories of society you have learned, in the audiences for which you write. But it also reflects a series of choices, almost always made with uncertainty, because, by definition, you do not know enough to make the right choices. Constructing an argument is an emotional as well as a cognitive process, a series of leaps of faith, sometimes grounded in hard evidence, sometimes in sheer speculation. You look about for support and for inspiration from books and articles, from colleagues and friends, from your inner resources of imagination.

Individuals bring to the research process widely varying material, emotional, and intellectual resources. How much time do you have for the project? How much money to buy books? How good is your library? Do you have a job? These mundane questions about material resources decisively affect the potential scope and depth of the project. Networks of colleagues and fellow students as sources of information are another important resource. How extensive your intellectual contacts are is partly a function of how much time and money you have, but not entirely. Emotional resources—your level of commitment to the problem, your capacity to concentrate intensively—are also crucial. Are you comfortable calling strangers on the phone? How long can you sit still poring over dusty archival volumes? Intellectual resources include how many languages you can read and how familiar you are with other cultures.

The injunctions to "Master the literature," "Formulate a theory," "Deduce a hypothesis from theory," "Look for relevant data," "Ensure validity and reliability of the data," and "Draw theoretical conclusions from the data" are of very little help in the research process. These Six Commandments of scientific method provide a moral framework akin to "Do not steal," "Love thy father and thy mother," "Do not covet thy neighbor's wife," or, to quote Robert Fulghum, "Hold hands when crossing the street." Such maxims are of little help in confronting the ambiguities and complexities of daily life. Similarly, knowing that you should "Do informant interviews" or "Conduct a regression analysis" does not provide much of a concrete guide to solving the daily dilemmas of research.

From the outside, however, if you have not gone through this process, a published article or book, particularly one that has become a "classic"—one that is assigned in courses and footnoted in other books—assumes an appearance of hard objectivity or an aura of inevitability that obscures its origins. The process of revision and rethinking, of editing and reorganizing, that is an inevitable part of that process is hidden by the smooth marching of words down the page, by the finality of the hard cover, the resounding title, the impressive publisher.

Individual intellectual works are produced within the context of specific institutional arrangements (courses, fields, departments, research organizations, publishers) that establish the legitimate language, the problem, the tools (empirical evidence, methods of inquiry) and the resources needed to carry out the project (library access, time, assistants, data, computers). If the work is to be accepted as a thesis or dissertation or to get published as an article or a book, it must conform to certain standards of writing, of logical presentation, of evidence. It must cite sources and the literature. Human beings associated in what are labeled fields, disciplines, or research programs have developed conceptual frameworks that legitimate the problem and the project.[1]

The intellectual product—the book, article, paper—that results from these complex social processes does not ordinarily reveal its own historical origins and context. It is easy to be mystified and to conceive of the product as stemming from one hardworking and intelligent human mind. The closer a field gets to a "science," the more the historical context is concealed and the more the argument of the work seems to be the direct outcome of rational generalizations from evidence.

COGNITIVE AND EMOTIONAL SOURCES OF ANXIETY

It is striking that the process of inquiry is almost always treated as a series of *cognitive* choices, not emotional ones. The emotional commitments that underlie the research process are almost never acknowledged. Yet, physical and emotional energies have to be mobilized to carry out the multiple tasks associated with intellectual work. The massive focusing of energy necessary to read the literature, write notes and drafts, talk to colleagues and interview "subjects," and analyze data seem to occur totally divorced from the body. These are only the external manifestations of this mobilization of emotional energy. Even more subtle are the internal mobilizations that must take place: The decisions to enter a field, to choose a problem, to study for years, to commit yourself to writing, involve choices that are often painful and draining. We all "know" that this is true, but little attention is paid to the emotional and physiological requirements for intellectual work, and even less to how these requirements enter into the formulation of the problem and the choice of theory and method.[2]

Anxieties are associated with every stage of a research project. Some of them are necessary, justified, and ultimately enlightening. Others are unnecessary, distracting, and ultimately paralyzing. The intensity of the anxieties depends on what you have already written, how new the project is, how familiar you are with the research literature on the topic, how much time you have or are willing to commit to the project, and whether you have the necessary resources—your own time or the time of a research assistant, money to gather the evidence (whether a survey, documents, interviews, travel to archives), and resources to analyze the data (computer time, transcribing, content analysis, coding). And, of course, you need the emotional commitment and stamina to see the project through to some written product.

These sources of anxiety are real and cannot be wished away or eliminated. The fears associated with these present and future difficulties might be called "first-level panic." You inevitably feel these tensions, and sometimes they are almost necessary to force your full attention on the various decisions that must be made. A research project typically has many stages; first-level panic can occur when a novice researcher compares her confusion and indecision at stage 1—when a research question is being decided—to somebody else's polished product in a journal or book. The authors of that finished work have somehow successfully managed to cover the signs of their own panic, as they struggled to develop their research question into a theoretically informed argument supported by evidence. Thus, this comparison is inappropriate, albeit almost inevitable.

A second type of anxiety, which is unproductive, results from an inappropriate handling of first-level panic. Persistent self-questioning of your choice of problem, your motives, and even your intelligence might be called "second-level panic." If you do not realize that first-level panic stems from the intrinsic complexities of the theoretical and empirical issues, you may start questioning your own competence and commitment to the problem. You may wonder why you picked the project in the first place. In these difficult moments, the research process may lead to a state of mind that some people pay others to help them get rid of: obsession, brooding, withdrawal, even despair. Such emotional states sometimes call for therapy, or at least the loving support of friends and family. Such self-questioning cannot help accomplish the real tasks with which you are confronted in the research process.

The working vocabulary is offered to help the process of research by reducing unproductive stress and wasted resources. You can move back and forth between empirical and theoretical "tracks" of inquiry. If you are temporarily blocked in thinking through your theoretical claims, you can stop and pursue the empirical questions: analyze a table, read through the transcript of an interview, review your field notes, study maps showing the geographical distribution of ethnic groups, reorganize your summaries of documents. Or, if you are baffled by a piece of empirical evidence that does not seem to fit, you can reread your notes on the basic concepts or study the latest articles on the topic.

The working vocabulary will help you cope with the intellectual sources of anxiety by providing some tools to help you think through the research question and other issues associated with your primordial choices. Moments of panic are almost inevitable in any research process. You must learn to be kind to yourself in this complex process of thinking—flexible in adjusting the theory to the available evidence and able to reinterpret the evidence in the light of your changing theoretical ideas.

It is time to confess that I am just as subject to anxiety about my work as everybody else. My experience leads me to "know" that I will somehow get through the process and finish this book. Because I am dealing with multiple paradigms of inquiry with hotly contested criteria for "good" work, I have been faced with criticisms that have been very hard to meet.

The long list of acknowledgments at the front of the book barely hints at the intensity of collegial reaction to the argument I make within it. At this moment, I am sitting at my computer rereading several inches of accumulated critiques from colleagues and friends who took the time to wade through drafts and to write detailed comments. Some points I have incorporated; others I have neglected; still others I simply cannot deal with in this book. It is too late to rethink my fundamental assumptions, but I have tried to patch some of the potholes.

It is anxiety provoking to realize that I have not justified all of the theoretical claims I make and have provided only a few examples and illustrations at best, rather than systematic evidence. And, if this book were a conventional research report, my own emotional "state of mind" would certainly not be mentioned, as I am doing now. But I think (note the uncertainty still!) that this reflexive comment (apology? explanation? rationalization?) is appropriate here.[3]

SELECTING A PROBLEM

You start a research project with a *problem*: a theme, an issue, or a concern, which at the beginning of the process is inevitably imprecisely defined for research purposes. Problems grow out of a combination of personal *experience* (your motives, interests, and life history); problems of the *discipline*, transmitted through the analytic tools, methods, and theories you have learned; and problems of the *society*, transmitted through your exposure to history, broader social theory, politics, and the media.

Possible problems might include the following: the economic welfare of immigrant workers in Western Europe; the causes of peace negotiations in the Middle East; the fate of homeless people in New York City; the global environmental crisis; the lack of funding for AIDS research; the political movement of disabled persons; the male backlash against feminism; the labeling of young black males as violent; American's economic decline; health care delivery in Canada; the differences in income between men and women who hold comparable jobs; the consequences of sexism for mental health; the relationship between homelessness and racism. The range of potential topics or problems is almost infinite.

A *problem* is not yet a *research question*. This point cannot be overemphasized. It is easy to assume that stating a topic or a theme or an issue is equivalent to asking a research question. It is not. A research question is literally a sentence that ends in a question mark and in which every word counts, one that points in two directions—toward the theoretical framework that justifies the question and toward the empirical evidence that will answer it. A research question is a commitment to a way of framing the problem for the research process to begin or continue, since research questions usually change in the course of the project.

Substantive problems must thus be translated into the vocabulary of social inquiry. You must ask yourself: What am I really interested in explaining? Which are the central and which the peripheral aspects of the problem? How can the relevant theoretical claims be justified? What are the necessary and possible kinds of evidence available? Perhaps most important: Why do the project at all—what intellectual, political, and emotional commitments can motivate an arduous, perhaps years-long project? If you want to *do* something, *change* something—to further the cause of peace, of equality, of freedom, of justice—or achieve any other goal by means of your research, then you have an *action agenda*.

An action agenda must be translated into both theoretical and empirical questions if research is to be potentially relevant to social action or social policy.[4] Action can be taken without research, of course, but it is more likely to have the desired consequences if the actors have knowledge of historically analogous situations and the potential consequences of action. Research directly focused on policy alternatives, administrative implementation, or popular mobilization will keep the action agenda in the foreground of the research process.[5]

RESEARCH QUESTIONS AS ENTRY POINTS

The importance of asking the right research question is widely recognized, of course, but is seldom treated as a central issue in the research process.[6] Very few books on either methods or theory deal with how to formulate research questions. The problem—and the appropriate concepts to analyze it—may be assumed to emerge from the data.[7] Formulating research questions commits you to a lengthy process of intellectual work. Since a research project may last for several years, it is easy to flounder, go down dead ends, and become paralyzed with self doubt. Working out a way of thinking through the choices and some appropriate sequence of tasks will allow you to answer a research question with a comprehensive *argument*. The process of defining research questions is essential to learning how to think critically about the research literature in relation to your own work.

There are two types of research questions: theoretical and empirical. An *empirical* question is one that is answerable from some kind of *evidence* or data. It is tempting to start with an empirical question, because it grounds you in a search for concrete evidence without worrying too much about what the answer might mean or what its significance might be. That can be a rational strategy, if you ask yourself frequently about the general significance of the empirical question. A "data-driven" approach has the danger of totally absorbing your intellectual energies in the problems of gathering precise measures and analyzing them with the most technically sophisticated methodologies.

A *theoretical* question is one that derives from an unresolved general conceptual issue in the field. Examples include: "What explains the universality of gender differences, or of social stratification, or of power relations?" Note that these questions presuppose some empirical or cross-cultural evidence that gives rise to the theoretical issue. The question can also be framed in terms of a theory of gender, class, or power that will then lead to such a study.

Either kind of question can be the *entry point* into the problem. Let us take the topic of gender inequality as an example of a problem. Suppose you are interested in the general *problem* of equality between men and women. If you are starting with a concern to reduce the inequalities between the genders in the workplace and at home, you are starting with an *action agenda*. However, the action question "How can gender inequality be reduced?" cannot be answered as such but must be translated into both theoretical and empirical questions.

You then need to ask yourself: "What is interesting about that problem?" and "Why is that an important topic?" You can answer in several ways, each of which constitutes a different entry point into the research process. A research topic that implies an empirical entry point might be the answer "Because I want to find out if it is true that men have higher incomes than women, even among men and women with similar education and skills." A research topic that implies a theoretical entry point might be "Because I want to understand why the same pattern of gender inequality ("patriarchy") exists in both wealthy and poor societies, in both traditional and modern cultures."

If you have observed in your own experience that women do more housework than men, you may wonder what happens if the wife is working and the husband is not. The question "Do unemployed men do more housework than employed men?" is an *empirical entry point* into the problem. (See the discussion of *The Second Shift* by Arlie Hochschild in Chapter 5.)

But suppose you have been reading some "human capital" theory in economics and "gender identity" theory in women's studies. Your entry point might be these questions: "Under what conditions do marriages constitute a contract between parties exchanging domestic services for economic support? Under what conditions do marriages become intimate relationships in which gender identities are displayed and reinforced?" These questions represent *theoretical entry points*.

The theoretical frame for the empirical question need not be human capital or gender identity theory. The theoretical questions that give significance to empirical observations of gender differences in housework might be "Under what conditions do different organizations of family life produce different personalities in male and female children?" "What are the relationships among work, leisure, and emotional life in modern families?" or "What are the different ways in which labor power is reproduced in capitalist societies?"

Conversely, if your entry point is the theoretical question "What are the conditions under which human capital-versus-gender identity theories are valid?," a wide variety of kinds of evidence will be relevant, in addition to (or instead of) gender differences in housework. You might ask, "What are gender differences in promotion rates in different industries?" or "How do men and women calculate the relative attractiveness of potential sexual partners?" or "How frequently do male and female doctors interrupt male and female patients?" Such empirical studies might in different ways cast some light on the theoretical issues raised by human capital or feminist theories. After that, whatever knowledge you have gained of the conditions under which gender inequality is reproduced *may* allow you to generalize about possible paths of action to change that situation. Your research thus responds to your *action agenda*.

Formulating research questions therefore involves a sequence of *choices*. The vocabulary I offer is a strategy for narrowing down the problem through a process that might be called *exorcism*. If you are obsessed with a particular aspect of the problem but know that you do not have the time or other resources to deal with it, you have to acknowledge its importance to you, write up something that defines it as a future project, and file it away. You may be able to convince yourself to separate that aspect of the problem from those aspects you can handle and finish.

Deciding on questions is a *rolling* (or "iterative" or "recursive") process of raising a series of them, discarding some, reformulating others, and then thinking (assuming your entry point is empirical) about their theoretical implications. Similarly, if your entry point is theoretical, you need to think about their empirical implications. The process of defining the research questions does not end with the formulation of a hypothesis, as the traditional image of scientific method has it. Instead, to repeat, the process must be a *rolling* one— as you learn more, the questions shift, become redefined, sometimes more focused, sometimes more general. Research questions are always successive approximations, as you learn more about the phenomenon being analyzed. And, there is always a gap (or *slippage*) between the theoretical and empirical tracks— the evidence never quite fits the theoretical claims; the concepts never quite grasp the complexity of the empirical phenomenon.

Defining a problem requires *mapping* the intellectual territory, tracking footnotes through the jungle of relevant books and articles, asking friends and colleagues about key works to read. You start formulating possible research questions and think about both the theoretical and the empirical implications of asking different kinds of questions. Before committing yourself to a research question, there is no substitute for broad and even playful "reading around" in a subject. You may criticize the arguments in the literature, both theoretically and empirically, as part of the process of defining the relevant theoretical and empirical issues and establishing your own point of view.

Here are some examples of bad research questions: "Is Max Weber's concept of 'verstehen' more useful than Durkheim's concept of 'social fact'?" or "Is field research better than statistical analysis?" or "Should feminists criticize sociology for a masculine bias?" None of those questions poses an analytic *problem*, that is, a potential relationship between theoretical and empirical questions. Better questions would be: "Does Marx's concept of the 'dialectic' assume a social psychological process that Weber called 'verstehen'?" or "What kinds of research questions are more easily answered by field research than by statistical analysis?" or "Do standard research techniques of sampling and questionnaire design make unexamined assumptions about gender differences?"

Consider two questions of historical fact: "How many suicides were there in France on sunny as compared to rainy days in 1850?" and "Did Louis Bonaparte come to the palace on December 2, 1851?" These questions may well be significant if located in the context of a theoretical issue, as I demonstrate later in my discussion of works by Durkheim and Marx. But as posed, without such a theoretical context, the questions have no research significance. Durkheim wanted to refute climatic theories of suicide, so the correlation of the number of suicides with the weather was significant. Marx was concerned with the political role of Bonaparte in the dissolution of parliament, and his movements on a particular day might well have been important. But without such a context, the "facts" have no significance.

THEORETICAL AND EMPIRICAL TRACKS OF ANALYSIS

The most fruitful way to think about the research *process* is to constantly move back and forth from reflective musings about the larger implications of concepts and theories to quite concrete, grounded analyses of observations, evidence, or data. I call this process of moving back and forth from the theoretical to the empirical *tracks of analysis*, in the course of following different leads in the research literature and in the evidence.

Sometimes it is important to come down to earth by immersing yourself in the evidence. You may observe a group for months, take extensive notes from a historical archive, or collect extensive questionnaire data on a population. Buried in data, you feel for a while that you are making progress. However, at some point, without the guidance of theoretical questions, you may lose sight of your purpose. You may ask yourself: Why am I doing all these interviews, recording all these field notes, computing all these statistics? You have fled to empiricism. Empirical explorations should always be related to theoretical interpretation, but, given the inevitable gap between theory and evidence, it is difficult, albeit important, to learn how to move back and forth between the two tracks of analysis. A skilled research process does not follow automatically from orthodox scientific procedures—specify a hypothesis, generate data, test the hypothesis.

Sometimes it is important to float in the "clouds" of conceptual abstractions. You may, for example, compare and contrast Marx and Foucault, Weber and Giddens, or Durkheim and Parsons, with respect to the significance of power, rationality, or class for your problem. Then you may ask how these concepts are constructed in the "life-world" and read Habermas. Searching for fundamental theoretical arguments that frame your inquiry, you may lose sight of the original problem that motivated the project. You have fled to theoreticism. The way out of either empiricism or theoreticism is to see the two tracks of analysis as dialectically interrelated throughout the process of inquiry.

Moving back and forth from the clouds of theory to the ground of evidence is thus central to the craft of inquiry. Three points can be made. First, your entry point opens up a range of theoretical issues to the "spotlight" that focuses alternatively on the evidence and on the theoretical implications of the evidence. Although your theoretical and empirical interests may be well defined, in my experience that is seldom the case in the beginnings of inquiry.

Second, trying to merge theory and evidence results in confusion and paralysis. Theoretical concepts and assumptions should not be reduced to empirical procedures and evidence. Rich data and rigorous evidence cannot replace a coherent theoretical argument. Nor should the empirical implications of theory be avoided. Brilliant, logically consistent theoretical claims cannot substitute for evidence.

Third, explanation and description are different. A theoretical question is a search for an explanation of something and answers the question "Why." An empirical question asks for a description of an association or pattern of the events, behaviors, activities, beliefs, perceptions, and interests that constitute social life. An empirical association becomes evidence that is relevant to answering the theoretical question.[8]

Even quite similar questions will lead you down quite different theoretical and empirical paths. Frequently during the course of a research project you will find that you have generated or discovered evidence that answers a quite different question from the one that began the inquiry. Sometimes you may realize that a quite different theoretical question is the crucial one and requires quite different kinds of evidence.[9] These are both the hazards and the challenges of the process of social inquiry.

The theoretical and the empirical aspects of a problem are thus always in tension with each other. Abstract concepts never perfectly fit the complexity of reality. Evidence never contains its own explanation. Actual research practices contradict the classical positivist theory of knowledge that deductive theory predicts empirical support for an hypothesis and that inductively derived empirical generalizations confirm or falsify theories. In the course of a given project, the research question will be reformulated many times as either new evidence modifies the theoretical formulations or the revised theory calls for new empirical observations.[10] Theoretical and empirical questions are thus not logically distinct "inductive" or "deductive" types of inquiry. The skills embedded in the craft of social inquiry entail moving back and forth between theoretical and empirical tracks of analysis, neither merging them nor isolating them from each other.

Technical issues of measurement are (or should be) intrinsically connected to the underlying theory you are using or developing. As you define empirical measures, you are simultaneously specifying the content of the theoretical concepts. Every concept in each question you pose has both theoretical and empirical aspects. That is, the questions point "up" toward abstract bodies of related concepts and "down" toward relevant evidence of various kinds (itself located and defined by means of concepts). For example, the categories "man" and "woman" both contain theoretical assumptions about "sex" and "gender" and point toward observable behaviors or attributes that constitute the empirical referents of the categories.

Evidence ("empirical indicators") is always given significance by theory. Water, ice, and snow become the "same thing" (i.e., different forms of H_2O) by a theory of chemical structure and by empirical predictions of transformations of form under specified conditions. Goffman's theory of "total institutions" (see Chapter 5) constructs similarities among elite boarding schools, mental hospitals, prisons, armies, seminaries, and totalitarian political parties that were not apparent until the theory abstracted from the empirical differences. "Total institutions" as a theoretical concept allows generalizations across widely different empirically observed entities (in this case, those organizations that attempt to observe and control every aspect of behavior and also to construct new identities for their students, inmates, clients, members, adherents, or patients).

The point is that concepts classify similarities and differences as part of the building blocks of theoretical claims. The "research question" is a strategic formulation that allows you simultaneously to draw on concepts and assumptions from the clouds of theory to help organize an argument that is also grounded in evidence.

CONCLUSIONS

To summarize, a good research problem must be broken down into its two aspects in order to define both *theoretical* and *empirical* research questions. The *theoretical* question orients you toward the theoretical concepts within the relevant literature and frames the empirical question with a theoretical justification. Why did something happen? What explains what exists? What are the causes of an empirical association between observations or correlations among variables? Why did these events occur or these behaviors develop?[11] The *empirical* question directs you toward certain kinds of evidence that is necessary to answer the theoretical question. What happened? What is going on? What exists? What is the association between two events? What are the patterns of behavior?[12]

Formulating "research questions" helps you focus on one particular aspect of the set of issues that is of interest. In a substantial research project, there will be more than one; in a thesis or dissertation, there will be many, at least one per chapter, perhaps more. A general research question contains a number of more specific ones, each of which points toward a different aspect of the phenomenon you are interested in describing and explaining.

Once a research problem has been identified and a theoretical or empirical entry point chosen, you will face a set of choices about the kind of argument you will make in your project. Chapter 3 presents a basic map of three distinct but related paradigms of inquiry in sociology.

CHAPTER

3

The Construction of Arguments

﷼﷼

Theoretical claims and empirical generalizations are combined in three research traditions that I shall call "paradigms of inquiry": multivariate, interpretive, and historical. *Multivariate* and *interpretive* paradigms are pervasive in the social sciences. The *historical* paradigm has an ambiguous status; it is seen sometimes as combining the others, sometimes as having a special identity. In any particular work, one paradigm is usually in the "foreground" of the argument—the focus of both theory and evidence—and others are in the "background," providing rhetorical credibility or simply taken for granted. The construction of a multivariate argument about correlations of variables often assumes symbolically meaningful relations among the actors and also frequently takes for granted the specific historical context within which the data are collected; the construction of an interpretation of the symbolic meanings of action may take for granted both historical processes and underlying multivariate relations; the construction of a historical narrative may presuppose symbolic meanings and multivariate relations among events. Each paradigm of inquiry thus "borrows" from the others. Mixtures of paradigms maximize validity claims for an argument.

Each paradigm is associated with an epistemological assumption about the meaning of "theory" and "evidence."[1] Such seemingly neutral categories "theory," "evidence," and "explanation" themselves contain contested assumptions. Every theoretical claim, like any other aspect of social life, is located within a historical context, refers to or implies multivariate relations, and resonates with symbolic meanings. The relative importance of each of these aspects of a theoretical claim depends on the particular research question being asked (the "foreground" of the argument), the kinds of assumptions being made (the "background" of the argument), and the kinds of evidence being sought.

Some argue that each paradigm of inquiry entails a characteristic and unique combination of theoretical claims, methodological procedures, and empirical generalizations that cannot be translated into the language of other paradigms. This claim of "incommensurability" might be held by those who see art and science as completely different worlds of cognition. This is not the way in which "paradigm" is used in this book.

Others see paradigms of inquiry as constructed from the standpoint of the analyst, whose choice of assumptions and perspective is not constrained by standards beyond his or her preferences and prejudices. Still others see paradigms as constrained by universal and impersonal principles of logic and coherence. In this view, the correspondence of concepts to reality derives from objective and neutral criteria for drawing inferences from empirical claims.

My classification of paradigms, like the working vocabulary, is a device to clarify different ways of grasping social phenomena. There are multiple ways of extracting evidence from what is "out there" and assembling them into meaningful arguments. My goal is a pragmatic one: to help clarify the sequences of choices to be made as you thread your way carefully through a minefield of political ideologies, scholarly traditions, professional norms, and career necessities.

Theoretical claims—in order to be recognized as legitimate—must be couched in the language used by the members of the intellectual community who are the direct audience for the work: readers, students, colleagues. The indirect audience in the mind of the writer is those ancestors to whom she is giving homage as well as those antagonists whose arguments she is challenging. The audience being addressed normally shares some basic assumptions about the character of human motivations and human needs that underlie the concepts of the argument. Theoretical constructions are like any other social constructions in this sense, and the theorist is part of the social process that establishes the cultural meanings of the concepts being used to describe and explain the phenomenon.

Concepts, the building blocks of theories, also exist in a comparative and historical context, in which they are given particular meanings. A rigid and fixed definition that isolates a concept from its social context and from its history prevents you from seeing these relations. Concepts are also "historical" in the sense that they derive from intellectual traditions in which their meanings have become customary. Constraints on the use of concepts derive from the traditions that have given them certain meanings in the literature of the field. These meanings cannot be arbitrarily and idiosyncratically changed by the next user, precisely because their use resonates with their history and affects how the reader will understand them. At the time you are designing a research project, you cannot possibly be aware of all the historical and conceptual traditions that lie beneath and beyond your work, and yet they have enormous consequences.

Multivariate explanations must be distinguished from "causal" explanations. Because of the legitimacy of "normal," unitary science, the language of causality underlies the research practices of multivariate analysis. Linear correlation models, regression analyses, path analysis, and the other statistical tools of the multivariate paradigm are suffused with the metaphor of "cause." Quantitative correlations of two or more variables are frequently described with the words "effect of," "influence of," "determinant of," "factor in," or "explained by," as if the data entail causality, despite persistent warnings by statisticians and methodologists.[2] It cannot be emphasized too forcefully that causality is always a theoretical inference from an empirical association. There is *always* another possible explanation in addition to the one that seems to make sense of the observed relationship. Causal explanations can be framed in terms of interpretations of the motives and intentions of actors or in terms of the historical processes that explain outcomes, or they can be inferred from residual correlations after the application of statistical controls. But, regardless of the paradigm being used, causation cannot be inferred directly from the evidence.

The claim that multivariate analysis is the only "scientific" paradigm is part of a challenge to the importance of historical and interpretive paradigms. If multivariate analysis of many cases, employing a carefully specified model with reliable and valid indicators, were the *only* legitimate goal of social science, then this language would be warranted. But that is certainly not the case. Good work in social science answers many kinds of questions, within the several paradigms, as you shall see.

EVIDENCE AND THEORY

The distinction between theory and evidence is drawn from the positivist philosophical tradition, although my own theory of knowledge assumes that the distinction plays a variety of roles in different kinds of paradigms. Without evidence, research cannot be done. Even works that do not analyze any evidence are grounded in other works that do. The availability of relatively cheap and usable evidence decisively shapes the kinds of research questions that can be answered. Libraries, data archives, censuses, historical archives, records of community organizations, and government repositories are currently available to most students and scholars. As the society changes, the availability of evidence changes, not only in the codified form represented by libraries and computer files but also in archives of, for example, movies or videotapes. Once in existence, these sources of evidence become collective resources for future social research.

The state of research technology—computers, statistical programs for both quantitative and qualitative analysis, libraries of data, citation indexes—decisively affects the possible choices of different kinds of evidence to answer different questions. The widespread diffusion of particular statistical programs (SPSS and SAS in the United States, for example) has meant that certain kinds of statistics can be computed very easily and others are difficult. Because of the availability of this technical resource, students learn to think about—and even formulate—their research questions in ways that are amenable to treatment by the particular statistics available to them. Around the techniques is built an institutional infrastructure—research centers, data archive organizations, criteria for a publishable article—that makes certain kinds of empirical analyses not only available and relatively cheap but also legitimate. As someone said in another context, if a hammer is available, uses will be found for it. The result is that the theoretical assumptions about the social world that are built into the empirical techniques become embedded in the practices of research.

The very existence of data formatted in particular ways also affects the historical situation. A good example is the impact of census categories on the funding of social programs in urban ghettoes, where funding is earmarked for certain "groups" identified by the census ("ethnic," "racial"). As the historical situation changes (for example, if racial intermarriage increases), those empirical categories become increasingly erroneous measures of the underlying social realities. And the empirical categories themselves have enormous consequences. A person might find himself forced to identify as "black," for example, if he has a black father and a white mother.

When surveys are reported in newspapers or other media, people may redefine their conceptions of themselves and their behavior may change. An example is the Kinsey surveys of sexual behavior that reported higher incidences of certain forms of sexual behavior than were commonly believed. Kinsey may well have changed future sexual behavior by convincing people that their sexual preferences were neither weird nor abnormal.

A great variety of *primary* ("first order") evidence is used in the social sciences. Some of these sources of evidence are what might be called "found" or "natural," because the scholar does not create them: government archives, journals, newsreels, travelogues, census documents, memoirs, minutes of meetings, correspondence, dictionaries, posters, newspapers, videotapes, photographs, programs, poetry, novels, "texts" of all kinds. Others are "constructed" or "created": field notes of naturally occurring human activities in real-life situations, interviews, questionnaires, videotaped conversations. Other types of evidence are *secondary* sources: accounts of historical events by historians, an interpretation of primary sources by someone else, a data archive holding other scholars' surveys.

Evidence is sometimes produced by technically trained observers who record their observations in ethnographic studies, conduct sample surveys of populations, obtain life histories from individuals, or dig through archives to find textual evidence of intentions and actions. Sometimes evidence is generated by the routine activities of bureaucracies, where agents in different locations throughout the society report at regular intervals the incidence of certain types of social behavior: births, deaths, marriages, divorces, crimes, arrests, suicides, work, purchases. In censuses of the population, individuals voluntarily report the ages, incomes, and occupations of themselves and the persons living with them (the "family" or "household"). More mundane evidence of human behavior includes garbage, advertising, theater posters, and graffiti. All of these social phenomena—whether summarized as a statistical table, presented as images, or collected as a sequence of words—constitute evidence for theoretical claims.

At the lowest level of abstraction, a working consensus exists about "facts" that almost no one will disagree about. A few examples suffice to make the point: Rodney King was hit more than once by more than one policeman on March 26, 1991, in Los Angeles; black unemployment was higher than white unemployment in the United States in 1991; females earned less than males in the same occupations in the United States in 1990; per capita energy consumption was higher in 1997 in the United States than in India; the concept of bureaucracy is more important in Weber's theories than in Marx's.

The actual evidence necessary to establish the truth or falsity of such statements may be difficult to obtain, and clearly the categories contained in the statements are theory laden (occupation, earnings, energy, bureaucracy). But that their significance rests on theoretical inferences can hardly be disputed. Was Rodney King "beaten" or "subdued"? Does being a "parent" mean the same thing for men and for women? Does living in a "racially homogeneous urban area" mean the same thing for blacks as it does for whites? These are examples of what may seem like simple empirical issues of measurement that can become theoretically problematic as well as politically charged "facts."

Truth is inversely correlated with substantive importance. The more verifiable a statement is, the less significance it has. Thus, the evidence necessary to "prove" a theoretical claim can never be completely specified. General statements that have significance are at a level of abstraction where the potentially relevant facts necessary to assess significance are not only almost unlimited but almost always contested.

What you make of such evidence is always socially constructed, because no product of human activity explains itself. All of these forms of evidence presuppose a society within which they are symbolically meaningful. "Second-order" texts—the interpretations of the significance of the primary "objects"—are themselves an aspect of the evidence.

The legitimacy of different claims to constitute evidence is frequently debated. What constitutes a legitimate "field observation," for example? How much bias or sampling error can be tolerated in a survey? What is the relative credibility of different historical documents about an event? Disciplines develop operating procedures that guide inquiry, including rules about the quality and the relevance of evidence. The development of a consensus (a so-called "warranting community") on the validity of procedures that construct and interpret evidence is central to all paradigms of inquiry.

Evidence is also historically contingent. As a discipline improves technically, as knowledge accumulates, and as generalizations previously taken for granted are criticized, the standards of evidence required to support a given argument are raised. And, as the evidence produced by the society changes (e.g., videotapes, e-mail messages, audiotapes), so does the historical evidence available for social inquiry.

Each type of evidence must be converted to the appropriate form recognized by a theory in order to be defined as appropriate for generalization and explanation. A multivariate paradigm does not recognize as primary data any evidence that has not been converted into a "variable" (i.e., a count of some aspect of human behavior classified into attributes of some entity) and regarded as a sample from a defined population. Texts or narratives of events are primary for a historical paradigm but must be converted to variables by a coding process in order to be available for a multivariate analysis.

Similarly, an interpretive paradigm must be able to convert primary evidence into something culturally or symbolically meaningful. Take field notes from a participant observation of a natural site, for example. Within an interpretive paradigm, they are then seen as first-order evidence, although they have been gathered on the basis of selective principles and initial abstractions from the raw notes. Field notes can be redefined as "texts" and used to infer something about an event in order to be available for a historical paradigm. Similarly, field notes must be coded into variables that can then be associated with each other and with other variables in order to be amenable to multivariate analysis.

Take a historical text as an example. Tocqueville's nineteenth-century classic *Democracy in America* was originally a work of cultural interpretation, based on interviews, field notes, and documents. It has become a text that could be used as evidence within different paradigms: evidence for categories of interpretation used by French observers of America, evidence about the nature of American political culture in the nineteenth century, or raw data that could be coded for a quantitative study of the frequency of occurrence of the words "justice," "equality," and "democracy" as representative cultural symbols.[3]

Take a census table that contains quantitative data on occupation by gender for several decades as another example. Within the multivariate paradigm, it is direct evidence for the relationships of the variables in the table. Counts of attributes of different units of analysis (e.g., the categories of gender, occupation, and residence over time) are primary for multivariate paradigms but must be located in temporal context and interpreted as meaningful to actors in order to useful for other paradigms. Within an interpretive paradigm, the table is primary evidence for the ways in which bureaucratic institutions construct categories, such as gender, that shape thinking and perceptions. Within a historical paradigm, the table is primary evidence for the changing production of data by the state to be used to help form public policies on affirmative action, for example.[4] Theoretical definitions thus *constitute* relevant evidence in different ways for the different paradigms, although they do not create the evidence. For one paradigm, a particular kind of evidence may be in the foreground, and background evidence is reinterpreted in order to become theoretically relevant.

HUMAN AGENCY

How can human agency be restored to theoretical constructions of social life? We know from the sociology of science that what we see in the physical world depends on what we are looking for, on the categories we bring to it. "Theorizing" is an activity, a conscious human process, but "evidence" (or data, or observations) sounds like *things*, like entities that exist apart from human activity and social processes. A botanist literally "sees" different things in a leaf than a lay person. If we are interested in whether or not a plant needs water, we may only see the wilted leaves, not the tiny worms covering the leaves. The point is that there are many aspects to a concrete object, situation, or event, aspects that are grasped only by those with an active interest in some of those aspects. Particular aspects are singled out by *categories*. Some categories are concrete: worms or wilt, or gender. Some are abstract, as when we look at a census table on occupations and incomes and see either "social mobility" or "class inequality" or when a botanist sees different types of "striations."

When should you gather or create new evidence yourself? C. Wright Mills's injunction in *The Sociological Imagination* (1959) was to assess the potential benefits of possible lines of empirical inquiry before actually doing the research. Mills emphasized that empirical "excursions" are tempting because they seem to be a way of paving the path of inquiry, thus easing the way through the jungle of interpretations. But he also warned that concreteness can be illusory, since the path may lead nowhere. Piles of empirical findings accumulate along the way, but they may have little relevance to the theoretical destination. The reason a particular theory is chosen at the moment to explain the evidence has cultural and historical roots: professional fashion, political correctness, political incorrectness, tribal loyalties, and—last but, one hopes, not least—a belief that the evidence supports the theory.

With these preliminary observations about the general relationship between evidence and theories, I move on to the ways in which different paradigms construct theoretical claims and empirical generalizations.

FOREGROUND MULTIVARIATE ARGUMENTS

The sheer empirical power of multivariate descriptions of social structure and its changes gives this paradigm some of its fundamental importance as a cornerstone of modern social science. A foreground multivariate argument assumes that a society is composed of relatively autonomous subsystems (or "units of analysis"): individuals, communities, families, states, markets, organizations, ethnic groups, genders, international systems. The attributes of these units of analysis are described as "variables."

The multivariate aspect of a theoretical claim is the model of the measured and unmeasured factors believed to explain a particular social phenomenon. Theories are clusters of factors that allow you to construct empirical "measures" of the independent, dependent, intervening, and control variables that constitute the theory.

Variables (something that varies or differs, like gender, education, income, existence of democracy, or amount of housework done) are classified into several types. "*Dependent*" (or "response," or "outcome") variables are those that are to be explained by another variable. "*Independent*" (or explanatory, or causal) variables are those that, one's theory argues, explain the dependent variable. If being male or female is correlated how much housework you do, or if the wealth of a country is associated with whether or not it is democratic, you can argue on the basis of a theory and an appropriate time order (the cause must precede the effect) that there is a valid relationship between the two variables. The empirical correlation, once again, does not itself establish causation; it provides only a basis for a theory of causal mechanisms that has empirical support or, even better, experimental controls.

"*Intervening*" variables theorize about the mechanisms that explain *why* the independent and dependent variables are related. Do men do less housework than women because of traditional sex roles or because women are exchanging their household services for economic support? Are richer countries more likely to be democratic than poorer countries because richer countries have better educated populations and better educated populations are more tolerant of political differences? Or do people in richer countries simply have more to lose from a dictatorship? Such "three-variable" hypotheses are the core explanatory model for a multivariate paradigm, regardless of how much the theory is elaborated by additional variables or by complex statistical models. Note that the inferences can be tested empirically. Do women who work and thus provide an equal share of financial support for the household do less housework? Do women with a feminist ideology do less housework? Do men with an egalitarian philosophy do more housework? For the other example, are better-educated persons indeed more tolerant of political differences than less-well-educated persons?

"*Control*" variables are those aspects of the societal environment that you attempt to "hold constant" or that specify the conditions under which the presumed relationship between independent and dependent variable holds. The relationship between gender and housework may be true only in modern societies where both men and women are free to sell or exchange their labor and also legally free to marry and divorce. The relationship between wealth and democracy may be found only in those societies in which political competition is limited to issues that do not challenge the rights of private property.

"Interaction effects" exist when the association of one variable ("X") to another ("Y") depends on (is correlated with) the value (or "state," or "condition") of a third variable ("Z"). Note how the seemingly neutral analytic language contains implicit assumptions about causality.

Once the variables are theoretically defined, the next step is the definition of empirical indicators, the development of measures, and the gathering of primary data or the analysis of secondary data. Data can be either quantitative or qualitative, although the language of the multivariate paradigm often presumes quantitative measures. At this point in the research process, the problems usually dealt with in "methods" courses arise: What population are you analyzing (white, middle-class households? all Western societies?). How do you construct an appropriate sample, or are you dealing with the universe of all cases? What are the reliability and the validity of the measures of housework (hours per day?

Per week? Is cutting the lawn housework? Repairing windows?)? Is democracy best measured by the existence of a party system? Free speech? A free press? For how many years must they have existed before a society should be labelled "democratic"?

Technical issues of measurement are connected to your underlying theory of gender relations or of democracy. As you define empirical measures, you are simultaneously specifying the content of the theoretical concepts. Every concept in each question I have posed has both theoretical and empirical aspects. That is, the questions point "up" toward abstract bodies of related concepts and "down" toward relevant evidence of various kinds (itself located and defined by means of concepts).

The point can be illustrated by posing an empirical question: Is the relationship between the number of hours worked per week by women and by men inside and outside the home correlated with whether the husband or the wife (or both) work for pay? How is the relationship between gender and housework "affected by" (with no causal inference intended) the level of family income, education, and number of young children? The statistical tables showing the interrelationships of all of these variables may allow you to say something about power in intimate relationships or how family structures are related to the economy.

If the foreground standpoint is that of a search for multivariate relations, then symbolic meanings and historical processes tend to appear within a constrained multivariate rhetoric of explanation. That is, not only are the independent and dependent variables assumed to be objective and external ("social facts" in the Durkheimian sense), but cultural and symbolic meanings embedded in social interactions are regarded as objective, as another set of "factors" to be taken into account in constructing an explanation. Alternatively, sometimes subjective meanings are regarded as less important than material and measurable factors.

Multivariate paradigms treat different kinds of meanings very differently, depending on how close the meaning is to actual behavior. An entire literature exists on the problem of unmeasured but presumably correlated variables and problems of validity and reliability of measures. Much of this work analyzes such subjective variables as "prejudice," "interests," "values," "aspirations," "purposes," or "perceptions" of almost anything. Because of the importance of measurement in this paradigm, there is pressure to develop replicable and comparable (by whatever criterion) empirical indicators of the theoretical variables.

The historical situations from which the data are generated may be seen either as "noise" (accidental circumstances that affect multivariate relations in random or irrelevant ways) or as a different kind of factor, to be taken into account in the research design as the "comparative context." Historical processes may be seen as a way of looking at how the variables change over time ("time series analysis"), as exogenous factors that can be ignored, or simply as the theoretically irrelevant conditions under which the data were gathered. Historical situations can, after all, be described in terms of types and structures and compared with respect to their major characteristics. Those who construct theoretical claims about multivariate relations usually subsume historical processes under a theory of general explanatory mechanisms.

Concepts are assumed to designate a fixed meaning (as well as the chunk of reality to which it refers) for a particular community of analysts. The aspect of reality that the concept comes to represent becomes associated with the concept in a way that becomes socially accepted. What is perceived is then translated by the brain into the concept. You see an "apple" and immediately think the word. This is the "representational" (or "positivist") aspect of a concept: Its meaning is found in its measures—the observations of the world that it represents. Those concepts that are not on the contested frontiers of social inquiry, those that form the unquestioned vocabulary of research practices, have this representative character, *until* some theoretical issue arises that calls this aspect of the concept into question.

The development of standardized and widely used measures is a decisive advance in a multivariate paradigm of inquiry. When measures of such concepts as GDP (Gross Domestic Product), or authoritarianism, or alienation, or democracy, become part of the established repertoire of concepts linked to empirical measures, a tool for inquiry has been created that is then available to the community of researchers. That community has come to accept a certain empirical indicator as adequately capturing the underlying theoretical concept. In the natural sciences, the equivalent is a consensus that a certain piece of equipment measures what it is supposed to measure (although case studies of natural science suggest how risky these assumptions are). A measure agreed on by a community of social scientists reflects the outcome of long debates that have been temporarily concluded, allowing research to proceed on the basis of assumptions about stable connections among theories, methods, and evidence (i.e., an established paradigm).

Other examples within sociology are occupational prestige scores (based on surveys that ask respondents to rank a list of many occupations in order of prestige), SES (or socioeconomic status, based on questions about income, education, and occupation), segregation indexes for cities (based on measures of the numbers of census tracts with particular proportions of whites and nonwhites). An even better example from psychology is IQ, still retaining its hold on testing and popular belief despite severe criticism from scholars who have demonstrated that "intelligence" comprises different and quite unrelated capacities. That such measures have been rightly criticized is irrelevant to my point that institutional mechanisms exist to establish and sustain empirical measures.

The generic empirical question for the multivariate paradigm is "Does X regularly occur with Y?" where X and Y are any activity, event or, behavior that varies. The generic theoretical question is "Is this relationship explanatory?" Or, "What are the antecedent, intervening, and consequent [feedback] mechanisms that produce and sustain the relationship between X and Y?"

FOREGROUND INTERPRETIVE ARGUMENTS

Interpretive arguments are constructed from theories about social interactions that become symbolically meaningful for human actors. Such arguments were dominant in the old "Chicago school" of urban ethnography and community studies, and they remain central to the "symbolic interaction" and "social construction" traditions in sociology and cultural anthropology. Such foreground arguments combine an empirical focus on the language and gestures of human interactions with a theoretical concern with their symbolic meanings and how the ongoing social order is negotiated and maintained.

Other kinds of arguments within this paradigm focus on ideologies, discourses, and cultural frameworks. A combination of theoretical assumptions about the social construction of meaning and empirical evidence drawn from ethnographic field work or participant observation is the normal raw material for an interpretive argument. Other kinds of evidence, including texts, surveys, documents, interviews, and even experiments, can be used to construct the symbolic meanings of social worlds or the cultural significance of discourse or ideology.

In many interpretive arguments the reader is shown the world of the actors so that he can understand their life "from within." When you read W. F. Whyte's *Street Corner Society*, you are with Doc and his companions on the streets of the city, fighting with the police, dealing with the social workers. When you read any of the older classics of the Chicago school of sociology, such as *The Hobo, The Taxi Dance Girl, The Ghetto,* and *The Gold Coast and the Slum,* you experience new social worlds.[5] Erving Goffman's *The Presentation of Self in Everyday Life*, on Scottish crofters, and William Kornblum's *Blue Collar Community*, which focuses on steel workers at work and home in South Chicago, are more recent additions to that genre.[6] Arlie Hochschild's *The Second Shift* (1989) tells the story (see Chapter 5) of how twelve different couples negotiate the balance among work, housework, and child care. Hochschild provides "thick" descriptions of each family and also presents in an appendix (as background data) the statistical studies that estimate the actual numbers of hours done by men and women in different family situations. The reader shares vicariously in the lives of the individuals and groups depicted in vivid detail.

Arguments within an interpretive paradigm explain by reconstructing the social processes of interaction that constitute the detailed texture of social life. It was not necessary for the Protestants feverishly accumulating capital to be aware of the consequences of their actions for Weber's interpretation of the meaning and consequences of their behavior to have analytic cogency. Goffman, to take another example, wants to "isolate some of the basic frameworks of understanding available in our society for making sense out of events and to analyze the special vulnerabilities to which these frames of reference are subject" (*Frame Analysis*, p. 10). That is, he wants to show the difference between perceiving "what is going on here" in a straightforward manner (a conversation, a lecture, a circus, a holiday) and perceiving it as a joke, a dream, an accident, a mistake, a deception, a misunderstanding, or a performance.

All these aspects of human experience can be interpreted from an identical stream of reported events. The methodological issue is how the observer can know whether "what is going on" is a dream, a joke, or a "real" conversation. (At the postmodern extreme, the difference is either irrelevant or nonexistent.)

In another book, Goffman explores the "individual's capacity to acquire, reveal and conceal information" (*Strategic Interaction*, p. 4). Thus, "theory" is used not only to reveal what actors think is going on but also shows that what they think matters in understanding how society functions. Whatever happens at higher levels of conceptual aggregation ("the family," "government," "corporations") cannot be divorced from these basic interpersonal strategies for making sense of the world. Failing to make these links reifies social constructions.

Foreground interpretive arguments may take into account both multivariate relations and historical processes but reinterpret them. By taking on the actors' perspective, the researchers assume that the actors have an understanding of the factors affecting their actions, whether personal conflicts, economic interests, or the possibility of arrest. Understandings (how actors "define the situation") of such factors influencing action are often partial, but they are nonetheless what actors take into account in their decisions to take a course of action. Actors, of course, differ considerably in their understanding of what constrains their actions. And actors may also take into account the historical context—the antecedent circumstances, the past motives and beliefs of other actors and *their* understandings. Historical processes tend to be foreshortened in interpretive arguments, however, reduced to their impact on the consciousness of contemporary actors.

The definition of the situation does not, however, override the actual situation out there. As Goffman puts it, "Defining the situation as real certainly has consequences, but these may contribute only marginally to the events in progress; in some cases only a slight embarrassment flits across the scene in mild concern for those who tried to define the situation wrongly. All the world is not a stage . . ." (*Frame Analysis*, p. 1). People construct their conceptions of reality within a community of meaning constituted through interaction.

Thus, interpretive arguments include those that attempt to get at meanings that are "beneath" or "beyond" the consciousness of actors. Language and a wide variety of texts carry cultural associations and meanings that actors as users of symbols are not fully aware of. Language, in particular, obviously cannot be reduced to interactions among individuals and how they negotiate communication. Institutions are thus not outside the process of social construction of meaning but are vital elements in the social processes that constrain and shape meanings. Although the constraints and the particular historical situation in which they exist may be external "forces" from the standpoint of human actors, they are also the target of time-consuming and costly strategic estimation. Cognitive "shortcuts" develop that Pierre Bourdieu has called a "habitus."[7] They operate in scientific inquiry, as well as in every other human activity.

Within the interpretive paradigm, theoretical claims are viewed as the language used by members of a scientific community to share ideas about a social situation being investigated, the conceptual constructions that explain "what is going on here," since theory is constituted by the general ideas that people use to communicate with each other. Partly because of this view of theory, interpretive paradigms are likely to be presented in more personal terms, taking the theorist herself into account as part of the presentation of the argument.

The symbols used by the community or the social world being studied constitute part of the language being interpreted, and the "translation" from one language to another is always problematic. Concepts are negotiated in their actual usages in the process of communication between any set of social actors, including scientific observers.

The theoretical assumptions of ethnographic descriptions are frequently left implicit, as, for example, in W. F. Whyte's *Street Corner Society* (1943) or Elliott Liebow's *Tally's Corner* (1967).[8] The rich descriptions of white and black street corner life contain many assumptions about the conditions under which friendship, loyalty, personal conflict, and family responsibility develop and can be sustained. Traditional anthropology assumed a stance of scientific objectivity, in works by Margaret Mead, Bronislaw Malinowski, and Ruth Benedict, among many others.[9] Interpretations of observations of other cultures were made as if the observer were a neutral and objective presence. The presuppositions of such anthropology have been exposed as social constructions by the new critical anthropology. On the cover of James Clifford and George Marcus's collection, *Writing Culture* (1986), there is a picture of an anthropologist sitting in the doorway of a hut writing something (presumably his field notes), while a native is silently watching him from behind.[10] The Western, white anthropologist is seen as actively constructing an image of "primitive" culture, while—in the published report—maintaining an aura of objectivity and neutrality.

Regarding the interpretive paradigm as the only possible one assumes that the world can be understood only through the symbolic meanings of action and their continuous renegotiation in the situations in which individuals interact. History has no meaning except insofar as it is represented in the cultural significance of ongoing interactions. Causation is found only in the intentions and the perceptions of actors about the consequences of action.

The generic empirical question is "What did (any human behavior, experience, activity) mean to the participants?" The generic theoretical question is "How can we understand and explain those meanings?" or, more elaborate, "How do the actors' understandings and interpretations of what goes on in social interactions be shown to constitute cultural identities or social worlds?" The answers to such questions do not necessarily entail appeals to objective external causes outside the cultural symbols available to both the actor and those doing the interpreting of action.

FOREGROUND HISTORICAL ARGUMENTS

Historical arguments analyze specific historical processes that explain a sequence of contingent events occurring at specific times and in named places. Such arguments combine an empirical focus on events located in specific times and places ("conjunctures") with theoretical inferences about the situational context and the entities (sometimes called the "totality") within which the events have significance. The typical evidence for historical arguments is drawn from texts, documents, and artifacts from the past. Historical arguments constitute a distinctive paradigm only in the field of "history," partly because of the arbitrary separation of that discipline from the other social sciences.

Certain sequences of events are dramatic and well known, even momentous, yet do not readily lend themselves to multivariate analysis—the French Revolution of 1789, the American Revolution of 1776, the American Civil War of 1861–1865, the collapse of the Soviet Union in 1991, the trial of O. J. Simpson in 1995, and the "sixties," to pick only a few. Attempts to reconceptualize these unique sequences of events as instances of a general class of phenomena ("revolutions," "regime transformations," "criminal trials," "cultural movements") in order to be able to classify their attributes as "variables" and thus incorporate them into multivariate arguments may miss their essential features *and* their unique social consequences. Systematic statements of empirical covariation are of course important, but they do not replace a complex description and explanation of a particular historical totality.

The appeal of a historical paradigm is seen in such examples as Robert Caro's *The Power Broker*, a narrative of the life of Robert Moses, the "master builder" of New York City's bridges, parks, and playgrounds and a consummate politician and bureaucratic entrepreneur. Taylor Branch's *Parting the Waters* tells the story of Martin Luther King's progress from a boy in a small Southern town to a public symbol of the black liberation movement of the 1960s. David Halberstam's *The Best and the Brightest* is the tale of what happened to some of the men and women who served in two Washington administrations.[11]

In all these books, there is a red thread of narrative—events are located in time and space, particular people are named and act, around a unifying theme: New York city and state politics, the civil rights movement, the Kennedy and Johnson administrations. Although the texture of a social world may be evoked (Tammany Hall, a black Southern church, the Democratic Party in the South, the political circles around Lyndon Johnson), the core purpose of the narrative is not to convey the essential qualities of a social world. Nor is the purpose to develop generalizations about the conditions under which electoral coalitions, bureaucratic entrepreneurship, elite ruptures, religious movements, or effective organizational decision making occur. Every historical narrative presupposes some knowledge about and makes assumptions about social structures and the conditions under which certain events are likely, but such abstract generalizations are not the goal of the argument. None of these works (like many others that might be mentioned) is "purely" or "only" a description of sequences of events, but the narrative is in the foreground.

The analysis of such events, as practiced by either "historical sociology" or "social history" (the disciplinary boundaries are both institutionally significant and intellectually relevant) combines a search for systematic patterns and an understanding of how contingent and converging events create different outcomes or make alternative scenarios plausible. For example, suppose the research question is: Did the Soviet Union disappear in December 1991 because of internal economic crisis, military pressure from the United States, conflict within the Communist Party, or growing political dissent? As phrased, that question could be either a multivariate or a historical one. A historical answer would look for the complex interrelationships of each "factor," seen as summarizing a distinctive set of events in time and place. "Economic crisis," for example, might be indicated by massive public debt at all levels of government, by dropping productivity in major industrial sectors, by ever lower standards of living. Inferring that such a crisis was a factor in the disappearance of the Soviet Union presupposes the conclusions of comparative studies of "similar" events, but in important respects there *are* no similar events. Although this is the apparent paradox of a historical paradigm, the opposite is true of multivariate argument: It ignores the distinctive features of each case from which data are generalized.

For a multivariate analysis of this case, you would have to find "comparable" cases of regime changes, governmental transformations, or system crises. Note that each of these labels frames the disappearance of the Soviet Union in different theoretical terms, and might lead to a different selection of "comparable" events.

To take another example, you might argue that the sequence of unique events that preceded the French Revolution and that traditionally are regarded as "causes" of the Revolution (the fall of the Bastille, for example) were largely irrelevant to the outcome, because the events that led to the political and economic crisis started decades before the Revolution. Those factors (or "processes") could be summarized as a complex combination of a tax-exempt nobility, declining agricultural productivity, the growing cost of war, chaotic political leadership, and a disaffected populace.

Sequences of events can thus be theorized as processes that happen simultaneously and converge at given historical moments. The convergence of separate processes is contingent, and not predictable, but each process is potentially explainable by itself. That is, economic crisis, a peasant rebellion, elite disaffection, and an emerging social movement can be thought of as simultaneous but relatively autonomous processes that happened to converge in 1789 in France. Each of these "processes" could be regarded as a set of "variables," if converted to a multivariate argument. The foreground concern is to integrate all of these processes into a complex narrative. In a crucial sense, "measuring" an event or process as if it were separable from its historical context denies the essential "historicity" of the phenomenon.

Within historical arguments, theoretical claims are seen as historically developed concepts used to produce social knowledge under certain conditions. If you are committed to historical explanations and thus use the language of contingency, situations, circumstances, or conjunctures, you are more likely to accept the importance of the interaction of multiple processes that combine to explain a specific outcome. Such a combination may or may not be unique to the particular time and place. And you are likely to assume that their symbolic meanings to the actors will be found embedded in your narrative of the important events that together lead to the outcome.

How unique are historical events? *All* evidence is ultimately "unique," in the sense that at the most concrete level it is based on records or observations of time- and place-specific actions of human beings from which we generalize and abstract. The concept of "economic development," for example, is a very abstract generalization from the actual activities of human beings working, producing, saving, buying, investing, trading, and so on, aggregated as a characteristic of all the persons living in a given territory. The data from which a number called the "1991 Gross Domestic Product of the United States" is calculated are all ultimately derived from the concrete activities of millions of human beings. Similarly, there is no such *thing* as "war," "capitalism," "the state," or "revolution." Human beings do many different things: kill each other, produce goods for sale, write proclamations, march with each other. Almost every general concept can be reduced to the individual level.[12]

In this primordial sense, we all must be "methodological individualists." Human activities in specific times and places—recorded, told, leaving residual traces—are the only evidence we have to answer any research question. All social processes, events, and historical systems are thus unique. World capitalism, the War on Poverty, the Holocaust, the Second World War, the election of Nelson Mandela as president of South Africa: Each in some respects is "one of a kind." But also unique is the meal you had at McDonald's last night, the fight with your wife or boyfriend last week, or the house you lived in as a child. Analogies can be drawn with other "similar" events, of course, and the very categories ("capitalism," "war," "election," "restaurant," "intimate relationship") used to characterize these events assume that similar processes exist. Comparisons in order to make historical arguments are therefore inevitably approximate. We can certainly deploy plausible arguments about the causes of unique historical events, but they cannot be reduced to linear multivariate measures without losing the substantive richness of the historical phenomenon.

Like narrative history, historical sociology is concerned with describing and analyzing temporality and events. But it also seeks to explain outcomes generated by the interplay among social structures, social processes, and contingent, unpredictable events. Unlike narrative history, moreover, historical sociology tries to provide meaningful theoretical explanations for the temporal patterns, continuities, and ruptures discovered in human history over the long term.

The generic empirical question when constructing a foreground historical argument is, most succinctly, "What happened, there and then?" or "What were the significant events, X, Y, and Z? To whom, where, and when did they occur, and in what sequence?" The generic theoretical question is "What explains what happened?" or "What were the circumstances, the processes, or the situations that provide the explanatory contexts for these events?"

In conventional historiography, the goal is to construct a narrative of events selected for their significance with respect to one hypothetical explanation of "what happened." Although evidence is usually derived from historical texts, documents, and other records, the kinds of evidence usually central to other paradigms (surveys or field notes, for example) can be analyzed as texts that document contingent events and processes within a historical context.

Although contemporary historical arguments lack the distinctive philosophical foundations of the other two paradigms, it is still practiced as an operating paradigm. For, unlike the multivariate and the interpretive paradigms, whose research is grounded in the philosophical traditions of logical positivism and phenomenology respectively, historical arguments are produced without an underlying theory of knowledge (i.e., epistemology).[13]

As practiced, historical sociology and social history are adrift from their former moorings in the philosophy of history. History seems more diversely grounded epistemologically, at least as compared to the other two paradigms. That historical sociology lacks a common epistemology and methodology is confirmed by the variety of methodologies contained in Theda Skocpol's anthology of influential historical sociologists.[14] There you encounter interpretive and positivist-multivariate approaches as well as holism, evolutionism, structuralism, and developmentalism. While the remnants of an integrated philosophy of history are evident, even influential on some of the historical sociologists evaluated there, one searches in vain for a unifying epistemological basis for the practice of historical sociology.

What happened to the philosophy of history once so prominent in historical discourse? As a body of theory, the philosophy of history originated as an intellectual project of Enlightenment philosophers during the seventeenth and eighteenth centuries, a project that attempted to discover in the social world the same systemic laws that they believed were being discovered about the natural world. Philosophers like Vico (1668–1744), Kant (1724–1804), Herder (1744–1803), Condorcet (1743–1794), and Hegel (1770–1831) provided comprehensive accounts of human history couched in the metaphysical and speculative language of laws and inevitable progress.[15] Typically, either linear or cyclical patterns of historical progress toward a valued end point were explained by the unfolding of teleological final causes or immanent forces such as the Deity, reason, natural law, or evolution.

Historical sociology's commitment to macrosociological concepts, units, and processes reflects the early modern European project of nation-state formation. The preferred units of analysis (the subjects of historical change and the objects of inquiry) were peoples, nations, and civilizations. The cyclical and/or linear movements of civilizations occurred through distinct stages of change in such a way that the rise and decline of peoples and nations could be compared according their position on a continuum of progress toward some ideal end. Hegel, for example, argued that history was a rational process whereby the absolute spirit (reason) expressed as an idea of freedom manifested itself in distinct historical stages: Oriental, Greek, Roman, and, finally, Germanic civilization. Further, the progressive realization of this historical evolution was manifested in the national state.

In the nineteenth century, such metaphysical philosophies of history were rejected in favor of positivist science (August Comte) and Darwinian theories of social evolution. Though theories of social evolution were rejected by Weber, they influenced Marx's dialectical theory of capitalist development and, later, Talcott Parsons's neo-evolutionary theory of structural differentiation and functional integration. What all of these philosophies of history share is the assumption that historical processes are moving toward a final end, one defined by the beliefs or ideologies of the contemporary author, looking backward.

To return to the lacunae in the historical paradigm, the theories and methods of modern science have devastated the metaphysical reasoning underlying the philosophy of history's search for an all-embracing explanation for historical change or for the "stages" of historical development. To be sure, because ideas of the past influence the minds of the living, elements of the various philosophies of history do influence historical sociological inquiry. Indeed, communities of scholars are researching "puzzles" defined by the Enlightenment theory of progress, Marxism's dialectical materialism and many forms of social evolutionism. But historical sociology still lacks a distinct epistemology, comparable to positivism and phenomenology, that can ground its theoretical claims.

However, the rejection of teleological historicism does not indicate the failure of a historical paradigm as a set of research *practices*. If anything, the seemingly more solid epistemological foundations for multivariate and interpretive arguments can become—particularly for the former—a dead weight, making it difficult to recognize dynamic, changing aspects of social life. Despite their contradictory or absent epistemological foundations, works with foreground historical arguments are being continually produced.

THE DIVORCE OF THEORY FROM EVIDENCE

As may be clear by now, I am limiting my discussion to those practitioners who make explicitly problematic the relationship of theory and evidence. "Abstracted empiricism" and "abstracted theoreticism" are not my concern here. Each paradigm has its version of this division.

Within a multivariate paradigm, theory divorced from evidence becomes abstract "systems" theory or "structural functionalism," specifying the "requirements" for the functioning of a social system. The theorist Talcott Par-

sons is the best exemplar of this intellectual tendency. Evidence divorced from
theory becomes what C. Wright Mills called "abstract empiricism" or, in the
contemporary dismissal, mere "number crunching." "Theory" is reduced to
statements of the relationships between empirical indicators.

Theory divorced from evidence within the interpretive paradigm (i.e., without references to concrete experiences of human beings in interaction or to
cultural themes and symbols) is found in phenomenological philosophy (e.g.,
the works of Alfred Schutz and Maurice Merleau-Ponty, or George Herbert
Mead). In more contemporary versions, it is found in postmodern discourse
analysis and deconstruction, where the world disappears into texts. Evidence
divorced from theory is a descriptive statement of a social world, social situation, or social interaction, in the words of the actors.

When evidence on a sequence of events is divorced from a theoretical claim,
a historical argument becomes a description of unique events: people, places,
actions. Narrative historiography is the self-conscious method of this theory,
privileging the sequences of actions of individuals in specific times and places,
but not attempting to theorize or explain them abstractly. Extreme historicism
of this kind is no longer a legitimate contemporary practice of scholars.

Theory divorced from evidence in a historical argument is a version of
"structuralism." Laws of social development are postulated, and individuals become the "bearers" or agents of historical forces. Conjunctures are contained
within and can be predicted by the convergence of multiple historical forces
that in principle can be known. The contingent and open-ended possibility of
change and historically new social forms is denied. Subjective meanings are seen
as the bias of the observer. Causation is embedded in the historical forces that
over-determine the outcome of events. This structuralist view of history is also
obsolete.

CONCLUSIONS

Three possible ways of combining theoretical claims and empirical generalizations from various kinds of evidence in answering research questions have been
labeled *paradigms of inquiry*. Multivariate, interpretive, and historical paradigms
can be in the foreground or in the background of a particular work. Since every
empirical generalization simultaneously is located within a historical context,
implies multivariate relations, and is suffused with symbolic meanings, the three
paradigms are mutually dependent. Each paradigm presupposes, and in some
sense is dependent on, the others. Table 1 gives the working vocabulary of the
three paradigms.

It must be emphasized once again that these are pragmatic distinctions.
Sometimes a field study develops some hypotheses that can be tested by means
of systematic samples of individuals or organizations. Conversely, some data
(e.g., census data on the relationship between divorce rates and marriage type)
can be given qualitative significance and insight by life histories and ethnogra-

TABLE 1
The Working Vocabulary of Paradigms of Inquiry

	Multivariate	Interpretive	Historical
Micro level	Behavior	Symbols	Events
Macro level	Structure (system)	Culture (interactions)	Totality (context)
Known through	Data	Observation	Evidence
Source	Behavior	Field notes	Texts
Unit of analysis	Variables	Interactions	Events
Result	Explanation	Insight, understanding	Narrative account
Observer	Neutral	Participant	Spectator
Core metaphor	Cause	Meaning	Process
Method	Correlated measures	Ethnography, discourse analysis	Historiography
Generic research question	What factors explain an outcome?	How are meanings constructed in interaction and in social worlds?	What processes lead to events?

phies of particular families. Histories of particular groups, events, or societies can sometimes be systematically compared, with historical attributes reduced to variables.

More generally, multivariate models have the appearance of externality (in Durkheim's sense of a "social fact") and of objectivity. They seem to be, in the particular form such abstractions take, external forces that act upon individuals. "Variables" presuppose human capacities to extract meaning and calculate courses of action and are abstracted from the historical particularity of each situation.

An ethnographic account of the symbolic meanings of an interaction presupposes assumptions about the historical context in which those interactions occur and also a set of structural factors that shaped and defined the circumstances under which the interaction occurred.

Finally, a narrative of historical events presupposes a comparison that provides an implicit theoretical rationale for the construction of the particular narrative account. A historical narrative also presumes symbolic interconnections between the individuals participating and "constructing" that event.

An explicit "foreground" argument of one kind thus presupposes assumptions about arguments (both theoretical claims and empirical generalizations) about the other kinds. The difference between a foreground multivariate argument and others can be summarized as follows. The former seeks variations within a *system* of interrelated variables. The unit of analysis and the variables must be assumed not to change during the period of measurement, and they must be free of time and place in order to exhibit the power of abstraction. That is, "liberalism-conservatism" (for example) must be assumed to retain the same meaning across all individual measures as a concept and construct, but it can vary among them. In a foreground interpretive argument, the meaning of a political attitude such as "liberalism" is constantly being renegotiated in the course of social action. Foreground historical arguments add the time dimension—the meanings change over time, as structural arrangements are transformed.

The analytic distinctions I have offered should not mislead you about how imprecise and intuitive the "methods" for moving from theoretical concept to empirical evidence are, particularly in the construction of multivariate arguments, which claim the most scientific generality. There are no rules for agreeing on the relationship between concept and empirical indicator. How "far" from a concept should an indicator be? When concepts and indicators are "too close" (as when "age" is indicated by the number of years one has lived, or "gender" by whether one is a male or a female), there is no significant difference between concept and indicator.

There is also the persistent problem of tautology. What is a "democracy"? Is it a political system that has elections, competitive political parties, and freedom of the press (among other things)? How do we know that elections, and the other practices are features of a democracy? Because they are part of the definition of democracy. Here the concept is not validated by the empirical test, because the theoretical concept ("democracy") and the indicators (e.g., elections) are identical.

The relevant point is, once again, that the three paradigms are different in their rhetorical claims and ways of marshaling different kinds of evidence, but they also are intrinsically related to each other. In the example of democracy, there is no way out of the tautology (except to say arbitrarily, "This is what I mean by democracy right now") except by recognizing the contextualized (i.e., historical) meanings of the term and its indicators while also appealing to a community of analysts who accept the appropriateness of those meanings.

There is no reason to make a decision about these alternative paradigms a priori. In the spirit of methodological and theoretical pluralism, you should entertain all of these paradigms as potentially useful components of a general explanation of a social phenomenon. Being aware of how your theoretical and empirical choices fall into one or another paradigm of inquiry does not help answer your substantive theoretical and empirical questions, but it may sensitize you to a wider range of choices, regardless of the content of the research question. This approach may help you reformulate your research questions, self-consciously locating them within foreground or background paradigms of inquiry.

In distinguishing different arguments, the three aspects of social life should not be regarded as potentially separate "causes." That is, historical processes, symbolic meanings, and multivariate relations are not alternative explanations of the same phenomenon. Rather, they are combinations of theoretical claims and empirical generalizations that flow from research questions that abstract from the social phenomena of interest in very different ways.

In Chapter 4, I present exemplary foreground arguments within the multivariate paradigm to show concretely how theoretical and empirical research questions have been raised in several classic and contemporary texts.

4

Foreground Multivariate Arguments

ॐॐ

In this chapter I analyze three major works that represent foreground arguments located within the multivariate paradigm of inquiry starting with a work by the founder of the field, Emile Durkheim. The multivariate paradigm is conventionally seen as beginning with Durkheim, who successfully institutionalized the field of sociology in France, actually holding the first such professorship.[1] Because sociology dealt with "*social* facts"—those rules or norms that constrain and influence individual behavior—it had a method distinct from psychology. The discovery of presumably objective and external causes of human behavior justified sociology's claim to being a science. Sociology's distinctive concern with societal integration—the causes of social order—gave it a subject matter distinct from politics, economics, psychology, or history. Durkheim's body of work was an attempt to establish what the philosopher Imre Lakatos called a "scientific research program," specifically to establish the field of sociology.[2]

Durkheim (1858–1917) became a member of the faculty at Bordeaux and began teaching "social science" at the age of twenty-nine.[3] His doctoral thesis, completed in 1893, dealt with the division of labor and later became one of his most important books. Durkheim was called to Paris to hold the first chair of social science in 1902. Later Durkheim started the first sociology journal in France, the *Année sociologique*, which is still published. Under his editorship, the journal reflected "his acceptance of the essential unity of all social phenomena and his belief that their structural characteristics may be studied scientifically, objectively" (p. 189).

The political goals that animated Durkheim's scholarly activities have been called those of the "liberal left," starting with the assumption that "the social order needs an integrating morality to complement economic life . . ." (p. 190). All his life Durkheim was concerned with how modern society could be reintegrated after being subjected to the disintegrative forces of capitalism, urbanization, and industrialization.

HOW DOES THE SOCIAL INTEGRATION OF GROUPS EXPLAIN SUICIDE?

Durkheim could have started with either a theoretical or an empirical entry point in his study *Suicide*.[4] Let us assume first that he started with an *empirical* entry point. If the high rate of suicide in France was of concern to French policymakers, Durkheim might have thought that his goal of establishing sociology would be advanced if he could demonstrate the new science's usefulness and therefore applied for a research grant to answer the action question "How can suicides be prevented?" Prowling through the French census, he might have discovered that Protestant suicide rates were higher than Catholic rates and tried to figure out an explanation that would justify an autonomous discipline of sociology.[5]

If, on the other hand, he had started with a *theoretical* entry point, he might have thought to himself, "What are the consequences for individual behavior of variations in the cohesion of a social group? Can I define 'cohesion' in a way that cannot be reduced to individual feelings of attachment to the group? What might be some group differences that would be predicted by this theory? Let's look at suicide rates."

Multivariate Relations

At first glance, Durkheim's theoretical and empirical questions seem to have nothing to do with each other. Why should the suicide rates of men and women or Protestants and Catholics be explained by variations in group integration? Durkheim brought the questions together with his theory of causal mechanisms that intervene between group characteristics and the relative frequencies of individual behavior. The gap between the theoretical assumptions and the empirical evidence is closed by eloquent rhetorical claims.

Durkheim assumes that groups differ in their degree of integration, but his data refer only to differences in suicide rates among diverse social categories in several countries at different times: for example, men and women, married and unmarried persons, army officers and enlisted men, Protestants and Catholics. For each category he constructs a theoretical argument about the level of normative integration that will bind the individual to the group enough to provide a sense of security. "Egoistic" suicide occurs when the norms prescribe individualism and autonomy. "Altruistic" suicide occurs when the norms bind individuals so tightly that they lose their sense of self. "Anomic" suicide occurs when there are no norms or rules governing behavior. Protestants commit egoistic suicide; army officers altruistic suicide; divorced men commit anomic suicide.

Two seeming exceptions to his general theoretical claim—England and the Jews—are important, because they illustrate how he deals with apparently inconsistent evidence. The case of England seems to contradict his general argument—it both is Protestant and has a relatively low suicide rate. Durkheim describes England as the "classic land of individual freedom" but also as a country with a "general and powerful . . . respect for tradition" (p. 160–61). Durkheim gets out of this theoretical dilemma by denying the reality of the alleged "religious individualism" of England. He argues that English Protestantism is "really" hierarchical and "strongly constituted," like the Catholic Church. Durkheim thus ingeniously saves the theory by reinterpreting the meaning of the evidence, although he presents no additional evidence to support his theory of the causal mechanisms. Additional evidence is not central to his theoretical claim because this particular historical instance is in the background. However, his successful attempt to explain the exceptions gives greater weight to his foreground multivariate argument.[6]

The seemingly deviant case of the Jews poses a different difficulty for Durkheim. Jews are highly educated and pursue "intellectual occupations"; thus, according to Durkheim, they have a "desire for knowledge" that should—by his theory—give them a high propensity for suicide. However, Jews were not as likely as either Protestants or Catholics to kill themselves. Durkheim explains away this inconvenient finding by making the specific historical argument (without any evidence) that the Jewish desire for knowledge stems from the struggle against anti-Semitism, which requires "severe discipline" and strong, traditional beliefs. Education thus has different effects depending on its institutional context. More technically, education is an imperfect empirical indicator (of the theoretical variable "commitment to knowledge") because of varying conditions.

Durkheim relies on a general cultural understanding of the historical situation of the Jews to render his account plausible. He gives no evidence of a special Jewish desire for knowledge, of the history of discrimination against Jews, or of the "severe discipline" of Jewish communities.

Symbolic Meanings

Although it is not his foreground concern, Durkheim makes some important assumptions about symbolic meanings. If individuals have no valued memberships (family, religion, community, work, profession) that provide a sense of identity and significance to them, they are more likely to feel disoriented, to have a sense of unhappiness with their life, and thus to feel that their lives may not be worth living. A research question involving a search for symbolic meanings might be phrased as follows: "Through what social interactions do some Protestants come to believe that their lives have no meaning to them?" This question does not suggest that there is a structural cause and a hypothesized objective or behavioral consequence. Rather, the identities, beliefs, and perceptions summed up by the social identity "Protestant" lead some individuals to interpret their life situations in certain ways.

In *Suicide* Durkheim gives many examples of the symbolic meanings of group memberships to individuals that add credibility to the multivariate inferences that are his foreground argument. Attempting to explain the lower suicide rate of Jews compared to Catholics, Durkheim argues that "the less numerous confessions, facing the hostility of the surrounding populations, in order to maintain themselves are obliged to exercise severe control over themselves and subject themselves to an especially rigorous discipline" (p. 156). The language of "obligation," "hostility," "severe control," and "rigorous discipline" suggests the variety of meanings of group membership to the members of majority and minority religious groups.

Another contrast between Protestants and Catholics conveys the symbolic meanings of interactions between the Protestant clergy and their flock: "Nowhere but in England is the Protestant clergy a hierarchy; like the worshippers, the priest has no other source but himself and his conscience. He is a more instructed guide than the run of worshippers but with no special authority for fixing dogma" (p. 158). One can imagine ethnographic descriptions of conversations between priests and worshippers in different churches. Other evidence might be drawn from sermons, church law, or church governance practices.

Another example: A "religious society . . . socializes men only by attaching them completely to an identical body of doctrine and socializes them in proportion as this body of doctrine is extensive and firm" (p. 159). Finally, "each community became a small, compact, and coherent society with a strong feeling of self-consciousness and unity. Everyone thought and lived alike; individual divergences were made almost impossible by the community of existence and the close and constant surveillance of all over each" (p. 160). Here the words "attach completely," "small," "coherent," and "feeling of self-consciousness" suggest specific meaningful interactions among believers. Yet Durkheim does not give any actual examples or evidence of symbolically meaningful interactions or of the cultural beliefs and practices that would reinforce them.

Historical Processes

Durkheim is not concerned about whether individual needs for integration into a group are historically specific to Western Europe in the nineteenth century. His research question is not "What explains the rate of suicide in Western Europe in the nineteenth century as compared to that in China and India?" If the variation in suicide rates between groups in Western Europe is small compared to, for example, that between Western European and other societies, the appropriate theoretical inferences might be quite different.

Nor does Durkheim ask questions about specific historical events in his own data, such as "Why did suicide rise sharply in France in 1884 as compared to 1883?" Although his evidence derives from specific times and places (France, Germany, Switzerland, the Grand Duchy of Oldenbourg, in 1880, 1887, 1890, and other years), Durkheim never discusses whether the findings can be explained by particular historical features of those societies at those times and places. Durkheim's theory could be used to explain why suicides increase both during economic depressions and periods of rapid growth, and he does give many examples of specific events and dates. But his concern is to explain these events by generic variables, not by events peculiar to the specific historical situation.

Durkheim dismisses the explanation of the decline of military suicide as "due to the laws reducing the length of service," a historically specific explanation. Instead, the decline in the rate of suicide among the military is due to the fact that "the habits of passive obedience . . . [are] more and more in contradiction with the requirements of the public conscience" (pp. 237–238).

This view of historical processes is consistent with his position on the relationship between sociology and history. Durkheim left historiography with only "the auxiliary role of finding, cleansing, and presenting the raw material for the generalizations of sociologists." In response, Charles Langlois and Charles Seignobos, authors of the "influential handbook of methodology" *An Introduction to the Study of History* (1898), praised documents as "the only remaining embodiments of and access to past reality" and "affirmed an independent historical science with its accent on the unique and the individual." Seignobos "tried to 'conquer' the new social science by making the historical approach its prevailing methodology" (Breisach, 1983, p. 277).[7] The effort failed; Durkheim's theory and method became the dominant paradigm of inquiry.

Durkheim's foreground multivariate question—"What are the consequences of variations in group integration for suicide rates?"—presupposes both meaningful symbolic links between the measured variables and historical processes from which the data derive. Durkheim gives no evidence for either the subjective meaning of group memberships for individuals or the historical situations in France in 1870 or Germany in 1890—one indication of their background character. The only data are statistical relationships between rates of behavior (suicide) and certain social categories.

I turn now to two works that have become recognized as contemporary classics. William Julius Wilson's *The Declining Significance of Race* asks the question "How does the interplay between 'race' and 'class' support the continuing subordination of blacks in the United States?"[8] The book is a powerful combination of multivariate and historical arguments. Douglas Massey and Nancy Denton's *American Apartheid* analyzes changes in racial segregation and theorizes the consequences of the ghetto.

WHAT IS THE IMPORTANCE OF "CLASS" VS. "RACE" FOR AMERICAN BLACKS?

William Julius Wilson poses the multivariate question "How has the development of a black class structure affected the importance of race for occupation, education, and income?" (paraphrased from p. x). The hypothesis is that once blacks are stratified economically, race per se is replaced by the advantages or disadvantages of class as the best explanation of a person's life chances. The independent variable is "class" position, as indicated by occupation, education, and income.

Wilson argues that one empirical proof of this hypothesis would be to show that the income differences between whites and black are now explained by differences in seniority in jobs. One could translate this into an empirical hypothesis: Controlling for age, one should find that among persons with the same occupation, seniority, gender, and education, incomes among blacks and whites are the same.[9]

Wilson recognizes the existence of "privilege and power" but treats them as the result of a system of stratification of income and other economic and political rewards to individuals.[10] There is no societal totality, whether a "democratic culture" or a "capitalist society," in which economic, political, and cultural institutions interact and change historically. Wilson suggests that "political changes" along with "economic changes" have affected "race relations," as if these were separable variables.

"Class" is defined in Weberian terms as a group that has a unique interest in the marketplace, that is, as "any group of people who have more or less similar goods, services, or skills to offer for income in a given economic order and who therefore receive similar financial remuneration in the marketplace" (p. ix).[11] Wilson's basic theoretical claim is that racial oppression of all blacks has become "class subordination for the less privileged blacks" (p. 23).

Multivariate Relations

In his chapter "Race, Class, and Public Policy," which discusses the reaction to the first edition of the book, Wilson says that many comments marshaled income statistics to show that "race was not declining in significance" (p. 167). Wilson says that he does not disagree that one historical consequence of discrimination was a substantial income disparity between blacks and whites. Wilson agrees with the Marxist argument that in the antebellum South, "racism and racial stratification were primarily the work of the ruling class . . ." (p. 46).

Wilson argues, however, that the significance of race for social mobility has declined, compared to that of class. He cites some empirical generalizations: "Before the mid-1960s sociological studies showed that race was so much of a dominant factor that very little of black economic achievement was determined by class background" (p. 167). A later study shows that "family background has only slight effects on the labor-market achievement of older black men but a sizeable impact on the position of young black men" (p. 168, quoting a study by Richard Freeman). This empirical finding has no meaning unless linked to two theoretical claims: first, the historical effects of racial discrimination on occupational attainment and income, and, second, a theory about the inheritance of class position. In effect, two multivariate theories are related here, both of which are necessary to make sense of these quantitative findings.[12]

One of his basic theoretical claims is that although in general "racial problems *were* [my italics] principally related to group struggles over economic resources" (p. 4), economic class theories, specifically orthodox Marxism and
split-labor market theories, do not adequately explain the history of black subordination in America.

The orthodox Marxist view is that capitalists try to divide the working class
and that racism is a main way of doing that. Reducing labor solidarity also reduces the labor costs of part of the working class, in this case blacks. It is a
weapon against the white working class as well, because blacks are always available to replace the whites or to act as strikebreakers. Racial antagonism is a
"mask for privilege." The split labor-market theory argues that normally business would support a laissez-faire ideology that "would permit all workers to
compete freely in an open market" (p. 5). White working-class competition
with blacks, however, leads to racial subordination.

Wilson frames his argument in multivariate terms, as a choice among different independent variables that best explain the mobility opportunities for
American blacks. In effect, he converts historical processes into variables. These
factors are:

1. Capitalist exploitation and the direct control of the economy *and* the state
   by a ruling class.
2. Competition between the white and the black working classes. The greater
   political resources of the former facilitated the exclusion of black workers
   from many occupations.
3. Racist norms and beliefs stronger than necessary to maintain exploitation
   and exclusion of blacks. The issue here is whether racist beliefs are a genuine independent variable or primarily an intervening variable, helping to
   reinforce and legitimate exploitation and exclusion.
4. State commitments to policies, such as Jim Crow or affirmative action, that
   "legitimate, reinforce, and regulate patterns of racial inequality" (p. 17).
   The issue here is whether the relevant state policies of exclusion and discrimination were influenced either by the capitalist class or by the white
   working class.

Wilson's argument that the life chances of individual blacks are now due
more to their economic situation ("class") than to their race is based on two
empirical claims: first, that urban blacks are now largely segregated into low-
wage occupations that nobody else wants or is forced to accept, and, second,
that affirmative action programs for professionals and service workers as well as
strong unions in certain high-wage industries have reduced competition between black and white workers and thus the pressure for exclusion of blacks
simply on the grounds of their race. The result is that racial conflict occurs now
more in the "sociopolitical order" than in the economy (p. 111).

Both multivariate and historical arguments are in the foreground in Wilson's book. In effect, he builds a historical argument on a succession of essentially two-variable relationships. One example: "Affirmative action programs have had little impact in situations where labor supply is greater than labor demand . . ." (p. 100). Another: ". . . High unemployment rates in the central-city ghettoes are directly related to high labor turnover rates in the low-wage or secondary labor market" (p. 105). These multivariate empirical generalizations are located within a set of historical claims about the changing significance of state policy and class strategies.

Historical Processes

Racism, according to Wilson, is now more manifest in the historical consequences of oppression for present economic status than in daily experiences of discrimination, mainly because of the impact of the civil rights movement (p.1). The new barriers confront mainly the underclass. As he puts it, the "new barriers have racial significance only in their consequences, not in their origins . . ." Wilson does not deny that racism per se is still present in limiting access to certain residential areas and private social clubs, but he maintains that "class has become more important than race in determining black access to privilege and power" (p. 2). Wilson's argument rests on the plausibility of his theory of class.

His multivariate findings are located within a linear historical model that he does not spell out explicitly, perhaps partly because his own empirical generalizations are more subtle than his rather mechanical formulation of three stages of race relations in the United States—preindustrial, industrial, and modern. This formulation allows him to present a complex theoretical claim about the changing importance of different "factors" in American history.

In the preindustrial period (characterized by a simple division of labor and a nonmanufacturing economy), a "paternalistic" form of race relations was dominant. The great social gap between the races meant that racist ideologies were not as important in maintaining racial boundaries as they are today. This is a historical "interaction effect": Under some conditions, racist ideologies are necessary for racial domination, but under other conditions such ideologies are not necessary.

Another important claim about the preindustrial form of race relations concerns the impact of white labor. Since white labor had little power, race relations between white and black labor were not an important factor in the total racial order (p. 14). White labor wanted laws to prevent the employment of slaves, but almost all such proposed legislation was defeated thanks to political control of the state by employers and slaveowners (p.44). Thus, "class conflicts were expressed in racial antagonism" (p. 45). Wilson argues that the Southern ruling class was able to use a variety of political tactics, including allying itself with black workers and using its disproportionate influence over the federal government to restore its control of Southern blacks after the abolition of slavery.

In the industrial and "modern" racial orders, there is competition between white and black workers, and thus racist ideologies are needed to maintain racial subordination. Because in the modern industrial era the black underclass is located in low-paying and dead-end jobs that are not in great demand, labor market conflicts are not great. Thus, economic class theories "which associate labor-market conflicts with racial antagonism have little application" (p. 16).

But the story is not a simple one of contending forces: the ruling class versus working class power versus the state. The "factors" cannot be isolated from each other. Each one influences the others, in ways that change historically. For example, Wilson rejects the "Marxist explanations that ethnic antagonisms were initiated by the capitalist class . . ." (p. 51). But his point is that within the context of capitalist ownership of the means of production, white workers tried to use their political resources to protect themselves from competition from black workers. As long as there were enough European immigrants for employers to hire, white workers were not concerned with either protecting or exploiting blacks merely because of their race.

This argument is far more complex than a simple linear multivariate statement that either white workers or employers were responsible for racial conflict. It is also more satisfying, because it seems to be more historically accurate. It seems implausible that *either* the ruling class *or* the white working class was *the* cause of racial domination. A linear multivariate model cannot deal with such complex historical processes: The efforts of both white and black laborers to gain some economic security were carried out within a changing context of employer strategies, North and South. Employer alliances shifted; employers sometimes sided with black labor, sometimes with white labor.

Wilson quotes from the historian C. Vann Woodward to the effect that the Farmers Alliance in the 1880s sought political power in order to reinforce racial divisions. Woodward calls it a "paradox" that "political democracy for the white man and racial discrimination for the black man were often products of the same dynamics" (p. 57). Again, the historical context is one of capitalist class relations. Racial subordination of blacks was both independent of and dependent on the changing patterns of class conflict. Wilson rejects the reduction of this complexity to an either-or multivariate explanation in terms *either* of "the work of the capitalist class" *or* the "victory of higher-paid white labor," saying that such claims "obscure the dynamics of the complex patterns of racial inequality in the postbellum South" (p. 59).

Historical arguments recur. Northern blacks were successfully excluded from urban political participation until the mid-twentieth century. "White ethnic control of the city machines was so complete . . . that blacks were never able to compete for municipal political rewards. . . . Accordingly, the racial conflicts that permeated the economic and social orders never really penetrated the political sector" (p. 85). To put the point in other language, the absence of racial conflict in the political sphere was an indication of class hegemony, not political consensus.

Wilson takes great pains to emphasize that class relations are not simply and directly translated into racial domination. Quite the opposite; the "polity," "political system," or "state" (Wilson uses all three words interchangeably) has recently acted to "promote racial equality." This change is, he believes, a result of increasing black political resources: the black vote, the black middle class, and the civil rights movement of the 1960s.[13]

Symbolic Meanings

Wilson has little to say about cultural or symbolic meanings, regarding them, by implication, as caused by more "powerful" economic and political forces. He does discuss the controversy among Stanley Elkins, Herbert Gutman, Eugene Genovese, and others about whether a slave culture developed that encouraged either canny strategies of survival or passive submissiveness.[14] He essentially agrees with Gutman, emphasizing the existence of networks of kin and a genuine slave community that developed alongside paternalistic relations with the slaveowners (pp. 34–35). Yet he definitively rejects the notion of an "underclass culture" or the essentially similar concept of a "culture of poverty" as the basic cause of the contemporary economic situation of blacks in America.

Conclusion

Although Wilson does not deny the fundamental *historical* importance of racial conflict and subordination in the emergence of modern economic and political institutions, his primary research question is "What factors explain the *contemporary* life chances of individual blacks?" For Wilson, the history of race relations viewed in the context of the several stages of capitalist development explains the accumulated deficiency of resources available to entire groups of blacks to support their chances for individual upward mobility. However, once those life circumstances are firmly established for the black population, race no longer predicts whether or not a given uneducated young black will be able to get a job at McDonald's. The tension between these two types of theoretical claims, empirically supported in different ways, gives both ambiguity and power to Wilson's argument.

WHAT ARE THE CAUSES AND CONSEQUENCES OF RACIAL SEGREGATION?

The epigraph by the pioneer black psychologist Kenneth B. Clark to the powerful book *American Apartheid*[15] evokes the deep commitment to racial equality underlying this work: "Racial segregation, like all other forms of cruelty and tyranny, debases all human beings—those who are its victims, those who victimize, and in quite subtle ways those who are mere accessories." The moral commitments of this work are indicated by the conclusion that "apartheid not only denies blacks their rights as citizens but forces them to bear the social

costs of their own victimization" (p. 16). The title of the book carries an even
more dramatic image, since the word "apartheid" conjures up images of Soweto:
starving black children in the wastelands of the South African ghettoes. The
emotional impact of the book is greater because of the calm, measured presentation of the data.

Massey and Denton's claims are supported by foreground multivariate census data for U.S. cities and by background analyses of historical works. If Massey
and Denton are right, their data support a radical critique of the racism embedded in American culture and social institutions. But do the data support
their argument? Does the argument support their action agenda?

Multivariate Relations

In their chapter "The Persistence of the Ghetto," the authors deal with changes
in indicators of segregation from 1970 to 1980.[16] The primacy of quantitative
data for Massey and Denton is indicated by their statement that "Hard evidence about segregation's ill effects requires statistical studies using nationally
representative data" (p. 178). Their positivist epistemology assumes that empirical measures (the "racial" composition of a census tract) correspond to an
external reality and are correlated with the unmeasured theoretical variables
("interracial contact") they presumably "cause."

Their empirical research question for one chapter is: "By a variety of measures, has racial residential segregation persisted in American cities up through
1980?" The unequivocal and dramatic answer, despite the passage of a series
of fair housing laws, is yes.

The chapter "The Continuing Causes of Segregation" investigates the
causal mechanisms that sustain segregation and attempts to dispose of alternative theories of the causes of segregation. From census data, Massey and Denton document the "racial" rather than "class" character of segregation, showing that middle-income blacks are just as segregated as poor blacks.

The conclusion of their multivariate argument is that

> concentrated poverty is inevitable when high rates of poverty and intense racial
> segregation are combined. The concentration of poverty, moreover, sets off a
> series of ancillary changes in the social and economic composition of neigh-
> borhoods. By concentrating poverty, segregation also concentrates other con-
> ditions that are associated with it. Deleterious conditions such as falling retail
> demand, increasing residential abandonment, rising crime, spreading disorder,
> increasing welfare dependency, growing family disruption, and rising educa-
> tional failure are all concentrated simultaneously by raising the rate of poverty
> under a regime of high segregation. (p. 146)[17]

In making this argument, Massey and Denton—if they are right—have ex-
ploded a theory that explains either poverty or segregation by positing a "culture of poverty." The institutional mechanisms that reinforce segregation and
poverty render unnecessary any explanations that depend on internalized values.
It is not necessary to resort to characteristics of individuals to explain their poverty

or their behavior. To put the point another way, the behaviors that everyone agrees characterize the ghetto—drug use and criminal activity, for example—are not variables explained by an underclass culture, but at best intervening consequences of far more important structural factors: economic transformations, racist institutions, and sheer poverty. Unfortunately, their authors' theory of a "culture of segregation" is almost a replica of the "culture of poverty" thesis.

Historical Processes

Chapters 2 and 7 of *American Apartheid* present background historical arguments, based on secondary analyses of historical studies, and deal with the formation of the ghetto in American cities and with the history of public policy on racial discrimination in housing. A concrete unit of analysis ("Philadelphia, "the ghetto," "suburb") is specified in time and place, which frames the boundaries of the historical events being narrated. Even though this unit of analysis is not "theorized" in a sociological sense as a definite "structure" or "system," the term establishes a frame of reference for a beginning, a life history, and an internal set of relationships between events and actors that provides criteria for the selection and arrangement of the historical evidence.

Massey and Denton show how black ghettoes were constructed in every American city. A complicated interaction of economic pushes and pulls (that could not be reduced to separate independent variables) led to black migration from the South to northern cities. World War I was a turning point, because the "war both increased the demand for U.S. industrial production and cut off the flow of European immigrants, northern factories' traditional source of labor . . ." (p. 28). At about the same time, the arrival in the South of the Mexican boll weevil devastated the cotton crop, and a series of disastrous floods reduced the demand for black tenant farmers and day laborers. Black migration to the North reached new heights, but the arriving blacks were largely penned up in urban ghettoes. Racial violence increased, as part of the white strategy to establish and maintain a "hardening color line in employment, education, and especially housing" (p. 30).

As some blacks managed to get into middle-class occupations and had income enough to buy into white areas, they were faced not only with violence but also with legal barriers: neighborhood "improvement" associations, restrictive covenants (not outlawed until 1948), deed restrictions, and discriminatory real estate practices. Blacks were forced to live in ever more crowded new ghettoes.

One real estate strategy for maintaining the ghetto while making enormous profits was "block-busting." Realtors would simultaneously encourage blacks to buy in white areas and conduct a scare campaign to convince whites that property values would decline if blacks moved in. Profits were made in both directions: Whites would sell at a loss, while blacks would buy at inflated prices. As this process continued, new areas became part of the black ghetto, including entire cities (Washington, D.C., was 71 percent black by 1970). The main

result of this strategy was that "the ghetto constantly followed the black middle class as it sought to escape from the poverty, blight, and misery of the black
slum." (p. 39).

World War II and the postwar economic boom brought millions more
blacks to the North, and the ghetto expanded enormously. Despite these "massive population shifts" the color line was effectively maintained: ". . . Racial segregation became a permanent structural feature of the spatial organization of
American cities in the years after World War II" (p. 46).

The federal government, through its mortgage loan policies, helped maintain residential segregation through a practice known as "redlining." Seemingly
universalistic, objective, and neutral property assessments were based on the
self-fulfilling prediction that poor and black areas were "unstable" and "risky."
Rapid suburbanization was also facilitated by racist private and public practices:
"The vast majority of [federally subsidized mortgages] went to white middle-
class suburbs" (p. 54).

As central cities became poorer, the demand for city services increased, and
thus taxes had to be raised, further increasing the incentives for residents to
move out to lower-taxed suburbs. So-called "urban renewal" programs and
public housing projects exacerbated the problem by simultaneously tearing
down what low-income housing did exist and building high-rise, extremely
dense government-owned housing, thereby perpetuating the ghetto, albeit in
another form (p. 56).

This historical explanation does not entail any appeal to individual motives,
prejudices, or interests as effective causes of behavior. Certainly, individual realtors benefited from redlining; individual whites benefited from moving to secure suburbs with good schools; individual middle-class blacks wanted to improve their housing. The institutional forces explain *why* those personal motives
led to certain selling and buying behaviors of individuals.

Symbolic Meanings

The most significant gap in Massey and Denton's study lies in the absence of
any foreground interpretive argument. While there are many references to the
ways that both blacks and whites have perceived the nature of the black ghetto,
interpreted its causes, and justified its continuation, none of these are theoretically developed or empirically supported. Instead, symbolic meanings are
rhetorical inferences that fill in the blanks between the historical narratives
and the multivariate statistical tables that construct the arguments of different
chapters.

Massey and Denton claim that their concept of a "culture of segregation"
challenges the "culture of poverty" explanation of the consequences of the
ghetto. They argue that lives organized (or disorganized) around drugs, crime,
unemployment, welfare, and teenage pregnancy have become endemic in the
ghetto. The most glaringly unsupported inference is that an "oppositional culture" has become normative and now constitutes a built-in expectation for both
male and female blacks in the ghetto (p. 170).

This argument is a *background* interpretive theoretical claim by Massey and Denton. They present no firsthand evidence of any kind, either qualitative or quantitative, and cite only a few participant observation studies to support the generalization that traditional institutions such as the family have been replaced by an oppositional culture: misogynist lyrics of rap groups, few shops selling goods about marriage, and other scraps of evidence (pp. 174–78).

A Dialectical Explanation

Massey and Denton draw from the craft traditions of both history and sociology. Both are relevant and necessary because of the broad way in which they have defined their research question. They are interested not only in the foreground multivariate questions that underlie their tables: "What are the dimensions of racial residential segregation, and how are these correlated in large American cities?" and "Through what structural factors is segregation reproduced and sustained?" They are also interested in historical questions: "How did segregation come into being in America in the past century?" and "What has been the fate of past attempts by the federal government to outlaw housing discrimination?" These questions rest on and have significance only within the framework of the findings about the extent and persistence of segregation. Without empirical knowledge that "the ghetto" (i.e., the variables correlated with the enforced concentration of a poor population in a small urban area) actually exists, the historical questions would have no significance.

One of Massey and Denton's main points is that race is intrinsically connected to class and that it is a theoretical (and political!) mistake to try to separate the "effects" of the two "variables." They criticize the work of William Julius Wilson on these grounds. Race and class cannot be entered into a multivariate analysis as if they had independent causes and independent effects.[18]

Massey and Denton cite studies that show that joblessness, low earnings, and teenage pregnancy are positively correlated with growing up or residing in the ghetto. But they do not present an argument about the causal connections between living in the ghetto and these alleged consequences (p.178). The measure of segregation assumes that segregation is comparable and meaningful in different cities, at different points in time. Yet, its significance rests on the existence of other evidence. For example, the authors' own analysis reveals that segregation is less prevalent in Southern cities. But racism is not less evident in the South, quite the contrary. Whites could live next to blacks in Atlanta precisely because residential proximity did not threaten white supremacy. The index of segregation is not necessarily an index of racist practices. It may seem paradoxical that desegregation in Southern cities indicated a stable system of racial domination, but not from a dialectical perspective.

An Action Agenda?

Most ghetto blacks "... live in a geographically isolated and racially homogeneous neighborhood where poverty is endemic, joblessness is rife, schools are poor, and even high school graduates are unlikely to speak Standard English with any facility" (p. 166). Massey and Denton are making the classic mistake of confusing correlations with causes, assuming that the sheer existence of a geographical concentration of blacks (what the authors' "segregation" concept measures) is the cause of these degrading conditions of existence. The identification of segregation as the underlying cause of these conditions of life leads to a politics that emphasizes integration rather than direct action to improve housing, provide employment, upgrade schools, and improve health care in the ghetto.

The importance of asking the right research question that fits an action agenda is dramatically illustrated by the example that Massey and Denton give of the sustained efforts undertaken by the Leadership Council for Metropolitan Open Communities, a Chicago organization that has "mounted an aggressive campaign against residential segregation in the Chicago metropolitan area" (p. 224). Filing complaints, mobilizing public and elite support, establishing fair marketing programs, prosecuting agencies for promoting segregation, and producing fair-housing rulings could quite reasonably be regarded as empirical indicators of the theoretical variable "success in taking action against racial discrimination" by the Council. Action implications could be drawn about the effectiveness of particular organizational strategies, leadership, and coalition building.

Unfortunately, Massey and Denton's quantitative data destroy that optimistic political conclusion. After all of those intensive efforts, Chicago "remains one of the most segregated areas in the United States. . . . Although Chicago's fair housing groups have pushed private fair housing enforcement to the legal limit, they have produced *essentially no change* [italics in original] in . . . racial segregation . . ." (p. 225).

What political action might show the way out of the ghetto? One could argue, following Marx's theory about the conditions of collective class action by factory workers, that an isolated and deprived group thrown into constant contact is in a good position to develop a collective consciousness and mobilize for collective actions. Why haven't ghetto residents organized for collective action to change the conditions of their lives?

Massey and Denton argue the opposite: Ghetto isolation has *reduced* the possibilities of effective political action, for two reasons. First, the conditions for political coalitions with whites do not exist. Second, an activist black leadership challenging racism does not exist. Because most urban blacks are concentrated in the ghetto, they are unable to create the kinds of political alliances with other groups around common interests that would enable them to make demands that would carry real political weight. And, as the black ghettos become worlds unto themselves, black businessmen and black political leaders come to have a stake in the continuation of the ghetto, because they monopolize black markets and black votes. Thus, in their view, neither the social base nor the leadership exists for a political coalition to effectively challenge ghetto formation and persistence. Although this is a plausible argument, it is not defended theoretically or supported empirically.

Instead, Massey and Denton substitute a belief, also not grounded in argument, that a combination of "moral commitment" and "political leadership" (p. 235) can change racial segregation. The federal Department of Housing and Urban Development (HUD) "must" act more effectively, public policies "must" change private housing markets, a staff "should" be created to scrutinize lending data, real estate agents "should" be instructed about fair advertising, Congress "should" adopt legislation about real estate listings. Since the legal framework to change segregation already exists, the problem, they say, is the lack of political will.

Their final chapter is an excellent example of letting action commitments substitute for an adequate theory of the conditions under which deeply embedded racist institutions might change. The authors give absolutely no argument about the conditions under which political will, moral commitments, or effective leadership might emerge. In absence of such a theory, the book ends on a romantic, if not despairing, implicit prediction that nothing will change. This argument is either a counsel of despair or a failure of analytic nerve, or both.

Framing a question with policy relevance in mind pushes Massey and Denton toward a multivariate argument, even when it is inappropriate for their research question. They attempt to isolate a causal factor about which something can presumably be done: federal action. Blacks are treated implicitly as passive victims, helpless in the face of self-interested realtors, objective bankers, and white racists. Because they present no evidence about the actual social worlds and identities of the black community, their argument is ultimately a self-fulfilling prophecy about the multiple factors that support a racist system. Their "culture of segregation" is almost indistinguishable from the "culture of poverty" they seemingly reject as a explanation of the subordination of blacks. Both disconnect ghetto culture from its structural and historical antecedents and thus by implication locate pathological individuals as the source of their own continuing oppression.

From a political as well as a policy standpoint, integration is presumably primarily a means to the end of provision to black Americans of decent jobs, housing, education, and health care. Massey and Denton assume that black Americans will achieve all of those things once equal opportunity to live and work wherever they choose is won. But they neglect the politics of segregation from both sides, that of whites and that of blacks. That is, they underestimate the resistance of whites to economic and political integration, and they overestimate the negative impact on the capacity for self-organization of the black community by the potential destruction of the black political base in the ghetto.

Functional mechanisms reproduce a system of racist institutions even if one or more factors within the system changes. That is the implication of Massey and Denton's pessimistic evaluation of the series of fair housing laws. Although they are cautiously optimistic about the increased power to enforce "fair housing" given to both HUD and the Justice Department by the 1988 amendments, they believe that racism is so deeply embedded in American institutions

that the "entrenched discriminatory processes that sustain the ghetto and perpetuate segregation" are not likely to change. "If history is any guide, they will
not. In the past each time that one discriminatory process has been suppressed
after a long and bitter struggle (e.g., legal segregation or restrictive covenants),
a new mechanism has arisen to take its place" (p. 211).

If this final judgment is true, more than either a multivariate or a historical analysis of the causes and consequences of segregation is needed. A dialectical analysis is needed of the multiple processes—structural, cultural, historical—which sustain a system that reproduces such inequalities and injustices and
of the potential forces of resistance and change.

CONCLUSIONS

In my analysis of the works discussed in this chapter you can see the differences among a *multivariate* analysis that attempts to discover and separate the
relative effects of different independent variables, a *historical* analysis that constructs a narrative of events, and a *dialectical* analysis that attempts to understand the ways in which multiple and interrelated processes combine in complex ways to explain a systematic pattern of outcomes. Foreground empirical
generalizations and theoretical claims within a multivariate paradigm, once
again, require the support of other kinds of argument for an adequate explanation.

The multivariate paradigm is the dominant one in sociology at the present
time. In almost every article published in the two core journals of the field, the
American Journal of Sociology and the *American Sociological Review*, independent and dependent variables are defined, empirical measures are developed,
and data are analyzed by means of various quantitative techniques. Quantitative techniques have almost become identified with the culture of the field,
sometimes to the regret of leading practitioners.[19]

The dominance of the multivariate paradigm has several causes: the legitimacy of science as a powerful array of techniques, the control of funding agencies by those who favor multivariate techniques for obtaining knowledge, the
historical legacy of victories in internal battles in the field. But the fundamental importance of the empirical findings that systematic multivariate research
has produced must also help account for its institutional power.

Our theories (as well as our social policies and our potential for effective
action based on knowledge) would be impoverished if we did not have such
multivariate findings as the following: Blacks in urban areas are less likely than
whites to get housing loans; women earn less than men in many different occupations, even with comparable education and experience; union members
earn more than nonunion members in the same occupation, black teenage girls
are no more likely to have babies outside marriage than white teenagers; violent crime is no more likely in central cities than in suburbs; and the total
amount of work-related theft is higher among the middle class than among

workers. Such multivariate findings may or may not be well confirmed, but certainly they have both theoretical and political significance.

Multivariate arguments are an excellent way of attempting to theorize about associated chains of variables, about what might be a genuine as compared to a spurious inference of causality; and to attempt to systematically separate out empirical relations among variables; and to explain the various relationships. As we have seen, multivariate relations always presuppose historical processes, even if the historical aspect of the problem is not in the foreground. Multivariate arguments also presuppose, whether explicitly or not, the symbolic meanings the variables have to human actors. In Chapter 5 I turn to arguments that foreground such symbolic meanings.

C H A P T E R

5

Foreground Interpretive Arguments

᎒᎒

Interpretive arguments focus on the symbolic meanings of human behavior as expressed in cultural assumptions, ideologies of conformity or resistance, and dominant or repressed discourses. The different languages of interpretive arguments refer to the fierce debates within the paradigm over the relative importance of "macro" aspects of culture and the "micro" world of the negotiations of meanings in interaction. The extreme "macro" aspect is represented by Michel Foucault's view of the pervasiveness of hidden power in social life; the extreme "micro" aspect is represented by the philosopher George Herbert Mead's focus on the internal conversations between the socialized aspect of the self (the "me") and the spontaneous and individual part (the "I"). Between those extremes are the kinds of sociological themes on which I focus in this chapter: the ways in which social institutions create motivations to act in prescribed and expected ways, construct and undermine personal identities, and define social roles that give meaning to life.

The symbolic meanings of behavior within institutions can be studied, as already argued in Chapter 3, through a wide variety of types of evidence. Although ethnographic observations are the traditional evidence within a "symbolic interaction" perspective, texts of various kinds can be used to infer cultural themes and dominant discourses.

In this chapter I present analyses of three very different works with foreground interpretive arguments: Weber's sociological classic *The Protestant Ethic and the Spirit of Capitalism* (1904), Erving Goffman's equally classic ethnographic study of a mental hospital, *Asylums* (1961), and a more recent multiple argument work by Arlie Hochschild, *The Second Shift* (1990), which analyzes the ways in which men and women negotiate who does the housework.

WHAT SYMBOLIC MEANINGS CONSTRUCT THE PROTESTANT ETHIC AND THE SPIRIT OF CAPITALISM?

Max Weber was not a sociologist by training or professional affiliation but a historian and economist. It is one of the strange quirks of intellectual and institutional history that his work is canonical in sociology. The work to be analyzed is not based on ethnographic field work but uses an interpretive theoretical perspective to analyze texts: Calvinist doctrines.

The Protestant Ethic and the Spirit of Capitalism was published in 1904 and 1905 as a series of essays but remained a "fragment," according to Reinhard Bendix.[1] The work was an exploratory essay, meant to be the first step in a research program that was then abandoned in favor of the unfinished project on the economic ethics of the world religions. It is Weber's "most famous as well as most controversial book." Weber was forty when it was published.

Bendix describes some of the personal history that led to the thesis, drawing on Marianne Weber's biography of her husband:

> Within his family Weber was able to observe a traditional entrepreneur, who combined individualism and an ethic of economic conduct. His uncle, Karl David Weber, was the founder of an enterprise based upon the domestic industry of the countryside surrounding the village where he lived. And Weber saw that his way of life was marked by hard work, frugal living and a benevolent but reserved manner, which appeared to reflect the period of the great entrepreneurs in the early phase of modern capitalism." (p. 50)

Weber was unable to work for a number of years because of severe depressions, but he began to recover by 1904 and published the first chunk of *The Protestant Ethic* before coming to the United States in September 1904.[2] While in New York, he "searched the library of Columbia University for materials to be used in *The Protestant Ethic.*" Gerth and Mills speculate that "perhaps the United States was for Weber what England had been for previous generations of German liberals: the model of a new society. Here the Protestant sects had had their greatest scope and in their wake the secular, civic, and 'voluntary associations' had flowered" (p. 17). After some three months in the United States, Weber and his wife returned to Germany, where he finished the work.

Symbolic Meanings

The foreground emphasis in *The Protestant Ethic* is on the social construction of meanings. Weber's theoretical question might be phrased as: "How did Protestant inner-worldly asceticism further, even if unintentionally, the spirit of capitalism?" His analysis assumes that meanings ("spirit" and "ethics") explain specific multivariate relations and historical events. Weber attempted to establish by means of religious texts that Calvinism gave people the "idea of the necessity of proving one's faith in worldly activity . . . [thus creating) a positive incentive to asceticism" (p. 121). People had to be motivated both to be economically active and not to consume the fruits of their labor.

Weber's argument rests on *cognitive* and *symbolic* interpretations: beliefs that interpret the world, create motives, and generate activities that arise from the beliefs. No evidence refers to factories, banks, churches, or any other institution where work, saving, or religious activity takes place. Nothing is said about mechanisms of social control that enforce the ethic. True to the title, the work is about an "ethic" and a "spirit," both symbolically constructed.

Weber has constructed a psychologically plausible set of meanings that might have been attached to Lutheran dogma about salvation and the ways people may become convinced that they have reached a state of grace. He sticks closely to the interpretation of *texts*, although they are used not to document sequences of historical events but rather to infer powerfully binding emotional and cognitive commitments to both religious and economic behaviors.

Historical Processes

The Protestant Ethic is, on the surface, a historical work. Weber prefaces the thesis by comparing the Occident to all other societies, noting its historical uniqueness—the aspects of Western society that set it apart from all others. And the argument that Weber eventually develops, as seen in his last chapter, is indeed a historical one. There he writes almost poetically about the way in which asceticism, once it had played its historical role in creating the conditions for capitalist development, was itself undermined in dialectical fashion.

> The Puritan wanted to work in a calling; we are forced to do so. For when asceticism was carried out of monastic cells into everyday life, and began to dominate worldly morality, it did its part in building the tremendous cosmos of the modern economic order. This order is now bound to the technical and economic conditions of machine production which today determine the lives of all the individuals who are born into this mechanism, not only those directly concerned with economic acquisition, with irresistible force. (p. 181)

However, I argue that a historical paradigm remains in the background for Weber, at least in this work, because he frames his historical considerations in a consistently interpretive manner. No specific events or their time and place are mentioned, although the basic terms of reference are historical totalities: the "West," "Protestantism," "capitalism," "the rationality of modern society."[3] These historical assertions about the changing role of religion in modern societies are neither empirically nor theoretically elaborated.

Multivariate Relations

Multivariate inferences are woven through Weber's argument. The very beginning of the book makes multivariate statements about the relationship of occupation to religion, supported by a quantitative table in a footnote that contains a statistical table from Baden in 1895 that shows the religious affiliation of the students in schools differing in their emphasis on a technical as compared to a classical curriculum. Catholics were underrepresented in the more "technical" schools. It is significant that the quantitative table showing the relationship between religion and type of school is not in the body of the text. Weber, in effect, is saying that these statistics are merely suggestive; one shouldn't place too much weight on them. The assumption of a causal relationship between religious affiliation and class motivation and achievement is his empirical entry point.[4]

Weber asserts that among both Germans and Poles, Protestants are more likely than Catholics to be business leaders and owners of capital, upper-level skilled workers, technical and commercially trained personnel in large enterprises, and managers. Weber does not go into detail about these skimpy empirical findings. He does not consider, for example, whether the apparent "religious effect" was really an "ethnic effect" possibly resulting from a similarity in the ethnic makeup of both the occupational and the religious groups.

Such prosaic methodological questions are central to the multivariate paradigm. By treating such empirical generalizations so casually, Weber is signaling to us that such multivariate assumptions are not his core concern. He does not investigate the empirical relations between religious beliefs and economic behavior.

Weber says that the explanation for the relationship between occupation and religion is that "the mental and spiritual peculiarities acquired from the environment, here the type of education favored by the religious atmosphere of the home community and the parental home, *have determined* [italics added] the choice of occupation, and through it the professional career" (p. 39). Here he speculates on the mechanisms that intervene between the Protestant ethic and the capitalist spirit. The complex data he might have collected illustrate a possible multivariate empirical generalization.

Weber could have drawn samples first of "communities" and then of "parental homes" and developed measures of the "religious atmosphere" of both the community and the home. He might have resorted to field work, visiting a number of communities in order to establish their "religious atmosphere." He could have visited Protestant and Catholic families on Sunday and observed whether they said grace, prayed at night, went to church. Would these behaviors constitute a "religious atmosphere"? Would a close connection between "religious atmosphere in the home" and "occupational motivation" be shown by the talk of mothers to sons about their aspirations for them? How would we know if the mother had a conception of a "calling" when she advised her son to become a capitalist? What evidence, in other words, would be necessary to establish a causal relationship between religion and occupational choice? Weber was silent about these multivariate inferences. His foreground theoretical claim concerned the interpretation of meanings, not the prediction of behavior.

In his very last pages, Weber suggests that the "next task" in a research project would be the construction of empirical generalizations that might lead to an "estimate" of the "quantitative cultural significance" of ascetic Protestantism. The problems for the "next task" are fully historical as well. He proposes a study of both the causes of ascetic rationalism in "the totality of social conditions, especially economic," and the consequences for "social ethics," the "organization and the functions of social groups," "technical development," and "philosophical and scientific empiricism," among others (pp. 182–183). They remain background arguments, in part because Weber has not yet established a firm empirical connection between the key events.

From the symbolic meanings of the "calling" and "ascetic rationalism," Weber makes numerous causal inferences that are not supported by evidence but are asserted as "obvious": for example, ". . . the exclusive search for the Kingdom of God only through the fulfillment of duty in the calling, and the strict asceticism which Church discipline naturally imposed, especially on the propertyless classes, was bound to affect the productivity of labor . . ." (p. 178). Why was it "bound" to have that effect? This multivariate argument is a shadow background inference from the foreground argument about "utilitarian interpretations" and "psychological sanctions" as a cluster of conceptions about the conditions under which life has meaning. And, as already noted, although this assertion is grounded in an assumption about specific events that take place in particular moments, there are no references to any laborers producing anything anytime or anyplace with any sense of duty or calling.

The sociologist Gianfranco Poggi says that no studies of the empirical correlation between Calvinism and entrepreneurship, for example, have been done. He argues that "Weber, with most of his contemporaries, simply *assumed* [italics added] a basic factual correlation between adherence to Reformed Christianity, on the one hand, and the formation of early entrepreneurship, on the other" (p. 298). Instead, he sought "exclusively to identify the precise link 'at the level of meaning' between the two by asking what aspects of what strands of Reformed Christianity fostered what changes in individual . . . conduct. This distinctive concern of Weber was further dictated by his *meaning-centered conception* [italics added] of the makings of action. In the context of *historical research* [added] on an event of the dimensions of the rise of capitalism, that conception inspired him to emphasize authoritatively proffered definitions of meanings and collective codes of conduct" (p. 298).[5]

To summarize, Weber presupposes a complex historical narrative about both the rise of capitalism in the West and the rise of Protestantism, and about their interrelationships as they develop. Barely any events at all are mentioned in *The Protestant Ethic*, which focuses on the presumed behavioral consequences of two kinds of symbolic meanings: a "spirit" of economic accumulation as a sign of the "ethic" of religious salvation. Though assumptions about multivariate relations run throughout the book, the power of Weber's argument derives from his unique interpretive focus on cultural meanings in an institutional and historical context.

HOW ARE INDIVIDUAL IDENTITIES UNDERMINED
IN TOTAL INSTITUTIONS?

Erving Goffman's classic work *Asylums,* a study of the threats to individual identity in mental hospitals, was published in 1961.[6] Goffman's ethnographic study asks, What are the organizational processes in "total institutions" that allow the destruction of "normal" personal and social identities? It is a tour de force of analysis, combining a focus on organizational structures and on the concrete interactions between the individuals who play different roles within and between them: "patients," "staff members," "doctors," "family members." Goffman's foreground argument is within one branch of the interpretive paradigm: The evidence is drawn from participant observation, and he is developing a theory of the self as symbolically constructed (and undermined) through interaction.

Asylums was Goffman's second book, following his dissertation, *The Presentation of Self in Everyday Life*, a field study of life among Shetland Islanders.[7] *Asylums* is based on a year's field work at St. Elizabeth's, a mental hospital in Washington, D.C. Goffman said that his object was to "try to learn about the *social world* of the hospital inmate, as this world is *subjectively experienced* by him" (p. ix, italics added). His basic theoretical assumption is that "any group of persons—prisoners, primitives, pilots, or patients—develop a life of their own that becomes *meaningful*, reasonable and normal once you get close to it . . ." (pp. ix–x, italics added). He describes his method as follows: "[A] good way to learn about any of these worlds is to submit oneself in the company of the members to the daily round of petty contingencies to which they are subject"— that is, *participant observation*. Goffman warns us that adopting the perspective of the patient is likely to provide a "partisan view," since the worldview of a group (here the patients) "provides them with a self-justifying *definition of their own situation* [italics added] and a prejudiced view of nonmembers . . ." (p. x).

Goffman starts the book with a thoroughly structural analysis of what he calls "social establishments," of which "total institutions" are a subset. He describes them in terms of variables: degree of openness, continuity of membership, source of status. Total institutions—those that encompass and control most of the lives of their inhabitants—are widely varied in content: prisons, mental hospitals, homes for the blind and aged or indigent, orphan homes, P.O.W. camps, concentration camps, army barracks, ships, monasteries, convents, colonial compounds, work camps. The category "total institution" is an ideal type—none of the examples have all of the attributes of the type (p. 5). In total institutions, people work, sleep, and live in the same place, unlike the normal institutions and lives of "civil society" (the contrasting category). The "handling of many human needs by the bureaucratic organization of whole blocks of people" is the "key fact" of total institutions" (p. 6).

Goffman's action question is implicit: "How can the integrity of the self be preserved in large scale bureaucratic organizations?" His most general *theoretical* questions might be phrased as follows: "How are personal identities ('the self') constructed and undermined in different kinds of organizations?" More specifically: "What are the processes in total institutions that first destroy the self created in civil society and then reconstruct the kind of self (and social world) possible under those conditions?" These questions do not focus on the relative importance of different factors, unlike multi-variate arguments.

Symbolic Meanings

Goffman is committed to an argument within an interpretive paradigm. He holds that social identities that have meaning for individuals are constructed in the course of interaction and that institutions are constructed from combinations of social roles ("social selves"). The power of Goffman's analysis of the impact of institutions on individuals, especially mental hospitals, rests partly on his *not* assuming any mental or emotional states, or even "crazy" behavior, on the part of the "patient." Goffman calls into question the assumption that the status of "patient" is necessarily associated with any subjective states of being or objectively describable behaviors. He assumes that much the same things would happen to anybody placed in such an institution: a sense of abandonment and of being deprived of the markers of personal integrity that "normal people" count on. Part of the dramatic power of his argument comes from this hypothesis.

In analyzing what happens to new patients, he argues that they learn the "limited extent to which a *conception of oneself* can be sustained when the usual setting of supports for it are suddenly removed" (p. 148, italics added). Here is another example of the interaction between the "I" and the "me" made famous by G. H. Mead: the socially supported conception of oneself versus the one that is no longer sustained by the social environment.

Goffman shows his foreground interpretive arguments very clearly in his analysis of the way the formal, rational goals of the institution are translated into a "language of explanation" that interprets "every crevice of action in the institution" (p. 83). A "medical frame of reference" is a "perspective ready to account for all manner of decisions" in a mental hospital, including even the hours when meals are served. "Each official goal *lets loose a doctrine*, with its own inquisitors and its own martyrs, and within institutions there seems to be no natural check on the licence of easy *interpretation* which result"; ". . . words and verbalized perspectives . . . come to play a central and often feverish role" (p. 84, all italics added).

Goffman refers to the "interpretive scheme" of the total institution. The assumption here is that the institution has a symbolic frame of reference, a language of interpretation, that assigns categories ("sick," "rebellious," "sinful") to behavior, no matter what that behavior is. The behavior is thus rationalized and normalized according to the meanings assigned by the ideology of the institution. "Legitimated objectives" are translated into "ideological phrasings" and into the "simple language" of the privilege system, for example (p. 85). These are the levels of symbolic meanings that justify the institution and "define the situation" for both staff and inmates.

The symbolic interpretation of behavior, and the consequences of applied labels, constitute a central *theoretical* claim for Goffman. He is dealing with a complex series of interactions among social roles with sets of expectations and identities, all defined symbolically. He argues at the end that one of the main functions of the mental hospital is not "treatment" at all but rather the reinforcement of the belief of the professional staff that treatment is indeed taking place and that they are responsible for it.

When an individual has a "primary adjustment" to an organization, "he *finds* that he is *officially asked* to *be* no more and no less than he is *prepared to be*" (p. 189, italics added). This is another example of the multiple conceptions of the self described in Goffman's work: The external demands on the self coincide with the internal expectations of the self, but there is also another self looking on, the one observing the relationship between being asked and being prepared. The institution's demands coincides with the individual's view of himself.

The contradictions inherent in the social role of psychiatrist are an excellent example of the integration of theory and evidence in Goffman's argument. There is a contradiction built into the service relationship between psychiatrist and inmate in a mental hospital (pp. 366–368). The psychiatric staff "are in a position neither to forego the fiction of neutrality nor actually to sustain it" (p. 366). The inmate must accept the appropriateness of being treated as a "patient" if "the psychiatrist is to be affirmed as a medical server." But accepting the patient role is not likely, because the inmate is usually not in the hospital voluntarily. Instead, the patient is likely to complain and treat the situation as if he were a prisoner with a jailor or a "prideful man declining to exchange communications with someone who thinks he is crazy" (p. 367).

The psychiatrist is in a double bind. To defend his professional role, he must treat the "outpourings" of the patient's anger not as information from a human being about her situation but as signs of the illness. But (and here is the contradiction), if the psychiatrist treats the "statements of the patient as signs, not valid symptom reporting, it is of course to deny that the patient is a participant as well as an object in a service relation" (p. 368). Similarly, when a patient expresses hatred for the hospital, that is evidence to the psychiatrist that "his place in it is justified and that he is not yet ready to leave it." In this way, "a systematic confusion between obedience to others and one's own personal adjustment is sponsored" (p. 385).

This is a very significant point. Because acceptance of institutional regimentation and social conformity are regarded as "healthy behavior," the ideological identification of institutional stability with mental health prevents an accurate assessment by the psychiatrist of what is really going on in the institution—and in the inmate. The enormous insecurities and traumas created by institutional life itself create and sustain "hostility" and "aggressive behavior," which are then systematically either denied or "translated" into the individual inmate, whose illness is made the "cause" of the behavior.

Goffman is here pointing to a critical internal contradiction in a professional service relationship with a client or patient who is being "treated" involuntarily. This is one of Goffman's most powerful and disturbing points, and one that would be difficult to translate into multivariate language.

Multivariate Relations

Goffman rejected the "usual kinds of measurements and controls," arguing that "the role and time required to gather statistical evidence for a few statements would preclude my gathering data on the tissue and fabric of patient life" (p. x). This assertion underlines the challenge of any research project—how to define the research questions as sharply as possible so that the results from any given empirical foray will be worth the investment of limited time and resources.

Asylums is full of generalizations among empirically measurable variables, but they are not explicitly defined as such, nor is evidence mobilized to test the hypotheses contained in them, as a few examples will show. A comparative study could be done of the different kinds of institutions Goffman theorizes about: prisons, army barracks, mental hospitals, boarding schools, concentration camps. Such a study could test his hypotheses about stratification, language, the privilege system, and the mortification of the self to see if the empirical evidence supports his hypotheses about the correlation between institutional arrangements and consequences for the self.

While the concept of "total institution" is an ideal type, one could also test for the empirical frequency of the correlation among such structural variables as spatial segregation, bureaucratic organization, labeling, use of admissions procedures that erase individual differences, rules for treating all people the same, loss of external status, degradation ceremonies, control of daily behavior via surveillance, and sharp stratification between staff and inmates.

Another possible multivariate hypothesis is: "Given the expressive idiom of a particular civil society, certain movements, postures, and stances will convey lowly images of the individual and be avoided as demeaning" (p. 21). To evaluate this hypothesis, one could videotape persons of different status and different institutional locations (patient or inmate vs. staff member or physician) and correlate their status with their posture and movements. Are such variables measurable? Is the status "conveyed" by the posture, "correlated" with the posture? These possible questions suggest the difference between multivariate and interpretive questions.

Evidence and Theory

Goffman confidently reports all of the patterns he describes as if they validly distinguish significant variations in social roles and behavior in the mental hospital he studied. Dramatic examples from the sociological literature and from novels and personal accounts, plus illustrative incidents and field notes from his year of observation of one mental hospital, support his generalizations.

Goffman says that when the private pursuits of inmates (singing, art, woodworking, card playing) get too engrossing, the staff will object, because "in their eyes the institution . . . must possess the inmate," not any other activity or membership (p. 69). But how does he know what the staff believes about the institutional goals? Maybe the staff is just as cynical about the "institution" as the inmates. It is interesting that he assumes that the staff's perceptions and beliefs are aligned with those of the "institution." No evidence for that supposition is cited, nor does he make any theoretical claim about how the staff gets imbued with the official ideology or their incentives for supporting it.

Goffman says that he does not want to rely upon "data" about "what the person *says* he *thinks* he *imagines* himself to *be*" (p. 127, italics added). Note the multiple levels of what the person is signifying to himself, again in the spirit of G. H. Mead. What the person *is* one thing; then he *imagines* himself as something; then he *thinks* about imagining himself as something, then he *says* that he thinks he imagines himself to be something. What Goffman omits here are the further levels of interpretation: the person being "said to," and the second person's interpretation of what the first person says (with the further and analogous complexities of the second person's thinking, imagining, being), and then the communication of these different interpretations back and forth.

Goffman also ignores his own participation in this nest of interpretations; he is the interpreter of all of these interpretations, constructing generalizations about the character of the selves and their moral careers. Goffman himself is absent in the smooth flow of his argument. He reports all of these interpretations as if they are social facts. The sheer literary quality of his writing pulls us along, gives his theoretical claims a sheen of coherence and credibility, regardless of their intrinsic theoretical or empirical merits.

Historical Processes

Goffman mentions almost no concrete historical events, and the only places he mentions are countries. Ironically, he probably got the fellowship at the National Institutes of Mental Health (and the support for the year of field work at St. Elizabeth's Hospital in 1956) because of the series of prison and mental hospital riots and disruptions that took place in the late 1940s and early 1950s, which led to the attempt to dismantle or reform those institutions. None of these riots is mentioned in Goffman, nor is there any attention given to the conditions under which collective resistance is likely (he argues that it is highly unlikely). Goffman does not pose the question "Under what conditions will inmates engage in collective resistance that disrupts the normal functioning of the institution and leads to change?" One knows nothing of such possible events from the book.

Although full of concrete references to specific situations (and in that sense not "theoretical" at all), the book is divorced from place and time. Goffman does give a few historical details. He mentions the "Western *history* of the interpretation of persons who seem to act oddly" (p. 350, italics added). He does refer to Britain at the end of the eighteenth century, when the "medical mandate" began, inmates began to be labeled "patients" and madhouses were retitled "mental hospitals." He notes that, in 1756, in the United States, a "similar movement" began at the Pennsylvania Hospital. And, referring to "today in the West," he discusses the differences between practitioners with "organic" approaches and those with "functional" approaches. On page 354 he mentions the "recent historical context" of the development of mental hospitals from a variety of other institutions.[8]

In describing activities in "Central Hospital" during his field work, Goffman makes many references to specific incidents, but they are not labeled by date. The place is identified, but not any specific individual by name, only by role (patient, guard, staff, doctor). There are many examples of "abstract" sequences of events, a narrative or story about some situation in which events occur over time. But none of these are concrete, dated events involving named persons in a specific place, in sharp contrast to foreground historical arguments.

Conclusion

All of Goffman's descriptions of the social processes that constitute the daily life of an asylum (of whatever kind) are based on implicit empirical generalizations about specific events and activities in specific times and places, but none are given in this work, because of the way his theoretical categories structure his presentation of the evidence.

What is striking about Goffman's general argument is the ways in which the concept of total institution finds similarities in organizations so seemingly completely different in their social functions and human values. Goffman's work demonstrates the power of a sociological imagination, its ability to find analogies and common patterns among such different types of social institutions as boarding schools, concentration camps, mental hospitals, and prisons.

HOW DO MEN AND WOMEN NEGOTIATE HOUSEWORK?

Arlie Hochschild's *The Second Shift* is a foreground interpretive argument about the emotional dynamics of relations between men and women over the knotty issues of housework and child care.[9] Hochschild interviewed 145 persons, spoke with fifty couples in greater depth, and observed the home life of twelve couples. Half of the seventeen chapters are devoted to an ethnographic account of the home life of eight couples and their children. The demographic transformation of the household frames the study: In the late 1980s, two thirds of all mothers were in the labor force, including fully half of all mothers with children under the age of one year (p. 2). Both husband and wife in each family in the study worked. As the title of the book implies, in most of the couples, the wife worked a "second shift." The heart of Hochschild's study is the complex emotional negotiations that go on between the husband and the wife over the household division of labor.

Symbolic Meanings

Hochschild herself frames the "deeply emotional issues" of her book in question format: "What should a man and woman contribute to the family? How appreciated does each feel? How does each develop an unconscious 'gender strategy' for coping with the work at home, with marriage, and indeed, with life itself?" (p. 3). Her empirical answers to these questions were followed by a chapter dealing with the question "How do men who share *differ* from other men?" (p. 216, italics in original). Nothing about men's own upbringings provided a clue, and "each story differed totally from the next" (p. 216). The number of hours the men worked or how much money they earned did not distinguish those who shared housework from those who didn't. Hochschild falls back on separate stories for each man who did and who did not share the household tasks.

The "gender strategies" Hochschild describes in her most general theoretical claims involve a complex set of interactions between the man and the woman and a cycle of reinforcements for women who work the "second shift." Her basic argument is worth summarizing:

> . . . because men put more of their 'male' identity in work, their work time is worth more than female work time—to the man and to the family. The greater worth of male work time makes his leisure more valuable, because it is leisure that enables him to refuel his energy, strengthen his ambition and move ahead at work. . . . The female side of the cycle runs parallel. The woman's identity is less in her job. Since her work comes second, she carries more of the second shift, thus providing backstage support for her husband's work. Because she supports her husband's efforts at work more than he supports hers, her personal ambitions contract and her earnings, already lower, rise more slowly. The extra month a year that she works contributes not only to her husband's success but to the expanding wage gap between them, and keeps the cycle spinning. (p. 254)

This summary of Hochschild's basic argument vividly conveys the combination of material circumstances and emotional dynamics that explains the core empirical finding—that even employed women must also work the "second shift."

Historical Processes

Hochschild's background historical argument focuses on the changing meaning of "patriarchy." As she puts it,

> [F]ormerly, many men dominated women within marriage. Now, despite a much wider acceptance of women as workers, men dominate women anonymously outside of marriage. Patriarchy has not disappeared; it has changed form. In the old form, women were forced to obey an overbearing husband in the privacy of an unjust marriage. In the new form, the working single mother is economically abandoned by her former husband and ignored by a patriarchal society at large. . . . The 'modern' oppression of women outside of marriage has also reduced the power of women *inside* marriage as well (p. 251 italics in original).

Hochschild here is going far beyond the evidence that she has in order to place the experiences of the husbands and wives negotiating the terms of housework and child care in the much wider historical context of the transformation of the economy and thus of households. Her dialectical argument emphasizes the pressures operating both to undermine patriarchy and to sustain it. In her words,

> ... two forces are at work: new economic opportunities and needs, which draw women to paid work and which put pressure on men to share the second shift. These forces lend appeal to an egalitarian gender ideology and to strategies of renegotiating the division of labor at home. But other forces—the wage gap between men and women, and the effect on women of the rising rate of divorce—work in the opposite direction. These forces lend appeal to a traditional gender ideology and to the female strategy of the supermom and to the male strategy of resistance to sharing. (p. 253)

This background historical perspective gives Hochschild's foreground interpretive argument a powerful analytic frame.

Multivariate Relations

Multivariate research by others on "who does the housework and childcare" also frames Hochschild's interpretive argument, mainly in Chapter 1 and in an Appendix that summarizes the research literature. A number of surveys have asked people to remember what they did the previous day. All of them found a "leisure gap" between men and women: differences in how much free time they had after both work and family responsibilities were done. The gap ranged from two hours in one study to as much as thirty hours in a 1981 study of professional women with children (p. 278). Hochschild's dramatic formulation of this states that on the average women work "*an extra month of twenty-four-hour days per year*" (p. 3, italics in original).

Hochschild cites a number of multivariate empirical generalizations that have significance only within her interpretive theoretical claims—for example, "the higher up the corporate ladder, the more home support a worker had," whether man or woman (p. 255); "a mother's employment has no consistent ill effects upon a child's school achievement, IQ, or social and emotional development" (p. 236); "... compared to the sons of housewives, middle-class boys raised by working mothers were less confident and did less well in school" (p. 236); "twenty percent of the men in my study shared housework equally. Seventy percent of men did a substantial amount (less than half but more than a third), and 10 percent did less than a third" (p. 8); men were more likely to speak about household chores in terms of "liked and disliked," whereas women spoke in terms of what needed to be done (p. 282); or "the less the wife earned (relative to her husband) the more housework she did" (p. 284).

These disparate empirical findings need a theoretical context to give them significance. They underline the importance of multivariate relationships in Hochschild's study. Her study would have been much less rich if she had not summarized the research literature and framed her own findings in multivariate language.

CONCLUSIONS

Foreground interpretive arguments focus on the theoretical importance of the symbolic construction of meanings in social interaction. Such meanings are inferred from observations of behavior in natural situations, from interpretations of texts, and from depth interviews that interrogate individuals about the way in which they interpret their experiences and social relations. The observer is seen as a participant in the co-construction of meanings, not as a separate, isolated, neutral, and "objective" scientific analyst.

Weber's key terms "capitalistic spirit" and "Protestant ethic" evoke the image of human beings attempting in a chaotic and uncertain world to find the certainty of eternal salvation by the hard labor of economic accumulation. Goffman's panorama of the relations among nurses, doctors, and inmates in and of mental hospitals shows the ambiguities of social roles in a precarious environment. Hochschild portrays the private dramas of family life as men and women negotiate their gender identities in the course of mundane struggles over washing the kitchen floor.

The strengths of interpretive arguments are found in their sensitivity to the complicated negotiations of meanings among human actors at the "micro" level and the ways in which deeply embedded cultural and linguistic symbols define personal identities, shape the legitimate boundaries of action, and channel potential resistance at the "macro" level. Their weaknesses, from the standpoint of the goal of constructing well-confirmed empirical generalizations linked to coherent theoretical claims, is their tendency to rely on the subjective insights of observers and interpreters. From "inside" that paradigm, such reliance is, of course, not a weakness but inevitable.

CHAPTER

6

Foreground Historical Arguments

❧❧

The separation between "history" as a discipline and analyses of the "historical aspects" of social, political, economic, and cultural phenomena has been a continuing problem for scholars committed to a historical perspective on the analysis of human societies. The power of established disciplinary boundaries as bureaucratic realities of modern university life have forced such scholars to try to set up interdisciplinary programs that have always been marginal and ill funded, and thus always vulnerable to cutbacks and changes of institutional priorities. Yet, the fundamental power of a historical perspective has persisted and is now as strong as it has been for many years.

Within sociology, the heritage of a historical approach goes back to Marx and to Weber and is now encompassed by the label "comparative historical sociology." Many works have been inspired by the legacy of Marx and Weber (see the selected readings for a partial list). The books selected here for analysis are only a few of such works.

This chapter presents analyses of three works that foreground historical arguments. Karl Marx's *The Eighteenth Brumaire of Louis Bonaparte*, (1852) is essentially a work of historical journalism. Written in white heat immediately after the events it analyzes, it is one of Marx's few analyses of specific historical events (another is *The Civil Wars in France*). Barrington Moore Jr.'s classic, *The Social Origins of Dictatorship and Democracy* (1966), helped establish and legitimate the modern field of historical sociology. It combines both historical and multivariate arguments, recognizing both the value and the tension between them. William Sewell Jr.'s *Work and Revolution in France* (1980) combines a narrative of events between the Revolutions of 1789 and 1848, an analysis of the symbolic meanings of the corporate language used by French workers, and empirical generalizations about the conditions under which ideologies mobilize political action.

WHAT HISTORICAL PROCESSES EXPLAIN THE COUP D'ÉTAT IN FRANCE BY LOUIS BONAPARTE ON DECEMBER 2, 1851?

On December 9, 1851, a week after the day Louis Napoleon Bonaparte abolished the French Second Republic, Marx wrote to Engels from London: "Dear Frederic, I have kept you waiting for an answer, *quite bewildered* [italics in original] by the tragi-comic sequence of events in Paris. . . . Now, what can I tell you about the situation? This much is clear, the proletariat has spared its strength. . . ."[1]

Whatever his initial reaction to the event, the final manuscript of his account, finished in March 1852 and published in New York by Joseph Weydemeyer, a radical émigré, is written in Marx's usual confident style.[2] In the foreground, it emphasizes sequences of contingent historical events, but it presupposes the importance of symbolic meanings and of multivariate relations. The book begins with the events of December 2, 1851, and recounts how the battle between political factions representing different class interests led to the downfall of the parliamentary republic.[3]

Marx's *theoretical* question was "How do different class interests in a society manifest themselves in political struggles between parties and factions?" In Engels's words, Marx's fundamental theoretical concern is to establish the "great law of motion of history, the law according to which all historical struggles, whether they proceed in the political, religious, philosophical or some other ideological domain, are in fact only the more or less clear expression of struggles of social classes . . ." (p. 13).

His *empirical* question was "What were the key political events in France from 1848 to December 2, 1851, that led to the overthrow of the parliamentary republic by Louis Bonaparte?" The argument of the whole book starts from the vantage point of the overthrow of the bourgeois republic on December 2. What were the political and class forces at work in France in this period? What events led up to and prepared the way for the coup d'état by Louis Bonaparte? Or, in the more vivid language of Marx himself: "How [did] the class struggle in France create circumstances and relationships that made it possible for a grotesque mediocrity to play a hero's part?" (paraphrased from p. 8).

Marx undertook *The Eighteenth Brumaire* as an attempt to show that his theory of class struggle and capitalist development could explain a given sequence of events. It was also important to demystify "heroes," to show that history was neither accidental nor only a sequence of actions by individuals. Nor should history be regarded as a morality play, a contest between good and evil. As Engels put it in his preface to the third edition, written thirty-three years after the original, the coup d'état had been "condemned by some with loud cries of moral indignation and accepted by others as salvation from the revolution and as punishment for its errors." Engels believed that Marx had reduced the "miracle of December 2 to a natural, necessary result" of the "whole course of French history" since the days in February 1848 when King Louis Philippe abdicated the throne (p. 111).

Marx's argument about the class basis for the Bonapartist regime is one of the most concrete expositions of what he meant by a social class in general and of how he uses such fundamental concepts in constructing his argument. First, he characterizes an entity as a whole; then he describes its internal differentiation and its relationships with other entities. This sequence is characteristic of Marx's method—to describe first the overall relationships that constitute the immediate totality (here the "small-holding peasants") and to introduce the internal differentiation (here the "conservative" versus the "revolutionary" peasants) and the relationships with other entities (here the state bureaucracy, the towns, the bourgeoisie), and, finally, to demonstrate how the changing relationships over time transformed the meaning and significance of a particular characteristic—small property itself, for example.

In *The Eighteenth Brumaire* Marx makes another famous and long-debated comment about the meaning of "base and superstructure" as causes of social relations:

> Upon the different forms of property, upon the social conditions of existence, rises an entire superstructure of distinct and peculiarly formed sentiments, illusions, modes of thought and views of life. The entire class creates and forms them out of its material foundations and out of the corresponding social relations. The single individual, who derives them through tradition and upbringing, may imagine that they form the real motives and the starting point of his activity." (pp. 60–61)

Almost all of the empirical references are to the results of actions by political leaders and state officials—a wine tax, a law putting schoolmasters under the clergy, the Paris-Avignon railway, a loan bank for workers, the deposing of General Changarnier, parliamentary votes on revising the constitution. The theoretical claims refer, however, to the strategies of various political factions (e.g., the "party of Order," the Orleanists, the Legitimists, the Social Democrats, the Republicans), class fractions (the peasantry, the bourgeoisie, the industrialists, the proletariat), and the state (the military, the executive, the parliament). Theoretical claims form the implicit framework for Marx's analysis of political events. For the most part, they appear only in the last chapter, where Marx advances his remarkable hypothesis that the bourgeoisie safeguarded its class rule by sacrificing its political rule.

Historical Processes

Marx relies on evidence from newspapers, private letters, and conversations with comrades in France, but in the main he does not cite primary sources (after all, this was a work of journalism!). Marx does give conclusions derived from economic statistics (not the actual numbers or sources)—grain prices, taxes, and mortgage debts—in the context of describing the preconditions for the political mobilization of the peasants. He assumes that these objective circumstances—summarized as the peasants' being "crushed . . . by the low level of grain prices . . . and by the growing burden of taxes and mortgage debts" (p.

85)—were enough to produce a political response not described in detail. He says only that the peasants "began to bestir themselves in the Departments" (p. 85).

The events recounted are organized around sequences of particular dates divided into periods. Each section begins with a narrative: "On May 28, 1849, the Legislative National Assembly met. On December 2, 1851, it was dispersed" (p. 53), or "In the middle of October, 1849, the National Assembly met once more" (p. 79), or "In the June days of 1848, [the social revolution] was drowned in the blood of the Paris proletariat, but it haunts the subsequent acts of the drama like a ghost" (p. 164).

However, when faced with awkward historical evidence, such as peasant support for Bonaparte despite "peasant risings in half of France, the raids on the peasants by the army, the mass incarceration and transportation of peasants" (p. 173), Marx resorts to a multivariate argument. Only *conservative* peasants, not revolutionary ones, supported Louis Napoleon. Marx theorizes a political and ideological division among the peasantry that correspond to the extent of their exposure to "modern" influences—the town, the school, elected officials. Political and class consciousness among some peasants was assumed to have been transformed by recent economic and political developments that had pulled the peasantry away from the routines of life on the land and from conservatism.

Symbolic Meanings

The disbanding of the National Guard illustrates how Marx deals with symbolic meanings as part of a background argument. Marx gives a brief history of the Guard's role in major political events and uprisings since 1830, when it had been "decisive in the overthrow of the Restoration." In February 1848 its "passive" attitude was key. In June 1848 it had put down the proletarian insurrection, furthering the "superstition" of the army regarding "civilian omnipotence" (p. 76). But on June 13 its "power was broken, and not only by its partial disbandment . . ." (p. 77). The "spell was broken." Up to the final moment, the Guard still appeared omnipotent.

How the meanings of certain events are socially constructed by different social groups helps explain for Marx when and why people take action and how they define the significance of their collective identities. Marx even uses such evocative phrases as: "The army convinced itself that [the National Guard] uniform was a piece of woolen cloth like any other" (p. 77). Marx is here saying that the social reality was that the solidarity and militancy of the National Guard had disappeared from the minds of the army along with the Guard's image of invincibility. "Bonaparte merely registered this fact when he subsequently signed the decree for its disbandment" (p. 77). The legal decree disbanding the Guard after December 2 was merely a confirmation and a public acknowledgment of its disappearance as a social force in the minds of citizens, not the "cause" of its disappearance. Bonaparte's decree abolishing the National Guard was the "cause" of its being disbanded only in the sense that a divorce is "caused" by the decree of a judge. It is a surface appearance, a proximate cause, not a "deeper" cause.

Marx's argument emphasizes the underlying social conditions of existence, not public and visible events, to "explain" outcomes. If you look only to the actions of political leaders or state officials as the "cause" of events, then you might interpret Bonaparte's decree disbanding the National Guard as the "cause" of its being disbanded. That is true, but only in a narrow, technical, legal sense.

Marx sets up the reader for a pathetic picture of French bourgeois consciousness and of the symbolic meanings of the events. This lengthy quote gives some idea of the theoretical interpretation Marx makes of the symbolic meaning of these events (for which he gives no evidence whatsoever):

> Now picture to yourself the French bourgeois, how in the throes of this business panic his trade-crazy brain is tortured, set in a whirl and stunned by rumors of *coups d'état* and the restoration of universal suffrage, by the struggle between parliament and executive power, by the Fronde war between Orleanists and Legitimists . . . by the advertisements of the different candidates for the presidency, by the cheap-jack slogans of the journals, by the threats of the republicans to uphold the Constitution and universal suffrage by force of arms [Marx continues . . .]—think of all this and you will comprehend why in this unspeakable, deafening chaos of fusion, revision . . . constitution . . . coalition, emigration, usurpation, and revolution, the bourgeois madly snorts at his parliamentary republic: *Rather an end with terror than terror without end.* (p. 152–3).

This dramatic list of the confusing political symbols that confronted the average bourgeois person conveys their presumed impatience with the seemingly meaningless activity of the parliamentary republic and explains why they could abandon a form of political representation presumably in their interest.

Multivariate Relations

Marx uses a combination of political and class concepts to describe the changing alliances and splits in France between 1848 and 1852, which he sees as the major causes of the events he wants to explain. The concepts "common interests of a class," "majority," "party," "faction," "coalition," "clique," and "following" move from more general to more specific levels of unity of interest and action. The "party of Order" represented the common interests of the entire bourgeoisie against the proletariat. However, the "bourgeois opposition," usually in the majority, stood against the "aristocracy of finance." Within each party, there were factions, corresponding to different class interests—the "pure republican," "industrial" and "petty" bourgeoisies—sometimes allied (when their interests as a class were threatened) but sometimes deeply split, as they were in the period after the Constituent National Assembly was formed in June 1849. Within each faction were "cliques"—groups of like-minded people temporarily associated in political situations for specific goals. The "republican bour-geoisie," for example, "was not a faction of the bourgeoisie held together by great common interests and marked off by specific conditions of production. It was a clique of republican-minded bourgeois, writers, lawyers, officers and officials that owed its influence to . . . personal antipathies . . . to memories of the old republic . . . to *French nationalism* . . ."(p. 33, italics in original). Class interests become causes of political action only in concrete circumstances, where action is contingent on the calculations of consequences.

Marx assumes that he can unambiguously classify the social bases for fac-tional alliances within the parliament, as for example, the votes around revision of the constitution. Modern political research would entail an analysis of a num-ber of votes, classified by their content (i.e., who benefits), and a correlation of how each faction voted with that faction's social base of support outside the parliament—who voted for it, which newspapers supported it, and so on. A large grant for textual and computer analysis would be necessary to test this hypothesis.

The analytic issue is how central these empirical assertions are for Marx's general theoretical claims. It is not clear how much his general argument about the relationship between class and political rule of the state and society would be undermined if any particular empirical generalization were to be proved false. That is, one might find that some of the Legitimists opposed revision, or even some of the Bonapartists, while some members of another faction supported it. Such an empirical finding would not necessarily undermine his general ar-gument, but it would complicate it. One might have to argue, for example, that the most powerful factions within a party took positions consistent with his argument. By assuming that the most powerful faction controlled the poli-cies of the party, Marx accepted an implicit theory about the conditions for the exercise of power in party organizations.

Marx's background multivariate hypothesis about the political leanings of the peasantry could be translated into an empirical study of the voting patterns of the peasantry in the different villages. If one took the percentage who voted for Bonaparte in the elections of December 10, 1848, and in the plebiscite that immediately followed the coup d'état on December 20, 1851, one should find lower votes for Bonaparte in more "modernized" villages, those with (to pre-sent a few possible indicators): 1) greater trade with towns, 2) closer proxim-ity to towns and with better roads, 3) higher incomes, 4) larger land-holdings, 5) a relatively high percentage of their production earmarked for sale rather than subsistence.

However, Marx, in the only actual report of voting patterns, has to con-tend with an empirical finding that seemingly contradicts a fundamental hy-pothesis. He admits that in the December 20 elections, which followed the coup, "the majority was still so prejudiced that in precisely the reddest De-partments the peasant population voted openly for Bonaparte" (p. 176). By "red" he means those departments that had protested against the December 2 coup d'état and demonstrated in defense of the revolution of 1848.

This is truly an awkward finding. Marx's explanation is that in the peasants' view "... the National Assembly had hindered [Bonaparte's] progress. He had now merely broken the fetters that the towns had imposed on the will of the countryside" (p. 176). This argument interprets the ideological consciousness of the peasantry as supporting an image of Bonaparte as a defender of traditional rural life against modernism and cities. Marx tries to find an explanation for a seeming deviant case, since his theory would predict that the peasant areas that protested against Bonaparte would not vote for him. This interpretation is what we would call today an ecological fallacy: predicting peasant consciousness from aggregate voting statistics. A multivariate analysis of the characteristics of the smallest voting units in France might reveal whether or not Marx's implicit hypotheses are supported by evidence.

Marx's basic assumption in this work (which focuses much less on economic and production relations than do his other works) is that a dense network of social relations—political, cultural, economic, and intellectual—forms individuals' consciousness and shapes their material interests. This assumption about the "social conditions of existence" is an unmistakable multivariate hypothesis, but it is at a very general level and cannot explain specific events.[4]

Marx poses a hypothesis: The political form of the parliamentary republic allowed the political representatives of the landowners and capital to unite and "thus put the rule of their class instead of the regime of a privileged faction of it on the order of the day" (pp. 62–63). But, although the republic made their "political rule complete ... at the same time [it] undermines its social foundation, since they must now confront the subjugated classes and contend against them without mediation, without the concealment afforded by the crown ..." (p. 63).

Sometimes open, explicit class rule is a target for challenging classes, and it is better to have class rule concealed behind a facade, either a monarchical one, where the monarch seems to represent the entire people, or a parliamentary one, where the parliament debates the great issues of the day. In any case, the sound and fury of factional combat—the *appearance of politics*—conceals the reality of class rule. This is probably the most general hypothesis about multivariate relations in *The Eighteenth Brumaire:* Parliamentary democracy turns popular attention away from the underlying class bases of rule, the state, and democracy and toward relatively superficial bargaining over incremental changes of one kind or another, toward symbolic politics of advantage, of identity, of status. The appearance, once again, is of popular democracy; the underlying reality is class rule.

Most of Marx's historical argument can be broken down into theoretical claims about the causal relations among political factions, class fractions, parliaments, organizations in which decision-making authority is fragmented, and other political subgroups. Marx assumed a whole series of these multivariate relationships and unified them as *background assumptions* for his analysis of the factors and processes that answer the empirical question "What important events led up to the coup d'état of December 2?" and the theoretical question "What explains the abdication of political rule of the state by the bourgeoisie?"—questions that when asked separately seem to have little to do with each other.

An adequate explanation of an event for Marx required consideration of the complex historical context. If, on the contrary, one attempted to isolate for analysis the events of a particular session of the French National Assembly and posed the research question "Why did the French parliament vote in favor of revising the Constitution?" and then interviewed all of the members about their motivations and interests (assuming that they responded honestly), one would find a vast array of conflicting accounts, which would undoubtedly add up to a "pluralist" explanation in terms of overlapping or conflicting interests, bargains, and coalitions that would "explain" the majority vote. Such a "micro-explanation" of a legislative decision would not necessarily be inconsistent with the broader one Marx offers, but it would not be answering the same research question.

To summarize, Marx's *18th Brumaire* presents a foreground historical argument about the processes that led to Bonaparte's parliamentary coup on December 2, 1851. Marx makes certain assumptions about multivariate relationships among political alliances, class interests, and other assumptions about the symbolic meaning of events to members of the bourgeoisie and of the proletariat. Interpretive questions (how did the 1848 massacre affect the Paris proletariat's perceptions of the potential for political action?) and multivariate questions (what are the consequences of different types of class coalitions for different degrees of state executive authority?) are thus in the background for Marx.

The distinctive feature of Marx's dialectical "method"—he does not call it that—is that the various social forces impinging on the immediate historical situation correspond to multiple and interrelated levels of abstraction. That is, historical actors are conceived of at different levels of abstraction. At each level of abstraction, different explanations apply. Within the *societal context* of the bourgeois form of class rule, for example, economic interests and political factions combine in various ways to form an *institutional or organizational* level of abstraction. This level in turn creates opportunities for and constraints on individual and group actions at particular moments, which might be labeled the *situational* level of abstraction.

WHY DID JAPAN BECOME FASCIST, CHINA BECOME COMMUNIST, AND BRITAIN REMAIN DEMOCRATIC?

Barrington Moore Jr.'s work *The Social Origins of Dictatorship and Democracy* is a classic of comparative historical sociology.[5] It combines multivariate and historical arguments (interpretive ones are explicitly rejected) in a way that is both eloquent and edifying. Moore's work is a foreground historical argument based primarily on secondary historical texts. Moore's work established an important tradition of work in historical sociology and has been followed up by a number of important works, notably *States and Social Revolutions* by his student Theda Skocpol. His commitment is to macrostructural historical transformations of total societies in global perspective.

The complexity of Moore's argument has often been noted. Moore himself says that "there is a strong tension between the demands of doing justice to the explanation of a particular case and the search for generalizations . . ." (p. xvii). Moore moves back and forth from a concern with multivariate relations ("generalizations") and historical events ("a particular case").

Moore's implicit action question could be understood as "How could the chances for democratic institutions under modern conditions be increased?" His empirical entry point is the question "What are the varying paths that certain large societies took toward democracy, fascism, or communism in the twentieth century?"

Moore's theoretical claims center on the collective action of the landed upper classes; they are the protagonists of his narrative. He argues a revisionist thesis: Rather than the urban bourgeoisie or the working class being the central actors who determine the political outcome during the process of industrialization, it is the landed upper classes.

Moore constructs a typology of three major political outcomes: democracy, fascism, and communism. He presents national case studies to show the role of the landed upper classes in determining the political outcome in each of the countries under consideration. In order to construct a narrative history, he reviews monographs and texts of each national history in order to show how the actions of the landed classes and their alliances interacted with material conditions and social arrangements inherited from the past. Here is where his method is visible. He introduces alternative explanations, Weberian or Marxist, and then rejects them; throughout, he is concerned to show the totality of the society undergoing the transition. Thus, he opposes a multivariate paradigm that emphasizes the separation of independent and dependent variables. Evidence about a particular "factor" must be seen in relationship to a whole. He uses statistical evidence, but only to provide an understanding of the society as a whole and the specific conditions that faced the landed aristocracy and their allies or antagonists.

After reviewing the major case studies, he returns to his typology, presenting a comparative analysis across the national cases considered. Here he is doing qualitative case comparison, abstracting from national case studies and discussing similarities and differences within each "outcome" or "dependent variable": democracy or dictatorship. His principle of selecting countries is thus by outcome.

Moore's explanation of the routes to modern politics, whether democracies or dictatorships, focuses on the alliances (or lack of them) of the landed classes with the peasantry, commercial agriculture, royalty, or the urban classes, especially industrialists. If they pursue commercial agriculture, ally themselves with the urban bourgeoisie, assert control over the state not by privilege but by liberal means, then the outcome is liberal democracy. England is the principal example here.

In France the revolution of 1789 was necessary to smash the reactionary alliance between royalty and the aristocracy and to create a commercializing peasantry and a weak but liberal democratic transition to capitalism. In the United States, an alliance between northern capital and labor on one hand and commercializing agriculture on the other successfully overthrew the reactionary plantation slave system.

In contrast, in the case of fascism in Germany and Japan, the aristocracy remained hegemonic in the state bureaucracy, and partially commercialized agriculture was based on a tenant peasant class dominated politically and culturally by the upper class. In these cases, the route to industrial capitalism was driven by a revolution from above and a reactionary alliance between landlords and industrialists still inspired by residual feudal values. Again, the central factor is the role of the landlord class: If it failed to commercialize agriculture and thus retained peasants as tenants and forged a reactionary alliance with urban industrialists, the political route to industrialization was through fascism.

Historical Processes

Moore argues that one must postulate a historical totality within which comparisons can be made and specific sequences of events explained. One cannot simply take a collection of states in the nineteenth century, measure their attributes (e.g., cohesion of the landed gentry, militance of the peasantry, political organization of towns), and then look at the consequences (emergence of democracy, fascism, or communism), as if a simple causal model "holding constant" various independent variables would suffice. The world system is a single system, and all nation-states are affected by that system's earlier history as well as by their relations to each other.

In his preface, Moore discusses his criteria for electing to study only England, China, Japan, India, France, and the United States and for including secondary analyses of Germany and Russia, rather than studying all "nation states" as the relevant "population" of cases. He explicitly rejected including the smaller democratic (Switzerland, Scandinavia, the Low Countries) and communist (Cuba, North Vietnam, North Korea) societies on the ground that he wanted to focus on those processes that "have made certain countries political leaders at different points in time during the first half of the twentieth century. The focus of interest is on innovation that has led to . . . significant power in world politics" (p. xiii).

Moore chose not to include smaller nations because "the decisive causes of their politics lie outside their own boundaries" (p. xiii). He also argues that the problems they face are not comparable to those of larger societies. This last argument, a deceptively simple one, offers a clue to Moore's argument about the difference between contingent historical events and multivariate relations. If one isolates the social units being investigated (in this case total societies, but the units of analysis could be social movements, groups, communities, or organizations) from their historical context, then one can compare "all democracies" (or a subset with similar or different sizes, population characteristics, and political and economic histories) by selecting attributes that one measures and then associates with other variables (such as the degree of development of a welfare state, the degree of political centralization, wealth, or degree of industrialization and urbanization). This is the classic multivariate model, in which the units of analysis are regarded as equivalent precisely because they are analytically torn from their historical context. Moore is arguing, on the contrary, that one cannot ignore the historical context, because the dependence of small, "weaker" societies on larger, more "powerful" ones so decisively affects the *internal* operations of the smaller societies that they cannot be lumped together for comparative purposes.

This argument is a *theoretical* one, making assumptions about some critically important features of the world system of societies in the twentieth century. Note that one does not escape theoretical assumptions about the nature of the world system of societies if one assumes that one can isolate all nation-states and compare them. The assumption then is that each society or state has "enough" autonomy that the variables measured are part of a causal subsystem that can be analyzed in isolation.

For the same reason, he rejects purely quantitative analyses. "The necessities of counting . . . make it necessary to ignore structural distinctions sooner or later." Also, "counting necessarily involves ignoring all differences except the one being measured" (p. 520). Moore is invoking the historical context again: "The same proportion between rural and urban population may have very different meanings in two different societies if one is like the antebellum South and the other a precommercial society" (p. 520).

An argument in favor of multivariate analysis, attempting to take into account such evidence, might be that the importance of a particular independent variable depends on other structural conditions that vary over time in their relations with each other. The ordinary practices of multivariate analysis depend on the independent variables (the hypothesized causes) being truly independent of each other, the context remaining unchanged, and the units to be compared remaining comparable while the data are being gathered. The linguistic complexities introduced in order to recognize the irreducibly contingent nature of multiple and changing relations among "variables" in particular historical contexts reduce the power of multivariate arguments to explain the common patterns that are its distinctive intellectual domain. Recognizing "interaction effects" is a partial and unsatisfactory way of analyzing such historical contingencies.

Multivariate Relations

Although Moore's primary commitment is to the distinctive patterns of historical developments in each of the countries whose history he analyzes, he uses multivariate language continually. However, he uses that language in a way that makes clear that he wishes to emphasize the contingent, problematic character of events. Phrases such as "routes to democracy," "led to," "favorable conditions for . . . ," "impetus to," "inhibits," "prerequisite for," and "dominant configuration" occur over and over again. The imagery is unquestionably multivariate, but the more important underlying metaphor is that of contingency, of constantly changing and multiple conditions that have unforeseen and unanticipated consequences.

One general statement will convey the flavor of his theoretical approach. Right after referring to three major "variables" (the relations of the landed upper classes to the monarchy, their response to commercial agriculture, and the relationship of the landed classes to the town dwellers), he generalizes as follows:

> The coalitions and counter-coalitions that have arisen among and across these two groups have constituted and in some parts of the world still constitute the basic framework and environment of political action, forming the series of opportunities, temptations and impossibilities within which political leaders have had to act. (p. 423)

Here, in one sentence, Moore has combined a multivariate argument about independent variable (coalitions among social groups) and a historical argument about the contingent and open-ended character of political situations faced by leaders who had real choices. This is not a difference in rhetoric that can solved by theoretical fiat or empirical indicators; Moore is grappling with the irreducible reality of *both* multivariate relations and the historical contingency of events.

Symbolic Meanings

Moore rejects explanations, offered by other scholars, of political transformation by symbolic or cultural meanings. He considers the possibility that commercial agriculture failed to develop because of "the inhibiting character of aristocratic traditions, such as notions of honor and negative attitudes toward pecuniary gain and toward work" (p. 421). However, he rejects the possibility that "among the English landed upper classes military traditions and notions of status and honor were substantially weaker than . . . in France" (p. 422). Moore simply says in rebuttal that "it is doubtful that the cultural difference is sufficient to account for the difference in economic behavior" (p. 422).

In many places, Moore does call on symbolic or cultural explanations, but always as intervening causal mechanisms. In the case of China, for example, "Massive poverty and exploitation in and by themselves are not enough to provide a revolutionary situation. There must also be felt injustice built into the social structure, that is either new demands on the victims or some reason for the victims to feel that old demands are no longer justifiable" (p. 220).

Similarly, for Japan, Moore gives a structural argument for the persistence of the "human sentiments" expressed in the "warrior tradition" of the samurai. "They have to be drilled into each generation anew and kept alive through social structures that make them seem more or less sensible and appropriate"

(p. 291). For Moore these "empirical" recognitions of symbolic meanings have no theoretical status.

Moore makes no serious effort to investigate possible cultural differences between—to take another example—the landed upper classes of France and England in their political identities, internal bases of social solidarity, and distinctive patterns of social interaction. Such evidence might have given some additional qualitative support to the structural factors he is most concerned with—but it might also have complicated some of his comparisons.

HOW DID THE LANGUAGE OF LABOR LEAD TO REVOLUTIONARY ACTION IN FRANCE BEFORE AND AFTER THE OLD REGIME?

An excellent example of multiple arguments is William Sewell Jr.'s *Work and Revolution in France.*[6] It was written during the author's five-year tenure at the Institute for Advanced Study at Princeton. Sewell describes the Institute as having an "insistently interdisciplinary atmosphere" (p. x), where he exchanged ideas not only with historians but with social scientists of every stripe.

Historical Processes

Sewell's book bursts the bounds of the traditional divisions of labor within the field of history itself. He argues that the trade corporations into which French workers were organized provided the organizational framework and the language that were then transformed into revolutionary rhetoric. As Sewell puts it, "the discovery that artisans created the nineteenth-century labor movement makes the problem of continuity with preindustrial forms and experiences impossible to escape" (p. 1). A tendency by historians to ignore the origins of the language and organizational forms of labor in the "old regime" was "reinforced by the organization of the French historical profession, which has made the old regime, the Revolution, and the nineteenth century domains of different specialists" (p. 2). Ironically, the very discipline presumably committed to a broad historical perspective on society and social change is itself trapped by a particular form of intellectual fragmentation of its subject matter.

Sewell started his work with an empirical entry point: his study of the "public discourse by and about workers" in Marseille in the nineteenth century. He says that he was "repeatedly struck by the use of such unambiguously corporate terms as *corporation, corps, état, corps d'état,* and *corps de métier* . . . the corporate terminology was particularly prevalent among left-wing republicans and socialists during the Revolution of 1848, the last place one would expect to find sympathies with the old regime" (p. 2).

This observation led him to investigate the persistence of "corporate" language as a source of working-class organization and solidarity. "But what these terms really meant in the nineteenth century, and what they implied for the experience and consciousness of mid-nineteenth century workers [his core research question] remained obscure. . . . I needed a much larger body of writing produced by and/or intended for workers than existed in the libraries and archives of Marseille" (p. 3).

Another source provided basic empirical materials, but his comment on it also shows the importance of a theoretical vision on a historical problem:

> Remi Gossez's study of Parisian workers in 1848 . . . is packed with quotations from documents written by and for workers . . . it confirmed my belief that corporate notions were central to the working-class experience of the Revolution of 1848. Yet Gossez did not solve the problem of the *meaning* of the workers' corporate idiom. His long immersion in the mental world of Parisian workers enabled him to display that world in the most vivid detail, but it also deprived him of the sense of distance so essential for formulating a critical interpretation. . . . [his work] did supply a body of evidence sufficiently rich and abundant to make an attack on that paradox possible. (p. 3)

The "paradox" that oriented Sewell's entire project was, to put it as a question, "How could a radical revolution be carried out in corporate terms?" His preliminary answer was that the answer was not simple.

> It soon became clear that the corporate content of workers' ideology in 1848 had not been delivered intact from the old regime but had been reshaped by the vast historical changes of the intervening years . . . corporate language and practices came to *mean* something very different in 1848 than they had meant before 1789. (italics added)

Sewell is not concerned only with the symbolic meanings of language. Precisely because meanings changed, "I had to consider a wide range of transformations that affected the meaning of corporate notions: changes in the legal system, in economic life, in political constitutions, in property relations, in moral and religious ideas, in conceptions of labor, and so on" (p. 4).

The "data" Sewell draws on are partly his own archival sources from a study of Marseille, but also "a large number of more specialized studies . . . ," synthesized from a theoretical standpoint based on " 'the new social history,' intellectual history, cultural anthropology, and certain new strains of Marxism" (p. 5).

Multivariate Relations

Sewell credits the extension of legitimate historical sources to include quantitative analysis of the data on the lives of ordinary people with broadening the scope of history. The "new social history," or "history from the bottom up," took advantage of "new methods" to raise "a whole range of new questions and theoretical perspectives" (p. 6). His summary of the transformation of theoretical perspectives as a result of the availability of new evidence is important.

> Before 1960 our knowledge had been restricted almost exclusively to three topics: the institutional history of the labor movement, the intellectual development of socialist ideology, and the declining, stagnant, or rising real wages

of the workers. . . . To these, the new, more sociologically aware histories of labor added urbanization, political mobilization, demography, occupational recruitment, voting behavior, social mobility, family structure, migration, kinship, residential patterns, the fine structure of work experience, and so on. Consequently, our knowledge of working people in the past is now immeasurably more complete, subtler, and more exact than it was in 1960. (p. 6)

The dialectical relations linking theory, method, and evidence could not be expressed more directly than in that quote, and Sewell's own account of the change in his research trajectory from his initial study of the workers of Marseille illustrates the process of the "rolling" reformulation of research questions as one learns more about the phenomenon. His "largely quantitative" dissertation was undertaken "with the intention of illuminating this great transformation of workers' consciousness": The workers of Marseille changed from conservative to revolutionary in 1848 and have remained "consistently on the left ever since" (p. 7).[7] Sewell summarizes his major empirical finding as follows: ". . . unskilled trades and those skilled trades that recruited mainly from within the native-born artisan community of Marseille remained politically apathetic or conservative, whereas those skilled trades that recruited their members . . . nationally . . . were also more receptive to national revolutionary politics" (p. 7).

But Sewell acknowledges that he "found [himself] quite incapable of explaining why such a movement had come into existence in the first place or why it took the form it did" (p. 7). His first response (changing his research question) coincided with his insight that "the process of ideological development transcended local communities." In order to understand changes in political consciousness in Marseille, he would have to investigate much broader social transformations in France, and particularly in Paris, since French society and politics are so highly centralized.

Symbolic Meanings

But Sewell points to a shortcoming beyond restricting his focus to local history, a shortcoming that points once again to the intrinsic connection between theoretical claims and methodological tools. Sewell says that "an inability to come to grips with workers' ideological experience is also built into the research procedures of the new social history. In borrowing methods and theories from sociology, historians have tended to pick up the sociologists' pervasive assumption that quantification yields 'hard' or 'scientific' knowledge, whereas other sorts of evidence are 'soft' or 'impressionistic' " (p. 8). Because of perhaps laudable attempts to develop new interdisciplinary tools of analysis, "social historians have frequently been led to emphasize those aspects of social experience that could be described quantitatively or systematically over such seemingly ineffable matters as consciousness, attitudes, currents of opinion, sentiments and the like" (p. 8).

But Sewell does not find the traditional methods of intellectual historians any more satisfactory for resolving research questions about workers' consciousness. In order to answer his new question, Sewell had to look at the most diverse kinds of evidence, "available only in the most heterogeneous forms—in manifestoes, records of debates at meetings, actions of political demonstrators, newspaper articles, slogans, speeches, posters, satirical prints, statutes of associations, pamphlets, and so on. In such situations the coherence of the thought lies not in particular texts or in the 'work' of particular authors, but in the entire ideological discourse constituted by a large number of individually fragmented and incomplete statements, gestures, images, and actions" (p. 9).[8]

With such an approach, certain methodological issues central to multivariate analysis—representativeness, sampling, definitions of the "population" of ideological discourses and of empirical indicators of collective beliefs rather than individual outbursts—cannot be easily dealt with. How can one infer typicality or generality from such fragmentary empirical materials as posters, slogans, and pamphlets? How much consistency must one find in order to infer a "collective belief"? Because of his break with conventional multivariate standards, Sewell does not deal with these complicated methodological issues.

Sewell goes even further in his hospitality to interdisciplinary explorations. After rejecting both the "new social history" and quantitative sociology as primary sources of methodological inspiration, he finds what he is looking for in the interpretive cultural anthropology of Clifford Geertz.

Sewell's summary indicates his dialectical perspective. His focus on the "language of labor" is "not only about workers' utterances or about theoretical discourse on labor, but about the whole range of institutional arrangements, ritual gestures, work practices, methods of struggle, customs and actions that gave the workers' world a comprehensible shape" (p. 12).

Sewell refers to the dialectical move between "tracks of analysis" in his most focused summary of his method:

> . . . a history of workers' actions and consciousness must constantly move back and forth between the particular experiences of workers and the changing patterns of the larger society—the form of the state, major political battles, the nature of relations between various classes or orders, the ideas that informed public discourse, and so on. [This book] ranges far afield when such excursions are required to set workers' actions in a proper context. (p. 13)

Sewell's book takes advantage of the broadening of perspectives to make full use of multiple paradigms of inquiry and to be both theoretical and empirical. Multivariate arguments are integrated into historical and interpretive ones. Two chapters "treat workers' economic conditions and the labor organizations they formed in response to their conditions" (p. 14). And the whole book is framed by a summary of a cross-national empirical regularity in the particular occupations that spearheaded labor movements: "skilled artisans, not workers in the new factory industries, dominated labor movements [in France, England, Germany, and the United States] during the first decades of industrialization." Whether the development of such movements is measured empirically by "strikes, political movements, or incidents of collective violence," craft workers or artisans were the leaders (p. 1).

This empirical finding, Sewell argues, has significant theoretical implications. The historical sources of modern labor movements must be sought in much earlier times than the period when factories developed, as the conventional view suggests.

CONCLUSIONS

Foreground historical arguments focus on events in time and place and on concrete actors, although they use theoretical concepts drawn from substantive theories of many kinds.

The differences between historical and interpretive arguments are clear from the examples of Moore (this chapter) and Goffman (see Chapter 5). There is no history in Goffman's analysis of the mental hospital—no context, no societal environment, no changing circumstances under which incarceration occurs. Conversely, in Moore we do not see the social world of the peasants, the aristocrats, or the bourgeoisie. No "mentalities," no concrete interactions that form identities, no ideological discourses that shape cultural meanings appear in the broad historical sweep of Moore's work. Yet, in each work, theoretical claims and empirical generalizations other than those that are foregrounded appear as background assumptions.

Sewell's comprehensive theoretical framework and methodology provide a model for studies that abandon the conventional paradigms that force the researcher to focus on either macro *or* micro levels of analysis, do historical *or* interpretive studies, and in general remain within the boundaries of conventional paradigms of inquiry.

All three of the works analyzed draw, broadly and selectively, from Marx, but they have abandoned his teleological view of history, his view of the working class as the driving force of progressive change, and his sharp distinctions between economic base and superstructure. As such, these works represent only one major tradition within a historical paradigm of inquiry, although one that is a central commitment for many sociologists who do "comparative historical" work.

7

The Theoretical Power of Multiple Paradigms

☙☙

In this chapter, I define two hypothetical problems, one concerning the "welfare state" and the other "revolutions," to illustrate how the use of different kinds of entry points and paradigms of inquiry contributes to the craft of inquiry. The analytic strategy I use here is to begin with the multivariate paradigm and then to show how interpretive and historical arguments strengthen and modify that theoretical and methodological framework. I begin with the multivariate paradigm because, as I argued earlier, it is dominant in the field, as well as often institutionally resistant to recognizing the legitimacy of other paradigms. I also begin with "macro" units of analysis—total societies—both to illustrate the applicability of multivariate theorizing to societies and to show how "micro" processes can be linked to "macro" ones.

Once again, the heuristic distinctions among different kinds of questions, theoretical claims, and empirical generalizations are intended to provide tools for the craft of inquiry, not a set of formulae to be applied mechanically. The projects I have imagined exhibit possible trails, false leads, and pitfalls of the research process. The smooth surface of a polished work—any published work—conceals the rough corners of many failed insights.

MULTIPLE PARADIGMS OF INQUIRY ABOUT THE WELFARE STATE

When you begin to define a research question, you have to find out what is already known about the general theme or topic. The problem is that it might take months or years to read everything known or relevant, precisely because you can't possibly know the boundaries of the problem at this point.

I begin arbitrarily with the selection of a topic: the welfare state. Suppose you have read somewhere that the United States has one of the least well developed welfare states in the Western world.[1] That is an observation, a topic, a theme, not yet a research question. If you frame the research question as "Does the United States have a less developed welfare state than other Western democracies?," you have defined the problem in comparative multivariate terms. In order even to pose that question, one would have to have some hunch (based, perhaps, on reading a few books or articles or hearing a lecture) about how Western countries differ in how many different kinds of public services and programs they make available to citizens without regard for their income: health care, family assistance, day care, education, housing subsidies, and so on.

At this point, you might begin to wonder whether any of these kinds of programs, whether state or private, are comparable. Are "health programs" similar enough to be compared? Can you define "health" the same way in every society? What about differences in cultural definitions of what constitutes "health"? Maybe a look at discourses about the body in different societies would show how different social groups or cultures construct the meaning of "health" and "sickness." Perhaps "health care systems" can't be compared, let alone "welfare states," until primordial definitions of "health" are clear.

All of these ruminations are appropriate and even potentially important, but note that they have deflected you from the initial research question. The process of deciding on a research question is neither neat nor straightforward, and you may well decide that the question you are really interested in is "How do different societies construct definitions of the 'well' or the 'sick' body, and under what conditions can an individual body be treated by health care professionals?"

If you make some assumptions about the answer to that question (or leave it implicit), then one kind of interpretive argument remains in the background. But if one of your theoretical claims is that cultural definitions of the body and of health are potentially vital aspects of the explanation of different levels of development (and different emphases) of welfare state programs, then you may wish to put that question into the foreground. You might decide to conduct some ethnographic observations of health clinics in several societies that differ in the scope and level of public services they provide. The language or discourse of treatment, the courtesy with which patients are treated, how much attention is paid to the "whole person" rather than only to physical symptoms, and the self-definition of staff members as "professionals" or as "employees" may all be related to the institutional context in which the clinics function.

But let us return to the other line of argument and potential choices. Given the initial question framed earlier, you could go either the comparative route or the case study route. A quantitative comparison of a population of "welfare states" complements a historical study of one case.

The initial concern is to discover why the United States is "different," but the research question may change as you learn more. The first step is to "map the terrain." Remember that I am attempting to reproduce a process of complicated reasoning about a project. At this stage, a playful attitude is appropriate, an attempt to deal with any and all potential issues before making a commitment to a research design.

The Unit of Analysis

If you decide to conduct a comparative study, you might proceed as follows. You would first have to decide on the population of societies to be included and whether or not to "control" certain variables. (Refer back to Chapter 3 for definitions of different kinds of variables.) Let's assume that you include every society that exhibits at least a minimum level of "modern welfare state" as measured, say, by the existence of a Social Security (or the equivalent) program for the elderly.

But why, you may ask yourself are programs for the elderly the touchstone for the understanding of the welfare state? Again, you reconsider the research question. If you decide that you are really interested in programs for the elderly, and not in the more general issue of the "welfare state," then you go down that track of analysis—with exactly the same problems and choices, except that the substantive focus has shifted.

If you decide to stay with the level of abstraction of the "welfare state," you still have to decide which programs best exemplify it. Your reading of the literature may or may not help. All too often, assumptions about which public programs are central are made without justification. But you are trying to be self-conscious about your assumptions and their consequences for the research process.

Why not infant mortality programs? National health insurance? Unemployment insurance compensation? Aid to dependent children? Family allowances for each child? Which of these programs are vital components of any "welfare state," programs that have to be considered in deciding on which side of the dividing line between "welfare states" and "non–welfare states" to place any nation. Setting the criterion too high means excluding a lot of important cases. The United States, for example, does not have national health insurance, nor does it have family allowances, both of which are taken for granted in most European societies. Shall you exclude the United States from the list of welfare states?

Note that you are simultaneously deciding on the boundaries of the inquiry, or the basic "unit of analysis" ("What is a welfare state?"), and on the attributes (variables, aspects, components—the language varies) of that unit of analysis ("What are the characteristics of welfare states?"). The two questions are organically related but have very different implications for the research design. The point will become clear after a moment.

The Dependent Variable

Still pursuing the multivariate comparative strategy, you must consider possible measures of a dependent variable that you define as "level of development of the welfare state." There are several possible ways of measuring that variable: number of different "welfare programs" a society has (according to some list that you derive from the literature), percentage of total Gross National Product (GNP) spent on such programs, percentage of the population that receives some kind of assistance through such programs, how early the country started different programs, how many of the programs are means tested, how easy it is to apply for and receive benefits, how much surveillance there is of welfare recipients, how easy it is to be deprived of benefits, eligibility rules for receipt of benefits.

Each one of these empirical indicators can be justified as "measuring" some aspect of "welfare state development," but obviously they refer to quite different aspects: extent, timing, difficulty, history, restrictions, distribution. Have these relationships been studied in the literature? An important part of the project may well be the empirical exploration of the interrelationships of these different aspects of the welfare state, before you even reach the question of the causes of variations between societies.

Suppose you find out that there is almost no association between these various attributes of what you thought of as "welfare state programs." If societies are so different in the number, quality, and distribution of various public services that they cannot be compared in these respects, you might conclude that the basic concept of the term "welfare state" that might allow a comparative study has been undermined. Your empirical excursion has shown very few substantive and historical connections among the various public programs you wanted to classify together as aspects of a "welfare state." The concept is purely ideological, you conclude. It has political functions for mobilizing public debate and creating visions of social possibilities but little analytic relevance. If you conclude this, then you may go back and redefine the theoretical and empirical questions once again. The questions might become "How does the vision and image of a 'welfare state' enter into public political discourse? How is the ideology of the welfare state associated with historical images of equality, justice, or freedom? How was that ideology associated with the development of working class movements?"

Note that you have again moved in the direction of an interpretive paradigm. Whether or not this paradigm stays in the background or moves into the foreground depends on decisions you make with respect to other lines of theorizing and other substantive assumptions you are willing to make.

Note also that these explorations are eminently *theoretical*. As you learn more about the different aspects of the welfare state and how closely they are related to each other, you are also deepening your understanding of the basic meaning of the concept "welfare state." Suppose you find, for example, that those countries that on the basis of their number and diversity of programs seem to have the most "generous" welfare state are also the countries that have the most restrictions on receipt of benefits and the most rigid rules for disqualification. Or perhaps the countries that spend the most on their welfare states are also the ones that distribute the benefits most unequally. These discoveries do not merely pose methodological issues (what are the "right" measures?); they are also conceptual issues that may affect the fundamental definition of the problem.

Let's move along this track of analysis and assume that you've settled these theoretical issues about the unit of analysis and the attributes of welfare states). You have devised some measure that allows you to rank a number of countries in order of "level of development of the welfare state." You might combine some of the empirical indicators I have suggested into an index or pick one measure that seems unambiguous and clearly comparable. The percent of GNP spent on a comparable list of programs seems objective and simple, as compared to restrictions on benefits, for example.

You may, on the other hand, decide that a typology is in order, because your preliminary investigation has discovered that societies differ in whether benefits are means-tested and thus whether benefits are universal, provided without regard for income. Or, you may discover that benefits and programs are disproportionately available to those people who have steady jobs, rather than the unemployed. You decide that welfare states can be divided into "universalistic" versus "particularistic" and into "class biased" versus "not class biased." You have complicated the dependent variable by making it not just an empirically (although not necessarily theoretically) simple continuum that ranges from a higher to a lower level of development of welfare state programs, but a typology based on attributes of various programs. Such typologies are somewhere between a multivariate analysis of many cases and a study of a single case.

Both independent and dependent variables can be defined as either *continuous* variables ("level of development" measured by number of different kinds of programs, "wealth" ranked in order of gross domestic product, or "size of population") or *dichotomous* variables (presence or absence of national health service, presence or absence of family allowances, presence or absence of unemployment compensation, wealthy or poor, large or small). How to handle each bit of empirical information available depends on both the theoretical importance of each indicator *and* the level of validity and reliability of the empirical indicator. These different criteria are not necessarily correlated, unfortunately. That is, you may decide that ease of access to high-quality health care guaranteed and paid for by public funds in the absence of private insurance is an indispensable criterion for an advanced welfare state. But the data required on quality and access may not be valid or reliable for a large number of societies. You may have to settle for, let us say, publicly available statistics on the proportion of tax revenues spent for health care, a poor "proxy" (substitute) for direct measures of quality and access. If no other data exist, you have to decide—again on theoretical grounds—whether to abandon this empirical focus of the study or to change the research question once again.

However, let us assume that after all of these theoretical and empirical quandaries, you have settled on a dependent variable that measures to your tentative satisfaction the "development of the modern welfare state." Your theoretical decision determines whether the measure is defined as a continuous variable, a dichotomy, or a typology. That is, do you define "modernization" as a continuous and gradual process? If so, your theory allows you to view the measure as a continuous variable.

Does a society have a welfare state, or doesn't it? Is it democratic or not? Does it allow abortion or not? If any variable is viewed by your theory as either present or absent, then you are defining the measure as a dichotomy.

Are there different types of welfare states? You might regard a welfare state as centralized or decentralized, perhaps as measured by the proportion of benefits allocated by national and local governments. It might be participatory or hierarchical, as measured by how many welfare programs have citizens' advisory committees. It might be generous or stingy, as measured by the ratio of the average benefit in a society to the per capita income. If you view welfare states as quite different in major dimensions, then you may be constructing your measure as a typology.

Note that these decisions are *both* theoretical and empirical. Your initial theory leads you to define a welfare state in a certain way, but your subsequent empirical explorations may alter that conception and thus the measures. The point of research is to *learn* something new, not to reproduce your own consciousness in the results.

The Independent Variables

The next task is to theorize what might explain welfare state development. Remember, however, you are still mapping the intellectual terrain of the problem, using the process of developing "rolling" research questions as a strategy for moving through possible choices. You review the literature and discover that some of the possible independent variables in the literature are as follows:

1. *Corporatism.* "Corporatism" is defined as the existence of binding agreements to negotiate wages and prices at the highest levels of the state, capital, and labor (as measured by the existence of wage-price agreements for the past decade). Case studies in the literature have reported that Germany, Sweden, and France have corporatist agreements and seem also to have relatively highly developed welfare states. Why expect that relationship? You reason that there may be a link because corporatism gives labor unions (presumably committed to the welfare state) access to high-level political decision making. Keeping or increasing welfare state programs may be one outcome of the bargaining process that keeps a degree of industrial peace.

If you decide to include an interpretive component in the foreground, you may look at the actual texts of the corporatist agreements and see to what extent the rhetoric of serving the interests of the public through various welfare programs is included in the documents issued by the several parties to these agreements. Or you might attend the high-level meetings or read the transcripts of the discussions and try to assess the extent to which there is a common cultural understanding of and a commitment to universalistic welfare. The theoretical assumption here would be that common cultural understandings, not self-interested negotiations, might both be created in and lead to corporatist arrangements. Going back to the multivariate track, you predict that the more corporatist a society is, the more developed its welfare state.

2. *Strength of organized labor.* But perhaps the strength of the labor movement is the most important factor and explains both corporatist agreements and the level of development of the welfare state. This independent variable might be measured by the proportion of the labor force in unions, by the proportion of the *industrial* labor force in unions, by the number of major strikes in the last decade, or by the number of strikes *won* by labor in the last decade. If you have all of these indicators, you might combine them into an index, or you might decide—on either theoretical or empirical grounds—that the number of strikes, for example, is a sign of the *lack* of power of organized labor in the state. (If labor were truly powerful, it would be able to gain a place at the highest level bargaining table, namely the corporatist agreements. If this were true, then participating in corporatist arrangements would better indicate the power of labor than the sheer number of strikes.)

Let us assume for the moment, however, that in some fashion the interests of workers and the poor in welfare state programs are expressed through organized labor and that a stronger labor movement is better able to represent and defend those interests than a weaker one. Again, you can move in an interpretive direction and look at the discourses of labor, the rhetoric of freedom and justice, in a particular historical case. Finally, returning to the multivariate track, you hypothesize that the stronger organized labor is, the more developed will be the welfare state.

3. *Power of the Left party or parties.* Left parties, you reason, are mobilizing agents for a welfare state majority coalition. Quite independent of the strength of the organized labor movement, how successfully liberal and Left political leaders have managed to forge an effective electoral coalition is plausibly related to the likelihood of a developed welfare state. Possible measures of the political power of that liberal coalition you consider are the proportion of votes received by candidates from that coalition in the four most recent elections, the proportion of seats held by the coalition in the four most recent parliaments, or the number of years the president or prime minister has come from the Left party or coalition.

But you have to consider whether the power of the Left coalition is really only another way of referring to the strength of organized labor (another proxy variable). How much of the Left coalition is composed of votes from sectors of labor? But perhaps you can leave this to the empirical evidence to judge. If both the "power of Left coalition" and the "labor strength" variables have an independent effect on welfare state development (i.e, remain correlated in a multivariate analysis, perhaps a regression), can you infer that each variable contributes to a comprehensive explanation? Not necessarily. Once again—and this principle can never be repeated too often, if only because it is violated so often in practice—one can *never* infer causation from any pattern of empirical correlations. Explanation is always a theoretical inference. But it is enormously tempting to assume that strong correlations can settle the theoretical issues.

But, returning again to the multivariate track of analysis: your hypothesis is that the more powerful the Left party coalition, the more developed should be the welfare state.

4. *Popular legitimacy of the welfare state.* This might also be called a "political culture of equality." You might argue that majority public opinion in a democracy has potential influence over parties and elites, and thus over welfare state policies. If solid majorities of the participating electorate support welfare state programs, then you surely should find expanded programs in such societies.

Possible measures you consider are the proportion of eligible voters who report in a survey that they support a variety of welfare programs or the proportion who agree with such statements as "Government should provide health care for those who cannot afford it" or "Government should act to reduce economic inequality."

You pause to consider all of the political processes and mechanisms that have to exist in order to make such general policy preferences tangible political demands that governing or opposition parties have to respond to. Is it relevant to your project to try to analyze how public opinion is translated into political demands? Again, this is another decision that may be peripheral or central, depending on how much weight you want to place on a particular process, a particular explanation. If your originating question is "What is the role of public opinion in the expansion of the welfare state?," then obviously a detailed and intensive exploration of the mechanisms through and conditions under which public opinion has policy impact would be a central issue. All of the ambiguities of definition of concepts and measures would rear their ugly heads in this new context of research questions. Just to mention one possibility: public opinion is probably both shaped by the actions of political parties and governing coalitions and influences those actions.

But, back to your multivariate question. You hypothesize that the more legitimate the welfare state is in widespread public opinion, the more developed it should be.

5. *Elite consensus.* The beliefs of elites about the welfare state may be an independent cause of their behavior, aside from the political pressures they are under from political parties or interest groups. You think of this possible independent variable after having read some of the theories about elite autonomy and the importance of political leadership. Are elites merely agents of organizations, acting on their behalf or being removed? Can the acts of political parties or labor unions be taken as the direct translation and manifestation of the beliefs and values of their leaders? How much continuity is there in organizational policies after a leadership crisis?

These ruminations lead, once again, in another possible direction, toward a possible focus on the history of elite recruitment to the highest offices and how those elites were socialized by family, school, and peer group. If you are interested in explaining the welfare state, however, this could seem like a diversion.

So, you decide to try to measure the degree of elite support for the welfare state by conducting interviews with a sample of political elites. You might ask them about whether they agree with the policy statements of the organizations they presumably represent and whether they can act informally against the explicit goals of the organization.[2]

You may decide to examine the public discourses of elites to assess how much consensus seems to exist around the philosophical and moral underpinnings of the welfare state. You analyze sermons, speeches at university commencements, editorials in leading newspapers, the memoirs of leading public figures. You have to decide which elites are important, in which institutions, and for what reasons.

However you arrive at these judgments, you still advance the hypothesis that the more elite consensus exists around support for the welfare state, the more developed that state will be.

6. *Social needs.* In a democratic society, social needs are often expressed in political demands for public services, like welfare state programs. You assume that in each society you have chosen there are legitimate organizational and political mechanisms for expressing needs for health care, housing, education, and so on. Social needs may or may not have an impact on welfare state development independent of Left or labor strength. Even more interestingly, perhaps *only* if the organizational instruments exist for such social needs to become politically effective does the "objective" level of social needs have any effect.

You look at several possible measures of social needs: an index of the percentage of the population with incomes defined as below the poverty level combined with the percentage of children under school age and the percentage of people over sixty-five, a measure of the health status of the population. As before, your hypothesis is that the greater the social needs of the population, the more developed the welfare state should be.

It now occurs to you that the causal direction may be the reverse. If the welfare state has been successful, it has met some of the needs of the population, and therefore welfare state policies may be a cause and not a consequence of the level of public welfare and social needs.

My brief discussion of each variable has assumed that they may be causally interrelated, but that there is some possibility that each has an independent effect. On the other hand, a given factor may act through another factor. A regression analysis of a correlation matrix can map the patterns of these relationships but cannot tell you which is the most important causal factor.

The variables discussed include a more or less standard array of possible causes of welfare state development. Since this example is just an illustration of a point, I will not deal further with the problem of developing more specific definitions and measures of each of these complex variables. Let us assume (although that assumption will become problematic later) that you have found comparable definitions and measures of each variable for each country with a welfare state.

Finally, you must decide on "contextual" variables you want to include on which each society will be quite similar (i.e., you are "controlling" for these variables). These might include a minimum level of wealth (indicating enough economic surplus to support welfare programs), ethnic and religious homogeneity (sufficient to allow mobilization of effective political majorities), and the length of time the society has enjoyed a democratic political system (presumably indicating the existence of governmental institutions with reasonable effectiveness). You can (and should) subject your decisions about each of these contextual variables to exactly the same reflections on their theoretical and empirical assumptions as the others mentioned.

You have now "mapped the terrain of the phenomenon," at least for the moment. You have defined the unit of analysis and both the dependent and independent variables. Before turning to how a historical paradigm of inquiry would complement your approach, a brief word on analytic strategy is in order.

The Analysis

I will skip over a critical stage in the actual research process: the actual gathering of the data. Because, recall, all of this discussion is part of the preconditions of research, part of a process of mapping possible theoretical and empirical research questions, you can proceed to make some additional assumptions about the data.

Having gathered the data, you compute correlations on the measured variables. Note that you cannot assume, given my previous discussion, that the variables are likely to be empirically, let alone theoretically, independent.

Let's assume that you find that, *all* of the independent variables are separately correlated with the dependent variable, with the sizes of the correlation ranging from 0.5 to 0.7 (i.e. between one-quarter and one-half of the variation is "explained"). This procedure tells you that all of the independent variables may be potential causes. On the other hand, the correlation may be spurious—the apparent effect of a given variable may be due to a third variable that is the "real" underlying cause of the outcome. That additional variable, you may realize later, after reading about a particular case, may not even be one of your theoretically derived and measured variables.

Let's assume further that when you run a regression analysis, you find that only the power of the Left party coalition remains highly correlated with the development of the welfare state. All of the other correlations drop below 0.1. What can you make of these empirical findings?

At this point, these relationships are merely empirical correlations. You cannot infer from this finding that the power of the Left party coalition is a "cause" (let alone the most important cause) of the level of development of the welfare state. The correlations only provide guides for the next step of the analysis: a detailed look at each case to see what processes "intervened" between Left political power and welfare state expenditures. You might look at both kinds of deviant cases (where the Left party was strong but there was little welfare state development, and vice versa).

In order to demonstrate causality, you would have to show that:

1. Detailed historical events and processes—specific actors and their activities—connect the Left party's behavior with the concrete decisions taken to expand welfare state programs, in those cases that provide the appropriate data for the positive correlation.

2. You can find some explanation in the deviant cases for reasons why Left party power did *not* result in welfare state development: political mistakes by leaders, and possible other factors not included in your comparative multivariate model. A detailed historical analysis (of Sweden, for example) might well show that Left political power was *not* the real causal variable, because that power was itself caused by a political culture of equality, manifested in majority public opinion that cuts across class and other social cleavages. This conclusion might follow from a detailed narrative that examined events over a long historical period. (Note: this would be a background historical argument contained within a foreground multivariate argument).

   You could then go back to the regression analysis and look at interaction effects to discover whether you have missed a significant relationship between public opinion and welfare state development. There might be an interaction effect that was not visible in your initial equation: support for the "legitimacy of the welfare state" might be inversely correlated with "Left voting," so that the underlying "true" cause—a political culture of equality—was hidden.

A Historical Argument

The more closely you examine a particular case, the more the multivariate model will become so complex that secure inferences about the causal role of particular variables become difficult.

First, the analytic separation between variables becomes much more difficult the closer you examine their complex historical relationships. In a detailed historical reconstruction of the events leading to the Swedish welfare state, for example, the emergence of political alliances between capital and labor coordinated by the state ("corporatism") will be very difficult to separate (as different "causes") from "Left political power" or from "elite cohesion," *even if the empirical indicators are not the same.* Part of the power of the Left party might be regarded as being indicated by the capacity of part of the party's electoral base (the trade unions) to gain influence over capital and labor in corporatist negotiations. Or, as indicated earlier, the "real" cause of Left political power might be a political culture of equality. Or, the reverse might be true: A Left party that had been in power for some time might have been able to shape public opinion and actually create a political culture that supports the party. The clarity seemingly established by separate empirical indicators may evaporate as you look closely at the historical relationships of seemingly "independent" variables.

Second, separating the independent from the dependent variables will become difficult. Once the "welfare state" has some institutional stability, it may be able to generate its own political base of support (as Social Security is supported by the elderly coalition in the United States). A particular party (as Swedish Labor has) may gain and sustain its political base as the welfare state's supporter and sponsor. In effect, the welfare state has become a cause of its own reproduction. This is an aspect of political and social reality that cannot be captured directly in statistical correlations and regression equations.

Third, when you look at a particular case in detail, the independent and dependent variables become transformed over time, and their relationships change in complex ways that will not be clear if you are doing a comparative study of many cases. This point is related to point one but is not quite the same, because it emphasizes the role of human action in transforming over time these social and institutional relationships and dissolving their clarity as separate "variables." Let me spell out the relations of these variables as a historical scenario:

> Leaders of the poor arise in a particular situation who generate a popular movement on behalf of an expanded welfare state. The Left party then moves to coopt the movement. The resulting shift in party coalitions undermines elite cohesion. The resulting attacks on the welfare state lead to the breakdown of corporatist arrangements. The Left party takes advantage of the new political situation to appeal to a more militant popular base on behalf of a further expanded welfare state. Competition among economic elites threatens the loss of international trade competitiveness. A significant sector of labor agrees and abandons the Left party. . . .

Such a sketch of a narrative is the core of a "historical" argument, but the relative importance of one possible "cause" over another cannot be disentangled in the analysis of that case. Note that the *language* of the paragraph utilizes the conceptual framework of the independent and dependent variables distinguished earlier, but the variables are treated not as separate "causes" but as descriptive and summary labels for clusters of events, human actors, and social or political processes. If I attach dates and the names of persons to each abstract noun, the point is even clearer that the empirical evidence is based on concrete actions in time and place:

(Newspaper story in the *METROPOLIS GAZETTE*, January 26, 2000)

> John Smith, leader of the Poor People for Justice movement that began in 1998, yesterday challenged the leadership of the Social Democratic Party to select a presidential candidate in 2000 that the recently organized Movement for Social Equality could support. Social Democratic Party leader Peter Jones faces a dilemma, because he had worked out a division of electoral districts with the Conservative Party that maintained both parties' core base of electoral support. . . .

Fourth, as you look at each case more closely, the apparent similarities that allowed classification of the different complex attributes of these societies into comparable categories of independent and dependent variables will unravel. Elites will differ in their composition, and the mechanisms through which they reach consensus will differ; thus, the variable "elite cohesion" turns out to be not quite comparable from society to society. The "political cultures" of societies, even homogeneous democratic ones, will be internally diverse, fragmented into different subcultures, and have origins that differ in their religious, ethnic, and philosophical bases. It is safe to say that close inspection of any two historical cases will uncover diversities that make any comparisons of "variables" problematic.

The point is not to set up an artificial and misleading opposition between "historical" and "multivariate" arguments. Quite the contrary. And I am not, despite the examples, challenging the use of systematic comparisons of different cases with respect to even the variables discussed. Rather, these two paradigms of inquiry can be complementary.

The opposite point is also worth emphasizing: A detailed historical narrative always presupposes a comparative multivariate model in which a theory—frequently only implicit in traditional historical narratives—is embedded in the narrative itself as the underlying principles of selection and arrangement of the historical materials.

At several points in this discussion, examples have been given of how a choice of an interpretive argument might have been made, although the thread of a foreground multivariate argument was followed. The same general problem could be redefined, of course, from the standpoint of a foreground interpretive argument.

You might start with a research question about discourses about equality and justice. The language used in the press, on TV, or in legislative hearings to justify or attack the welfare state you would be part of the construction of a foreground interpretive argument. The language of entitlement, of privilege, of human rights, of fairness and equality, might be seen embedded in the same kinds of documents and reports otherwise used to construct measures of the variables of access, quality, and coverage. Or, ethnographic and participant observation in professional offices, welfare agencies, waiting rooms of clinics, planning committees for demonstrations, and nursing homes would enable an understanding of the social worlds that constitute the actual human meanings of the "welfare state."

MULTIPLE PARADIGMS OF INQUIRY ABOUT REVOLUTION

The ways in which multiple paradigms of inquiry complement each other can be illustrated with another example drawn from a possible study of revolutions. Another substantive focus may help understand the same general points. I again start with a multivariate frame and then subject the theoretical assumptions of that paradigm to a critique from the standpoint of the other paradigms.

Suppose you read the following (fictitious) statement in a book by some leading political scientists:

> Revolutions are likely in wealthy societies that have experienced recent histories of severe poverty, particularly among the stable working classes. However, revolution is likely only if the ruling elites have also lost their capacity to govern: They are weak, unstable, insecure, and split. In addition, revolution is likely only if opposing elites have the resources to mobilize a challenge to the ruling elites: strong leadership, an effective organization, and realistic strategies.

As stated, these conditions for revolution are empirical generalizations, that is, they are statements of a *correlation* or association of different attributes of these cases. The authors are not claiming that poverty *causes* revolution, only that revolution has frequently followed extreme poverty. Similarly, they have noticed that revolutions have occurred if, in addition, ruling elites have lost their capacity to govern and if opposing elites have resources. These are all only statements of observed empirical associations, not yet causal hypotheses.

The reason that you do not know yet whether any of these relationships is causal is that perhaps a completely different factor accounts for or explains your observed relationships. Or, perhaps the relationships are reversed; perhaps, that is, revolution causes poverty by destroying the stable social order and political system that has allowed the economy to function productively.

Further, considering the other two variables: Perhaps the mobilization of opposing elites destabilizes the ruling elites, rendering them weak and insecure. Or the reverse: Perhaps a weak and insecure ruling elite emboldens opposition elites, causing them to organize a following, using slogans of poverty ("Bread! Land! Work!") as a rallying cry.

These arguments are all at this point completely *theoretical*. They are statements of possible relationships between the four variables that constitute this little "model" of a revolutionary process: poverty, ruling elite capacity, opposing elite resources, and, of course, the occurrence of revolution itself. You could go on to elaborate all of these possible causal directions; all of them are plausible, once you think in terms of mechanisms and the possible direction of effects.

Tracks of Analysis

The important point in the present context is that the development of an argument about the relationships between these four variables and their indicators is a way of moving back and forth between theoretical and empirical "tracks" of analysis. You do not simply decide on a "theory": The empirical specification of the evidence you regard as relevant is part of the intrinsic process through which you work out a theoretical argument. Conversely, a particular piece of evidence—say, an observation that in a particular society riots followed a famine but that in another society no riots followed a famine—will give rise to some theoretical speculations about what might account for the difference.

The language of variable analysis—"independent," "dependent," "intervening," and "control"—helps you to think through the possible significance of these various relationships, whether or not you actually choose to measure them. At this point, you might regard "occurrence of revolution" as the dependent or "response" variable (what you are trying to explain) and "poverty" as the independent or explanatory variable. "Elite capacity" and "opposition resources" you tentatively think of as "intervening" variables. That is, your hunch is that once there is a situation of extreme poverty, revolution will happen only if economic deprivation triggers political mobilization among deprived groups, that is, if a process of mobilization "intervenes" or occurs after poverty causes real suffering.

A further issue arises of the "control" variables. What factors are you allowing to hold constant? Are you considering the conditions for revolution only in highly (or marginally) industrialized societies? Only highly ethnically homogeneous (or heterogeneous) societies? You may wish to exclude a variable from inclusion in the design precisely because you think it is a highly important causal variable, but a theoretically trivial one. If you knew already that there was a near-perfect correlation between a country's wealth and its likelihood of a revolution, you might want to "control" for wealth by picking only societies similar in that variable.

You would do that only if you regarded the strong correlation as theoretically trivial (like one between height and weight, or even perhaps one between the size of a city and its number of drugstores, or between gender and physical strength). Or you might make this correlation the centerpiece of the analysis if you decided that it was precisely the relationship between wealth and revolution that had to be explained. Again, your theory, as derived both from your reading of the literature and your own critical reasoning about specific cases, would lead you down one particular analytic path rather than another.

Why do you expect the relationship between revolution and poverty, for example, to be a causal one? From the quotation just given, you have grounds to assume that societies that undergo serious economic declines are more likely to see their citizens revolt against their government. Why is this so? Perhaps people whose expectations that their government will provide some economic security for them have been frustrated become willing to act, in some cases violently, to change their government.

Note that you can define the problem in both causal "directions." That is, you can ask, "What are the consequences of poverty? Does economic deprivation lead to revolution or not?" Or, you can ask, "What are the causes of revolution? Is one of the causes of revolution poverty?" This switch of analytic perspective—even though the basic research question concerns the same variables—has important consequences for the conduct of the research, but you will deal with that later. For now, let's deal only with the second relationship (the causes of revolution).

You gather data on a number of societies, first trying to figure out what evidence (or "empirical indicators") of revolution would be appropriate. You look at cases where there has been an unlawful overthrow of the government, others where there have been serious outbreaks of civil violence, others where there has been total breakdown of law and order, others where a new regime was elected but proceeded to abolish the constitution and parliament.

Consideration of the complications of these possible meanings (and consequential "measures") of the concept of "revolution" forces you to be clearer about just what you mean by the concept. If you include all of the types of events just mentioned (e.g., overthrow, violence), you have decided on a very broad concept. If you include only instances of "unlawful overthrow of the government," you have narrowed it.

The choice is a theoretical one, neither right nor wrong. The general point, applying to every study, is that the process of considering what specific evidence you will accept for the occurrence of an event cannot be separated from the process of defining the concept, which is itself part of theorizing the "meaning" of the concept (and its relation to other concepts constituting the theory).

You also have to decide whether you can include different time periods in one society or have to consider only different societies. You might, for example, look at every ten years in the United States and see if a revolution took place, and code your findings as 0 or 1. Could you, that is, assume that all of the conditions every ten years in one country can be regarded as an independent observation and thus add to the number of cases you have available for comparison? This procedure is problematic, precisely because the different time periods are not independent "samples" of different "populations" of "periods of time in which a revolution did or did not occur." The same processes that did (or did not) produce a revolution in each decade in the United States are probably operating continuously, decade after decade.

Or do you have to consider only autonomous societies as independent cases? If so, you run into the problem of comparability. Each historical case of "revolution" will be quite different—different social groups will be involved, the actual revolutionary events will be different, and it is only by heroic abstraction that you will be able to force the differences into comparable categories. Again, this is a *theoretical* decision, to regard or not to regard various attributes of different cases as similar "enough" to warrant comparison.

Then, you have to decide what evidence you will regard as appropriate for establishing the degree, type of, and distribution of "poverty." Should you include those historical cases where there has been a sudden decline of per capita income in one year or a gradual decline over ten years? Or, should you count only those cases where the consumption of food by the population has risen steadily for ten years but then dropped drastically the next year? Or should you combine "sudden drop in per capita income" and "sudden drop in food consumption" into an index?

Suppose that you compile data showing the distribution of income and food for the whole society, for the 10 percent of the population with the lowest incomes and food consumption, and then for the lowest 20 percent of the population. The last two calculations stem from the theoretical hunch that the most economically deprived population may be the most likely to revolt and that indicators for the whole population will not be revealing.

And, of course, you compile data not only on changes of income and food consumption but also on the absolute level of income and consumption, with the hypothesis that it is the comparisons people make between their own society and others that lead to revolution. That is, perhaps relatively poor people in rich societies are less likely to become revolutionaries because they realize how much better off they are than poor people in poor societies (if they are indeed relatively better off).

A Historical Argument

The multivariate component of the argument can be complemented with a historical argument, using the same variables but now visualizing them as "processes." Each "case" of revolution has its own history and its own culture: meanings to the participants, a legacy of memories of courage, songs, reminiscences, of feelings of anger and frustration, of dramatic and oft-told events. The story or narrative of the revolution can be told in a variety of different ways, depending on the angle of vision and what is highlighted or downplayed. The dramatic unity of the narrative presupposes an underlying and different kind of argument: Why did a particular event happen? What significance did that event have in the unfolding process of the revolution?

You might also construct an interpretive argument: What did these events mean to the participants? How did they interpret their participation to themselves and to others in order to construct meaning and a significant identity from it? What cultural symbols were available to participants to provide a vision of a new world?

Note that in a foreground historical argument, it is neither necessary nor possible to make a definitive judgment about the precise direction of the causal relationship. One process can influence another, in turn affecting the original process. All four "processes" (and others, or various combinations and subtypes) are seen in complex interrelationship and interdependence, as the "story" of the revolution is told: the accidents, the unexpected developments, the new connections. The analytic separation of "variables" becomes a narrative interplay of "processes."

More concretely, if you were telling the story of a particular revolution, you could show how all these processes—the fortunes of the economy, the gradual erosion of the stability of the ruling elites, the emergence of a revolutionary movement, the beginnings of direct and militant challenges to the government, the responses by political leaders—developed simultaneously and interdependently. The events that make up the revolution would constitute an integrated narrative of all of the processes. If a particular opposition protest was squelched, that might have emboldened the ruling elites and discouraged the opposing elites, reversing the "causal" factors and reducing the chances that further militant actions would be mounted. The factors that explain the success of that particular demonstration might be quite random and accidental, like the factors that explain a particular person's suicide for Durkheim, or a particular capitalist's decision to invest for Marx, or a particular bureaucrat's decision to implement a rule for Weber. Yet, if the larger "forces" at work were strong, a particular action, whether successful or unsuccessful, would not matter in the long run.

CONCLUSIONS

Two examples, the welfare state and revolution, have been used to show how components of the same general theoretical framework can be used to integrate multiple paradigms of inquiry in the course of confronting a series of choices in the research process. An explanation of the mechanisms that link an initial set of conditions and an outcome are actually *more* likely to be understood if you have a detailed understanding of the history of the events and of the processes that have occurred in a single case. On the other hand, detailed and extensive exploration of a single case may call into question the analogies and contrasts that allowed the comparison to be set up in the first place.

A comparison of many cases allows a description of empirical correlations of variables or attributes and provides clues to the possible mechanisms that might explain those correlations. There is a dialectical relationship between the delineation of patterns of relationships among measured variables for many cases and the discovery of the complex interrelationships of events, behaviors, and processes in a single case. A combination of different theoretical claims coupled with multiple kinds of evidence allows the construction of powerful arguments in social inquiry.

I have not yet shown how the process of moving back and forth among historical, interpretive, and multivariate arguments is central to an integrated or "dialectical" explanation and how one can understand the research process as a *social* phenomenon. In the next and concluding chapter, I will step back from the strategic choices of entry points, research questions, and paradigms to locate social science within a historical and institutional view of how knowledge is produced and to demonstrate how this social production is related to the sources of the sociological imagination.

CHAPTER
8

Dialectical Explanations and the Sociological Imagination

❧❧

Focusing on individual strategic *choices* overemphasizes the autonomy not only of the academic enterprise within the society but also of students as "free agents" within academia. Student dissertation projects are constrained by their advisers; undergraduate paper topics may be designed to please the instructor. I have made a number of implicit assumptions that you—the reader—are making choices about your theory, method, and evidence in response only to individual constraints (time and money) and to biographical experiences. Individual freedoms are real, of course, but research choices are also shaped by how "social science" relates to the society around it.

MULTIPLE PARADIGMS OF INQUIRY

The current configurations of power and resources in the field make it difficult to combine different paradigms of inquiry, although—paradoxically—outstanding works that achieve such combinations are sometimes rewarded with the highest prizes of the discipline. But there are also inherent practical difficulties associated with the pursuit of multiple paradigms of inquiry. Simply marshaling the energy to search archives *and* to do depth interviews *and* to conduct a large survey would tax anyone's resources, not to mention his or her sociological imagination.

Multiple paradigms of inquiry must remain legitimate in social inquiry. The tensions among them need be neither dissolved or reified. Isolating them from each other is a loss to each, since each one depends on and presupposes the others. "Multivariate" reasoning does not necessarily require quantitative data, although these kinds of theoretical claims are a prerequisite for selecting or creating the appropriate quantitative measures. This way of looking at the relationship between multivariate theories and evidence is almost the reverse of what the standard textbooks recommend. That is, rather than using qualitative observations as the basis for developing quantitative indicators—the presumably "scientific" procedure advocated in many textbooks—I recommend the reverse. Quantitative data should be used to "map" the basic empirical correlations between what are thought of (on the basis of preliminary observations and reading "the literature") as the key theoretical claims that will be "tested" by historical or qualitative case studies.

The language of multivariate analysis presupposes that the aim is to discover the relative importance of different possible causal factors for an "outcome." A "dependent variable" is the hypothesized "effect" of a variety of "causes" (the independent variables). Yet, the paradox is that this theoretical language is frequently translated mechanically and tautologically into a particular statistical operation: regression analysis and its variants. Regression analysis, in one of its several forms, is used almost without question.[1] Techniques such as regression are used precisely because they are standard, not because the specific data or the theory behind a particular problem warrant their use.

The solution to this fundamental issue is: Pay attention to multiple kinds of arguments. Don't confuse statistical summaries and reductions of the data with causal inference. Do pay serious attention to the historical context of the data and the actual social processes and interactions that constitute the meaning of the data to human actors.

Defining your research question in terms of all three paradigms of inquiry will clarify aspects of the problem that you might not otherwise think about. Redefining the problem in each way does not necessarily mean that you do research within all of the paradigms of inquiry; it requires only that you theorize the problem more broadly. Thus, I have presented a theory of method, not a set of techniques for research. Paradigms of inquiry provide heuristic guides to the complex process of deciding the grounds on which you can make certain kinds of theoretical claims and empirical generalizations. The theoretical and methodological assumptions embedded in these categories correspond to actual practices of inquiry, although because they are ideal types, no one person or work corresponds to all of the elements of each.

Not every argument must contain (explicitly or implicitly) elements of all three paradigms of inquiry, although it is tempting to argue that a silence is theoretically meaningful. Extreme claims within each paradigm reject the others. When structures overdetermine action, the outcomes of strategic interactions are not seen as problematic. When every interaction is seen as socially constructed and negotiated, structural determination simply cannot be recognized. The problem of human agency within social structures should not be defined away by assuming that every factual assertion is only a matter of interpretation, taste, the standpoint of the observer, or bias. If all history is a narrative of unique events by individual actors in specific times and places, comparisons of social structures cannot be made. If all qualities are reduced to measurable variables, dialectical processes within historical totalities cannot even be seen.

Within and between each paradigm there is a division of labor and a necessary tension between the "theorists" (those who study the conceptual framework, the underlying assumptions, the historical and analytic links between concepts), the "methodologists" (those who analyze the rules governing legitimate evidence and determine how and under what conditions inferences can be drawn and empirical generalizations made), and "researchers" (those who gather the data, conduct the surveys, do the participant observation, or ransack the archives). Within this division of labor, even more particular intellectual identities and roles develop: "sociologist," "free-lance writer," "journalist," "editor," "teacher." Debates, sometimes highly contentious, frequently take place between persons identified with each paradigm of inquiry. Knowledge is also produced within a functional division of labor, where there are markets·for the knowledge which is produced, consumed, and exchanged. Investments are made in paradigms, and they compete on a relatively open market.

Although there is a historical and traditional affinity between each theory and "its" method, the theory does not logically *entail* the method, or vice versa. However, within the institutional constraints and the intellectual and professional identities which constitute the sociological reality of a "paradigm of inquiry," theories do *constrain* the choice of method, in the sense that evidence must fit certain theoretical expectations in order to be recognized and accepted.

DIALECTICAL EXPLANATIONS

It is time to expand on the standpoint from which the working vocabulary for the craft of inquiry has been developed. My own approach might be labeled a "dialectical" (or "multiple" or "integrative") explanation, because the three traditional ways of integrating theory, method, and evidence are incomplete, internally contradictory, and historically changing. Each one alone cannot be an adequate framework for social inquiry.

The term "dialectic" has a long and honorable history of its own, going back to Aristotle and meaning "rational discourse." Obviously I use it in a more specialized and particular sense, to refer to an integrated approach that recognizes the relative power of the three paradigms to answer particular research questions and also their partial and incomplete characters. A dialectical approach recognizes the tensions or contradictions between macro and micro analyses, between case studies and comparative studies, between an emphasis on culture and one on structure. It tries to understand the ways in which historical change transforms the conditions of intellectual work and constrains the very possibility of formulating certain kinds of research questions. It refuses to accept as hard and fast the classic oppositions between understanding and explanation, between history and science, between objective and subjective.

A dialectical approach brings together theories, methods and evidence in a way that allows much more complex relationships to be analyzed. In effect, a much broader set of research questions can be asked and answered, because a broader set of theoretical tools *and* types of evidence can be marshaled.

The basic assumption of a dialectical approach is that social reality is being constantly produced, reproduced, and transformed and can be influenced by conscious human action but, under historical circumstances not completely controlled by human actions. Because social reality can be transformed by human actions, a merely "objective" description of or explanation of relations between variables may miss the potential for human intervention to change those observed relationships. However, one of the paradoxes of sociological research is that the research that is most passionately committed to social justice and social equality must simultaneously be committed to achieving a close approximation to "truth" and "objectivity." A dispassionate assessment of the evidence must be sought if the research is to have a significant and valid social impact. Thus, research on racial or gender inequalities of income, or on the extent of housing segregation, or on which industries benefit from a war economy, or on the impact of a work requirement for mothers on welfare on the mental health of their children may have been undertaken out of deep beliefs in equality, justice, and peace, but the truth value contained in the theoretical claims and empirical generalizations of the research must be judged by independent standards of coherence and evidence.

Part of the strength of sociology has always been its openness to the innovations in both theory and method needed to understand the "real world," whether defined as meaningful human experience, social structures, or the historical relationships of institutions within and among societies. Sociology has not become transfixed, unlike much of economics, by theoretical assumptions of rational choice that almost blind practitioners to the complexity of the relations between our concepts and the phenomena we seek to understand. Most sociologists, fortunately, have not wanted to ignore complexity in favor of predictive models. Sociology has never become, unlike much of political science, a direct ally of policymakers, and it cannot easily become turned to the needs of the society, paradoxically, despite the legacy of "applied sociology." Sociology, precisely because of its openness, tends to be critical and dissenting, not only from social norms but even within itself. But what may look like chaos to the outside observer—or even to the insider who wishes to impose order and consistency—is really a sign of intellectual health, in my opinion, precisely because of its diversity.

Thus, various ways of integrating theory, method, and evidence are constituted in the production of particular sociological works. Multiple paradigms of inquiry are available for use in constructing sociological arguments. Ignoring those intellectual resources impoverishes our sociological imagination.

A dialectical approach is not yet, and may never be, a paradigm in the sense of an institutionalized community of practitioners following an established set of procedures for the production of social knowledge. Part of the reason the development of such a paradigm is unlikely is that in some intrinsic sense a dialectical approach is a critical and dissenting one, in the spirit of C. Wright Mills, Robert S. Lynd, and Alvin Gouldner.[2]

INSTITUTIONAL CONSTRAINTS ON THE PRODUCTION OF SOCIAL KNOWLEDGE

Social science as we know it today is institutionally embedded within what might be called either the "liberal public order" or the "modern state." Most social science research is conducted within public institutions (or private institutions chartered by the state). Social scientists function in roles that are uniquely empowered to certify the nature of social reality. Economists develop measures of prices, productivity, and values and combine them into measures of "inflation" and "Gross National Product." Political scientists assess the level and significance of "voting turnout" and "partisanship." Sociologists analyze the relationships between social "behavior" and categories of "race," "gender," "class" (and its subcategories of "income," "education," "occupation," and "prestige"), "ethnicity," and "age."

Those by now conventional concepts are put in quotation marks to underline how much they are saturated with theoretical assumptions. But those concepts, the empirical evidence that buttresses them, and the works for which such theories and evidence form the analytic framework are also suffused with moral and ethical assumptions about the consequences of research. Social science is *public* scholarship, performed in the public sphere, with identifiable effects. The processes through which choices are made about research questions sometimes systematically obscure this relationship because of the appearance (and thus ideology!) of "objectivity." Sociologists, if they are to recognize the actual way that their work relates to the society, need an ethic of responsible choice of research questions.

S. M. Lipset has argued that sociology is in a crisis because of the political objectives of the people who come into sociology.[3] There is indeed a crisis, both in society and in sociology, but it is not of sociology's making. Separating action questions from theoretical and empirical research questions is a way to respond intellectually to the crises of society without becoming overly politicized in the way that Lipset fears. Lipset's premise is true—sociology does attract people with a commitment to social change—but that energy can be turned toward important intellectual ends without necessarily sacrificing the political and moral implications of knowledge.

As is probably clear by now, in my view "theory" and "method" should not be regarded as distinctive types of inquiry; their integration is the most useful means to producing significant research. The selection of particular kinds of evidence should be determined by exploring the methods best suited to assessing the particular theoretical claims under consideration. Attempts to answer a research question should not be based solely on traditions that have become isolated within fragmented "subfields." However, this position, however convincing it may be in "theory," does not take account of the powerful incentives and sanctions that create fragmented specializations in the theories and methods recognized within the boundaries of particular research paradigms. Academic institutions are constrained by cultural assumptions about scientific authority and by definitions of the legitimate role of public institutions, not to mention political constraints on funding.

Researchers on a particular problem typically summarize the background literature, stake out a theoretical position by routine citations to the canonical works, and proceed to use their favorite statistical or analytic technique. All too often they fail to consider the implications of the theory for the method and then for their analysis of the evidence.

Individuals are clearly not to blame, nor can they solve the problems created by specialization. Constantly narrowing substantive and methodological specialization and the explosion of publications in every area means that individuals cannot possibly master all of the relevant material in the several fields that bear on their problem. They must stake out a claim within the narrow territory in which they can establish expertise, in a research tradition linked to a theoretical standpoint and associated methodological "culture."

Significant institutional pressures are associated with the constraints on individuals to operate within a world of specialization. The pressures to publish are increasing, even in schools mainly devoted to teaching. The result is unquestioning and often inappropriate uses of standard methodological tools such as regression analysis. Also, large problems must be broken up into small publishable chunks to increase one's yearly publication harvest. The individualization of rewards—research grants, merit raises, tenure—further works against genuine interdisciplinary research groups. Even if funds or other resources have been obtained, the costs in time and energy—the intensive conversations, the reading of relevant works across several disciplines, the negotiation of complex research designs, the allocation of credit for publication—are high. One such costly experience may discourage a researcher interested in maximum productivity from repeating the effort, even if the intellectual payoff is significant. There are good structural reasons why most research is contained within the boundaries of one discipline, its journals, its concepts, its standard methods.

The institutionalized power of particular paradigms of inquiry that have incorporated particular forms of theorizing *and* the empirical techniques associated with those theories explains why a particular methodology is used, whether regression analysis, depth interviews and field observation, or investigation in the historical archives. When an article is submitted to a journal editor that bears the telltale marks of a particular tradition (footnote citations, core concepts, analytic techniques), it is usually sent for review to other persons who work within that research program for review. If it isn't sent to someone like that, the editor of the journal is quite appropriately subject to criticism for being partial and discriminatory, arbitrary in his or her judgments.

The solution for the editor is to be "pluralistic"—to accede to the standards of theoretical coherence and empirical plausibility accepted at the moment by those working within a particular research program. This way of routinizing decisions and avoiding conflict reduces intellectual confrontation among different paradigms and thus the possibility of changing ingrained research practices (such as using regression analysis); it also eliminates "maverick" submissions that do not fall into any currently legitimate research program and that can be rejected by referees within different research programs on the grounds that they are "not sociology," "not appropriate for this journal," "not scientific," or "not a contribution," whatever their merits on less parochial grounds.

Although action commitments are embedded in the selection of a problem (such as whether to reform the welfare state or instigate or prevent a revolution), this relationship is only obvious in new, not yet legitimate fields. The knowledge mobilized by powerful fields, those connected to legitimate power (as argued by Foucault) are called "professions" (medicine, law, accounting).[4] The lower status semiprofessions (teaching, social work, nursing), less connected to power, have been associated with producing knowledge that serves the excluded and the relatively powerless, that is, ordinary people.

Recent attempts to develop legitimate analogs to professions within traditional scholarly disciplines are called "applied research" or "public policy programs." Other attempts to institutionalize programs that embody responses to action commitments are still not quite legitimate—"women's studies" or various versions of "ethnic studies"—partly because they are not affiliated with dominant institutions. However, because these incipient "fields" are within the academy, they are under pressure to legitimate their commitment to either "theoretical" or "empirical" problems and a method of inquiry. Precisely because they are not yet legitimate, they can be accused of being "politicized." However, in the sense of being linked to external interest groups that define the context and parameters of the problems they study, these new "disciplines" are no different from law, economics, or accounting. They are more fragile because of their historical circumstances and political location.

These newer attempts to integrate action, theoretical, and empirical questions in institutionalized research practices face the contradiction between openness to evidence (prescribed by the values of science and free inquiry) and the need to develop a community of persons committed to certain goals and assumptions about the world. In the former guise the empirical specialties legitimate the scientific enterprise, because they are indeed finding out new things about the world—the newer "fields" such as women's studies can legitimate themselves the same way.

In the phase of theoretical development, "scientific" specialties may resemble political or religious communities: A charismatic leader mobilizes followers. Dissenters are excluded, and the authority of the leader is maintained, until a new schism occurs.[5] This internal contradiction in the "scientific" enterprise is denied by the image of the objective and rational unity of theory, method, and evidence as simultaneously differentiated but integrated parts of "science." The extent to which evidence actually shapes or "disciplines" arguments, despite personal competition and factional alliances, is an empirical question with important theoretical implications.

Both old and new social movements have had their impact on the institutionalization of research programs and disciplines. The rise of democratic participation and working class mobilization led (not directly, of course, but through many mediations) to "labor history," "social history," "critical theory," "stratification," and "political sociology." Their theories and methods have lost most of the traces of their origins, as the "subfields" have developed an internal intellectual momentum of their own, gaining institutional resources in the process.

The same process is recapitulating itself as the "new social movements" of excluded groups attempt to gain access to the resources of various institutions. For various historical reasons, the universities are more vulnerable to these claims than others. "Women's studies," various forms of "ethnic studies," and "gay and lesbian studies" enable the definition of a political and social identity and mobilize participation. They are not just the reflections of a social movement but part of it. If this institutionalization process succeeds, these programs will either disappear into an already established discipline or become another "factor" alongside the established ones. Gender, ethnic, and religious "factors" will be added to "economic," "political," "social," "cultural," and "historical" factors, each of which has its own discipline in the array. These factors will each be studied theoretically and empirically: "The role of gender in . . ."; "The theoretical construction of ethnic identity. . . ."

The environment of social and political conflict is thus intrinsically related to the emergence of new "fields" and "disciplines." The relative importance of certain action commitments in a given field can be explained partly by how close a given set of research questions is to the cultural, economic, and political struggles taking place in the wider society.

This brief argument about the emergence of fields and subfields is intended to give some historical perspective on the rather abstract and bloodless categories of "action commitments" and "theoretical" and "empirical" research questions. Individuals face real choices—of problems, theoretical framework, methodology, and evidence—but these choices are constrained by the structure of their discipline, the historical situation that presents certain problems at a particular moment, and the specific resources to which individuals have access.

The relationships between action commitments, theoretical claims, and empirical generalizations are complex. The former cannot be easily translated into the latter. Theoretical insights and empirical discoveries have an important impact on your moral and political commitments. The discovery of empirical complexity and institutional resistance may cause you to change your image of social possibilities, in either a more radical or a more conservative direction.[6]

SOURCES OF THE SOCIOLOGICAL IMAGINATION

The sources of the sociological imagination—drawing from C. Wright Mills—are as diverse as the legitimate traditions that link theory, methodology, and evidence. The three classical thinkers who constitute our intellectual heritage give us alternative explanations for the existence of multiple paradigms of inquiry. From a Durkheimian standpoint, different paradigms of inquiry are functionally differentiated units that constitute a division of labor among fields of knowledge. From a Weberian standpoint, the bureaucratization of knowledge requires multiple organizations (universities, research firms, publishers) capable of rationalizing the allocation of scientific resources. From a Marxian standpoint, the accumulation of intellectual capital may require intensive competition for both the use value of data, libraries, theories, and the exchange value of books and articles in the market for knowledge. "Science", similarly, is simultaneously a culturally significant identity, a set of institutions commanding resources and controlling the behavior of those subject to its authority, and a unit of intellectual commodity production in a capitalist economy.

The first source of the sociological imagination, drawing now on Durkheim, is in the experiences of different social groups, as represented in the language of everyday life. Membership in a discipline such as sociology constitutes a intellectual identity, and with that identity goes obligations to master the "literature" and to locate one's argument within contemporary debates. The sociologist as participant in society has access to the rules and norms that influence behavior, both verbal and nonverbal, public and secret. This is a profoundly important source, partly because it goes deeper than the academic abstractions of purely disciplinary concerns. But, access to experience also creates illusions, because the hypotheses within common sense about the social causes of behavior are limited by cultural stereotypes and parochial experiences.

Knowledge is produced by communities of scholars with intellectual traditions. You become a member of the community by participating in its rituals, observing its customs, and taking on the identity of a member of the clan, absorbing the tribal culture of theory and method. Many of the understandings central to a particular intellectual tradition are unwritten, passed on by mentors to protégés, by masters to apprentices.

Certain core symbolic meanings construct the social worlds of sociology. Multiple microsocial worlds constitute the "discipline": "symbolic interactionists," "rational choice theories," "world system theorists," "feminist theorists," "demographers." Each of those social worlds accepts certain beliefs and languages as appropriate ways of producing knowledge. Investigating those social worlds, you might ask: Who talks and writes to whom? Which people perceive themselves to be members of a sociological subcommunity? What metaphors of theory and method are used to describe and identify membership in a subcommunity? What are the lines of conflict within and between sociological subgroups? What symbols, practices, and communications convey loyalty to or betrayal of the solidarity of such a community?

The second source for the sociological imagination, drawing on Weber, is the discipline itself, as a set of organizations that command and allocate the resources for the professions and occupations of social science. As intellectual producers, we are limited not only by time, energy, and resources but also by disciplinary location and the authority of the specialized intellectual elites who have defined the boundaries of legitimate research questions and the acceptable ways of answering them. The ideology of professional specialization defines certain problems as legitimate and excludes others from investigation. Some problems are simply not recognized as within the bounds of "sociology." Career incentives for conformity and sanctions for deviance exist, since the authority of the discipline is expressed in rules that govern the allocation of rewards within it. As with any organization, the result is both to silence some theoretical alternatives that have not yet found a legitimate place and to provide a language, a set of problems, exemplars of "good work," that constitute "paradigms of inquiry." It is easy to flounder without a framework within which to conduct inquiry.[7]

Knowledge is produced by the rational organization of elite professionals in the special sciences. These elites control entry and access to resources that enable intellectual work to be performed; enact and enforce standards of judgment, publication, and promotion; and control and direct the research activities of students, trainees, and novice scientists. This *power* dimension of the production of social knowledge is consistent with Weber's view of the conflict between status groups for power and prestige. Science is a powerful status group in society, with its charismatic figures and its legitimating traditions of rational discourse.

The third source, drawing on Marx, is the intellectual capital that becomes potentially available to any sentient adult as a result of the enormous accumulation of knowledge across all fields of intellectual production. Sociology is merely one unit in a complex division of intellectual labor, and you cannot understand the part without understanding the whole.

To carry the metaphor further, human beings make their own intellectual history, but not under conditions of their own choosing. We are faced with an anarchy of intellectual production: theories, facts, concepts, arguments, problems, and questions, in the form of essays, monographs, reports, articles, and books. Whatever role you are playing at any given moment—intellectual, scholar, student, professor, researcher, policy analyst—you function as an individualized unit of intellectual labor power. The ideological process of the production of knowledge defines your choice of problems to analyze as a *consumer* choice. You behave as if you have a supermarket of research questions to choose from and enough intellectual capital to "buy" a problem and make it your property.

But some people have more cultural capital and political resources than others, because of the way the institutions that produce knowledge are stratified and organized. You inevitably become a commodity in an intellectual labor market, but—and here this extended metaphor breaks down—you are a craft producer of individual works, not an assembler in a factory (although some books—romance novels, for example—are indeed mass produced). Alienated intellectual labor, in which you control neither the process nor the product, exists side by side with the potential for seizing control of the means of intellectual production. The point of the metaphor is to assert, following Marx (although he never developed this analog of intellectual labor to capitalist production), that innovating new social relations of intellectual production requires mastering the existing forces of production (i.e., existing paradigms of sociological inquiry) and then transforming their use.

From the standpoint of the historical totality of the social relations of intellectual production, there is a contradiction in the very notion of a "sociological" explanation. On the one hand, sociology can be seen as in a sense a "bourgeois ideology." Not the totality of a capitalist society, but rather "fields," "problems," "research questions," and "topics" are ordinarily the starting point for social theory. The analogy is looking at the "economy" as if it could be understood as entirely composed of investors, entrepreneurs, managers, workers, and other economic actors. In this view, the divisions of intellectual labor among "theorists," "methodologists," and "researchers" are endemic within every social science field.

On the other hand, the present community of students, teachers, and scholars provides a continuity of intellectual traditions and thus one possible basis for a transformation of the institutions that produce knowledge about social structure and social change. Given a relatively open and pluralistic set of institutions that produce social knowledge, conformity to tribal demands, repression of certain problems, and domination by intellectual elites committed to certain paradigms must be incomplete. Room is left for dissenting definitions of the relations between theories, methods and evidence.

These sources of the sociological imagination constitute the academic cultures we represent and defend, the theoretical and methodological resources we can mobilize, and the disciplinary capital we have accumulated.

THE PROMISE OF SOCIOLOGY

Over the past two hundred years, sociology has offered humanity the promise of insight and knowledge derived from scientific research on the social forces that shape modern life. From Comte, Marx, Durkheim, and Weber in the nineteenth century to Parsons, Goffman, Merton, Lipset, Habermas, and others more recently, sociology has produced a powerful tradition of theoretical insight and empirical research that has enriched our intellectual culture and public life. Sociology has seemingly offered us an integrated and comprehensive "science of society" that could reform and even redesign the social world.

Few sociologists today have the confidence of their forefathers (there are no mothers in the canon) in the potential impact of social knowledge. Sociology's great intellectual promise has largely gone unfulfilled, and the discipline is in a profound institutional crisis that is partly due to its own success. The academic reputation of the discipline is precarious even though historians, literary critics, market researchers, criminologists, communications departments, and free-lance social critics and journalists have made extensive use of sociological methods and theories. We as sociologists have lost much of the intellectual prestige we had only thirty years ago, even as such concepts as status, alienation, and role have entered popular consciousness.[8]

Sociologists' perspectives are marginal to contemporary political and social debate, despite the ambitions of sociology's major thinkers and despite the fact that sociologists have insightful things to say about most of the important social issues of the day, including crime, the family, poverty, race relations, and education. Everyone has borrowed our language and many of our methods, yet few politicians, scholars, or journalists look to sociologists for ideas about how society can deal with the social problems all too evident around us.

Many reasons for the contemporary crisis of sociology lie outside the field itself. Sociology has neither the academic and cultural prestige of the humanities, nor the resources and practical utility of the natural sciences and various technical fields. Sociology is an "impossible science," partly because it raises profound questions about how the society is organized without directly serving the interests of powerful groups that would support the intellectual enterprise. Unlike much of psychology and most of economics, for example, sociology challenges many common assumptions about how social life operates. For example, much sociological research about the persistence of racial, gender, and class inequalities contributes to the unmasking of power and privilege in our society, resulting in active attempts to delegitimize its findings and their interpretation. These persistent concerns tend to marginalize the field in a political climate dominated by individualism and voluntarism as well as market determinism.

Sociology majors and graduate students at this moment in history are squeezed between alienating and demoralizing forces. Postmodern theorists are promoting despair by denying that anything can be known or be generalized in a way that can become a guide to action. Global competitive forces are pushing the production of knowledge toward individualistic "rational choice" explanations of social life in terms of calculations of individual interests. Structural and historical explanations are abandoned in favor of individualistic and psychological explanations and associated research techniques that fit the demands for marketable skills in bureaucratically organized "policy research" organizations. Research training in quantitative analysis may or may not provide a dignified living as a researcher in the face of a shrinking job market for sociology as public support for higher education erodes.

Sociology students, my audience for this book, thus face cruel choices. Your desires for social change—for community solidarity, for gender and class justice, for an end to racial discrimination, for peace and disarmament, for an end to environmental degradation—have inspired me to create tools for the craft of inquiry that will enable the creation of significant knowledge about such pressing issues. The research strategies presented in this book are intended to help construct theoretically coherent and empirically grounded knowledge that can be used to influence public opinion, shape intellectual debates, and affect social policy in a variety of arenas where such knowledge is crucial.

CONCLUSIONS

Sociology is a *craft*, a set of skilled *practices* that occur in a social context. The craft of sociological inquiry is both part of a liberal and humanistic education and a set of tools for the production of social knowledge. The sociological imagination deepens your understanding of how theory influences intellectual work and how research is done.

Sociology should be committed and relevant but not politically dogmatic, philosophically sophisticated but not trapped in epistemological debates, concerned with broad theoretical issues but not so abstract that connection with the real world is lost. Disciplinary specialization has limitations, but disciplines are here to stay.

I want to end with a quotation from my first sociology teacher, Robert Nisbet, taken from his classic *The Sociological Tradition*, written more than thirty years ago but still relevant:

> What sociology, at its best and most creative, has done is to lift [fundamental ideological conflicts of the past century and a half] in which they made their appearance during the age of the industrial and democratic revolutions and to convert them and refine them—in a host of theoretical, empirical, and methodological ways—into the problems and concepts that today give sociology its unique position in the understanding of not only the development of modern Europe but of the new nations that are now undergoing some of the same kinds of social change. . . . So long as these conflicts continue will the sociological tradition remain the evocative and relevant tradition that it has been for more than a century."[9]

Nisbet's emphasis in that book on ideological conflicts must, of course, be coupled with economic, political, and cultural conflicts, but sociology has something to say about all of them.

Sociologists can study diverse problems with a variety of methods, while remaining legitimate within the discipline. The diversity of sociology—its contending "paradigms," its hospitality to both quantitative and qualitative research—is one of its main strengths and not a source of weakness, as some suggest. The attempt to purge sociology of all except its most "scientific" theories and methods is potentially destructive of its most appealing and creative aspects. The "soul" of sociology lies in its location at the intersection between the humanities and the sciences, between historiography and systematic theory, combining art, science, and craft.

Notes

INTRODUCTION

1. For samples of my own writing in various genres of research see *Powers of Theory: Capitalism, the State and Democracy* (with Roger Friedland) (New York and London: Cambridge University Press, 1985), as well as *Health Care Politics: Ideological and Interest Group Barriers to Reform* (Chicago: University of Chicago Press, 1975); *Bureaucracy and Participation: Political Cultures in Four Wisconsin Cities,* with the collaboration of Harry M. Scoble (Chicago: Rand McNally, 1969); *Party and Society: The Anglo-American Democracies* (Chicago: Rand McNally, 1963); "The Political Language of the Nonprofit Sector," in *Language, Symbolism and Politics: Essays in Honor of Murray Edelman,* edited by Richard Merelman (Boulder: Westview Press, 1992); "Bringing Society Back In" (with Roger Friedland), in *The New Institutionalism in Organizational Analysis,* edited by Walter W. Powell and Paul DiMaggio (Chicago: University of Chicago Press, 1991); and "Orpheus Wounded: The Experience of Pain in the Professional Worlds of the Piano," with Andras Szántó, in *Theory and Society* (1996), vol. 25, no. 1, pp. 1–44.

2. See Robert Nisbet, *The Sociological Tradition* (New York: Basic Books, 1966) and his *Sociology as an Art Form* (New York: Oxford University Press, 1976).

3. See Reinhard Bendix, *Max Weber: An Intellectual Portrait* (New York: Doubleday, 1960). See also his *Kings or People: Power and the Mandate to Rule* (Berkeley: University of California Press, 1978) and *Work and Authority in Industry* (New York: Wiley, 1956).

4. See Robert K. Merton, *Social Theory and Social Structure* (New York: Free Press, 1957) and subsequent expanded editions.

5. See various writings by Paul F. Lazarsfeld and others: *On Social Research and Its Language,* edited by Raymond Boudon (Chicago: University of Chicago Press, 1993), *The Varied Sociology of Paul F. Lazarsfeld,* edited by Patricia L. Kendall (New York: Columbia University Press, 1982), and Paul F. Lazarsfeld and Morris Rosenberg, eds., *The Language of Social Research: A Reader in the Methodology of Social Research* (Glencoe: The Free Press, 1955).

6. See Robert S. Lynd, *Middletown* (New York: Harcourt Brace, 1929) and his follow-up study with Helen Merrell Lynd, *Middletown in Transition* (New York: Harcourt Brace, 1937). See also Robert S. Lynd, *Knowledge for What? The Place of Social Science in American Culture* (Princeton: Princeton University Press, 1939).

S. M. Lipset, later my dissertation adviser, also found Lynd's critical perspective on American democracy important. Lipset pays tribute to Lynd in his Ph.D. thesis on the Cooperative Commonwealth Federation, the socialist party and government of Saskatchewan. See *Agrarian Socialism* (Berkeley: University of California Press, 1950).

7. See C. Wright Mills, *The Sociological Imagination* (New York: Oxford University Press, 1959), and his *The Power Elite* (New York: Oxford University Press, 1956. An excellent collection of articles critiquing the theory and evidence of the latter book is G. William Domhoff and Hoyt B. Ballard, *C. Wright Mills and the Power Elite* (Boston: Beacon Press, 1968). For a biography of Mills, see Irving Louis Horowitz, *C. Wright Mills: An American Utopian* (New York: Free Press, 1983).

8. For various of Goffman's writings, see *The Presentation of Self in Everyday Life* (New York: Doubleday Anchor Books, 1959); *Asylums* (New York: Doubleday Anchor Books, 1961); *Strategic Interactions* (Philadelphia: University of Pennsylvania Press, 1969). *Frame Analysis: An Essay on the Organization of Experience* (Boston: Northeastern University Press, 1986; Originally published 1974); and *Stigma: Notes on the Management of Spoiled Identity* (Englewood Cliffs: Prentice Hall, 1963). All further references to Goffman's work are to these editions.

   See the following for summaries and analyses of Goffman's work: Tom Burns, *Erving Goffman* (London and New York: Routledge, 1992), and Philip Manning, *Erving Goffman and Modern Sociology* (Stanford: Stanford University Press, 1992).

9. I follow grander examples here, Robert K. Merton's introduction to the second edition of *The Focused Interview* (New York: Free Press, 1990) and Clifford Geertz's quasi-autobiography, *After the Fact* (Cambridge: Harvard University Press, 1995). Geertz's title is a wonderful triple entendre, referring to his search for evidence, reflections on his career, and his critique of scientific positivism. See also William Foote Whyte, *Participant Observer: An Autobiography* (Ithaca: ILR Press, 1994), the autobiographical interview with anthropologist David M. Schneider, *Schneider on Schneider* (Durham: Duke University Press, 1995), and Norbert Elias, *Reflections on a Life* (Cambridge: Polity Press, 1994).

   For less personal reflections on autobiography, see Jerome Bruner, *Acts of Meaning* (Cambridge: Harvard University Press, 1990), Phillippe Lejeune, *On Autobiography* (Minneapolis: University of Minnesota Press, 1989), and, for a historical approach, Paul John Eakin, ed., *American Autobiography: Retrospect and Prospect* (Madison: University of Wisconsin Press, 1991).

10. I shall not deal with the larger epistemological issues denoted by the terms "positivism," "historicism," "phenomenology," or "postmodernism." Nor shall I deal with matters of research technique: sample and questionnaire design, tests of statistical significance, techniques for interviewing or doing field work. Such techniques must be learned in order to answer empirical questions and are also resources to consider in deciding which questions to ask.

11. It perhaps also needs to be noted that I consider each work by itself, and not in relation to other works by the author. The argument of a work has to stand on and be judged by its own merits.

CHAPTER 1

1. See William Outhwaite and Tom Bottomore, eds., *Dictionary of Twentieth-Century Social Thought* (Oxford: Blackwell, 1993).

2. My critique is by no means new. Robert K. Merton, referring to a 1906 book by Pierre Duhem, argued that the instruments as well as the "experimental results obtained in science are shot through with specific assumptions and theories of a substantive order." *Social Theory and Social Structure* (Glencoe: Free Press, 1957), p. 87.

3. Whether or not the evidence offered in any of the works adequately supports the theoretical claims that are made is obviously critical for a substantive assessment of the arguments but not relevant in the present context, because I am concerned with how to *ask* research questions, not with the quality of the answers

   See Richard Hamilton, *The Social Misconstruction of Reality* (New Haven: Yale University Press, 1996), for a critical analysis of the empirical foundations of some standard works, including *The Protestant Ethic*. In addition, I am focusing on the construction of the argument in a particular work and not on how that work fits into the life work of each thinker.

4. By "background" I remind you that I do mean that an argument may be important but that it is not the central focus of theoretical claims or empirical generalizations.

5. Emile Durkheim, *Suicide: A Study in Sociology*, translated by John A. Spaulding and George Simpson (Glencoe: Free Press, 1951; originally published, 1897). For a thorough personal and intellectual biography of Durkheim, see Steven Lukes, *Durkheim: His Life and Work* (New York: Penguin Books, 1975).

6. Max Weber, *The Protestant Ethic and the Spirit of Capitalism* (New York: Charles Scribner's Sons, 1958. Originally published as "Die protestantische Ethik und der Geist der Kapitalismus," *Archiv für Socialwissonschaft und Sozialpolitik*, 1904–5.

7. *The Eighteenth Brumaire of Louis Napoleon* was published in German in several successive 1852 issues of *Die Revolution*, a New York revolutionary magazine. Page numbers are taken from the edition published by the Foreign Languages Publishing House (Moscow, 1954), as are the quotes by Engels from the Preface to the Third German Edition, 1885. The most recent corrected edition is in Marx and Engels, *Collected Works*, Vol. 11, pp. 103–197 (New York: International Publishers, 1978).

   Marx's action question was: "How can the events in France between 1848 and 1852 be explained in a way which will give workers of the world an understanding of the conditions under which revolutionary action is possible?"

8. Another classic theorist, Georg Simmel, can be regarded as a founding father of studies of social interaction, although he played no institutional role. See *The Sociology of Georg Simmel*, edited by Kurt H. Wolff (Glencoe: Free Press, 1950), and *Conflict and the Web of Group Affiliations*, translated by Kurt Wolff and Reinhard Bendix (Glencoe: Free Press, 1955). An application of Simmel's theories is contained in Lewis Coser, *The Functions of Social Conflict* (Glencoe: Free Press, 1956), and a more recent reflection on the continuing relevance of Simmel's work is David Frisby, *Simmel and Since: Essays on Georg Simmel's Social Theory* (London: Routledge, 1992).

9. Equivalent phrases commonly used are: "process of inquiry," "social inquiry," and "social research." I emphasize the word "process" because I am primarily concerned with the quandaries faced in the course of deciding the topic, the research question, and the appropriate theories, methods, and evidence appropriate to answer the question.

CHAPTER 2

1. See for this use of the term "research program" Imre Lakatos, "The Methodology of Scientific Research Programmes," in *Philosophical Papers*, vol. 1, edited by John Worrall and Gregory Currie (Cambridge: Cambridge University Press, 1978).

2. See Barry Glassner, "Fit for Postmodern Selfhood", in Howard S. Becker and Michael M. McCall, *Symbolic Interaction and Cultural Studies* (Chicago: University of Chicago Press, 1990), pp. 215–243.

3. It helps me to recall Erving Goffman's famous multilevel self-commentary in his Introduction to *Frame Analysis* (1961), pp. 13–20. Goffman says that writing an introduction "allows a writer to try to set the terms of what he will write about. Accounts, excuses, apologies designed to reframe what follows after them, designed to draw a line between deficiencies in what the author writes and deficiencies in himself, leaving him, he hopes, a little better defended than he might otherwise be" (p. 16).

4. The underlying epistemological assumption is eloquently stated by Michael Polanyi: ". . . Into every act of knowing there enters a passionate contribution of the person knowing what is being known . . . this coefficient is no mere imperfection but a vital component of his knowledge." See Michael Polanyi, *Personal Knowledge: Towards a Post-Critical Philosophy* (Chicago: University of Chicago Press, 1962; originally published 1958, p. viii. Polanyi's scientific expertise as a physical chemist is reflected in the otherwise odd word "coefficient" in this quote.

5. This brief comment does not do justice to the long history of the debate over "value-neutrality" in the social sciences. For an important historical discussion, see Robert Proctor, *Value-Free Science: Purity and Power in Modern Knowledge* (Cambridge: Harvard University Press, 1991), and for the relationship of this issue to "irrationality," see Alan Sica, *Weber, Irrationality, and Social Order* (Berkeley: University of California Press, 1988).

6. Stanley Lieberson, for example, says that an "elementary principle about the linkage between theory and research" is that "the nature of the question determines the nature of the data that are needed" (in *Making It Count* [Berkeley: University of California Press, 1985], p. 102). An equally important principle is that the research question also determines the theoretical concepts that are needed.

7. This is the problematic assumption of Anselm Strauss and Barney Glaser, *The Discovery of Grounded Theory* (New York: Aldine, 1967).

8. For a variety of philosophical views, see Daniel Little, *Varieties of Social Explanation* (Boulder: Westview, 1991), Alan Goldman, *Empirical Knowledge* (Berkeley: University of California Press, 1988), Paul K. Moser, *Knowledge and Evidence* (Cambridge: Cambridge University Press, 1989); Lawrence BonJour, *The Struc-*

ture of Empirical Knowledge (Cambridge: Harvard University Press, 1985); and John Dupre, *The Disorder of Things: Metaphysical Foundations of the Disunity of Science* (Cambridge: Harvard University Press, 1993).

9. See Jack Katz, "A Theory of Qualitative Methodology: The Social System of Analytic Fieldwork," in Robert Emerson, ed., *Contemporary Field Research* (Boston: Little Brown, 1983), pp. 127–148. Studying legal aid lawyers, Katz first asked the question "Was there, I wondered, a common process of leaving the institution, or 'burning out,' as the lawyers put it?" He says that "it quickly became apparent that I could not hope to explain the difference between those who did and did not stay more than two years. . . . So I changed the definition of the explanandum to 'desiring to stay two years'" (p. 131). In effect, he reversed the research question from studying why people left to why they stayed.

10. This process is also different from "grounded theory," because the concepts do not "emerge" from the data unmediated by conscious or unconscious theoretical predispositions. See, again, Barney Glaser and Anselm Strauss, *The Discovery of Grounded Theory* (New York: Aldine, 1967).

11. My theoretical questions are "What explains the emergence of paradigms of inquiry about the relationship between theory and evidence in the social sciences? and "What are the grounds for linking particular kinds of theories to particular kinds of evidence?" These questions are in the background for this project but will emerge into the foreground in another book focusing on issues in the epistemology of social inquiry.

12. My empirical questions are: "What are the actual practices of social scientists? How do sociological works regarded as excellent pieces of scholarship use theories, select evidence, construct explanatory arguments?"

CHAPTER 3

1. Multivariate arguments are more likely to use the term "data," interpretive arguments the term "observation," historical arguments the term "evidence." The three terms will be used interchangeably to refer to any kind of information available to human beings about the external (or internal) world.

2. See the exchange between the statistician David Freedman and several sociologists who specialize in methodology (Hubert M. Blalock Jr., William M. Mason, Richard Berk) in the 1991 volume of *Sociological Methodology*, published by the American Sociological Association. Despite other differences, all of them agreed that statistical correlations never directly imply causation. Conversely, the *absence* of a statistical correlation does not mean the absence of a causal relationship, since equal but opposing forces may be canceling out the empirical manifestations of those causes.

3. See Alexis de Tocqueville, *Democracy in America* (New York: Vintage Books, 1955, in two volumes; originally published 1835).

4. Note that this concrete example requires substantive theorizing about the meaning of different kinds of evidence. These are not the only possible interpretations of the census table.

5. For a complete bibliography of these "Chicago style" studies, see Lester R. Kurtz, *Evaluating Chicago Sociology: A Guide to the Literature with an Annotated Bibliography* (Chicago: University of Chicago Press, 1984). For analyses of the impact of the Chicago tradition on American sociology, see Martin Bulmer, *The Chicago School of Sociology: Institutionalization, Diversity and the Rise of Sociological Research* (Chicago: University of Chicago Press, 1984), and Jennifer Platt, *A History of Sociological Research Methods in America: 1920–1960* (Cambridge: Cambridge University Press, 1996).

6. See William Kornblum, *Blue Collar Community* (Chicago: University of Chicago Press, 1974).

7. See Pierre Bourdieu, *The Logic of Practice* (Stanford: Stanford University Press, 1990), and Bourdieu with Loic J. D. Wacquant, *An Invitation to Reflexive Sociology* (Chicago: University of Chicago Press, 1992). For critical assessments of the concept, see Craig Calhoun, Edward LiPuma, and Moishe Postone, eds., *Bourdieu: Critical Perspectives* (Chicago: University of Chicago Press, 1993).

8. See William Foote Whyte, *Street Corner Society* (Chicago: University of Chicago Press, 1943), and Elliot Liebow, *Tally's Corner* (Boston: Little Brown, 1967). More recent work in this genre includes Elijah Anderson, *A Place on the Corner* (Chicago: University of Chicago Press, 1978).

9. For samples of their approach, see Margaret Mead, *Male and Female: A Study of the Sexes in a Changing World* (New York: Mentor Books, 1955, originally published in 1949), Bronislaw Malinowski, *Sex and Repression in Savage Society* (New York: Meridian Books, 1955; originally published in 1927); and Ruth Benedict, *Patterns of Culture* (Boston: Houghton Mifflin, 1989; originally published in 1934).

10. See James Clifford and George E. Marcus, eds., *Writing Culture* (Berkeley: University of California Press, 1986).

11. See Robert A. Caro, *The Power Broker: Robert Moses and the Fall of New York* (New York: Vintage Books, 1975); Taylor Branch, *Parting the Waters: America in the King Years: 1954–1963* (New York: Simon and Schuster, 1988); and David Halberstam, *The Best and the Brightest* (New York: Random House, 1969).

12. For reviews of the controversy over methodological individualism and its link to the issue of the relation between "macro" and "micro" levels of analysis, written from various standpoints, see Joan Huber, ed., *Macro-Micro Linkages in Sociology* (Newbury Park, Calif.: Sage Publications, 1991); Jeffrey C. Alexander, Bernhard Giesen, Richard Munch, and Neil J. Smelser, *The Micro-Macro Link* (Berkeley: University of California Press, 1987); and Michael Hechter, ed., *The Microfoundations of Macrosociology* (Philadelphia: Temple University Press, 1983). See also Donald P. Green and Ian Shapiro, *Pathologies of Rational Choice Theory: A Critique of Applications in Political Science* (New Haven: Yale University Press, 1994).

13. Several journals include important work on the epistemological foundations of historical inquiry, notably *History and Theory, Historical Methods,* and *The History of the Human Sciences.*

14. See Theda Skocpol, ed., *Vision and Method in Historical Sociology* (Cambridge: Cambridge University Press, 1984). The historical sociologists or social historians

whose work is analyzed include Marc Bloch, Karl Polanyi, S. N. Eisenstadt, Reinhard Bendix, Perry Anderson, E. P. Thompson, Charles Tilly, Immanuel Wallerstein, and Barrington Moore Jr.

15. See Talcott Parsons, *The Structure of Social Action* (New York: McGraw Hill, 1937), for his classic attempt to integrate Weber and Durkheim, among others, into his "voluntaristic theory of social action" within integrated value systems. His more substantive essays are collected in *Essays in Sociological Theory* (Glencoe: Free Press, 1954). A more recent attempt to resuscitate Parsons's reputation as a major theorist, contrasting him with Durkheim, Weber, and Marx, is Jeffrey Alexander, *Theoretical Logic in Sociology*, vol. 4, "The Modern Reconstruction of Classical Thought: Talcott Parsons" (Berkeley: University of California Press, 1983). The most important collection of critical writings, with a rejoinder by Parsons, is *The Social Theories of Talcott Parsons* (Englewood Cliffs: Prentice Hall, 1961).

CHAPTER 4

1. For histories of American sociology as an institutionalized mode of production of knowledge, see Robert C. Bannister, *Sociology and Scientism: The American Quest for Objectivity, 1880–1940* (Chapel Hill: University of North Carolina Press, 1987); Dorothy Ross, *The Origins of American Social Science* (Cambridge: Cambridge University Press, 1991); and, for more general historical overviews, Dorothy Ross, ed., *Modernist Impulses in the Human Sciences, 1870–1930* (Baltimore: Johns Hopkins University Press, 1994), and Geoffrey Hawthorn, *Enlightenment and Despair: A History of Sociology* (Cambridge: Cambridge University Press, 1976).

2. Knowing that Durkheim was trying to institutionalize sociology, partly by distinguishing its subject matter from psychology, his action question might be defined half facetiously as follows: "How can I construct a theoretical argument and supporting empirical evidence that will convince French academic elites that a chair of sociology needs to be established in Paris?" Less personally, "Will the claim that 'social facts' are independent of individual motives and psychology help justify a separate academic discipline called sociology?"

3. See Edward A. Tiryakian, "Emile Durkheim", in Tom Bottomore and Robert Nisbet, ed., *A History of Sociological Analysis* (New York: Basic Books, 1978), p. 196.

4. See note 5, Chapter 1, for the reference.

5. Durkheim sidesteps completely the problem of differential suicide rates between Protestants and Catholics in France, which is treated as a "Catholic" nation, disregarding the Protestants. It is conceivable that he might have discovered a *lower* rate among French Protestants if they were a closely knit "defensive" community like the Jews—another seemingly deviant case.

6. The English Reform church questioned not hierarchy, liturgy, or dogma but only the authority of the Pope (to forbid Henry VIII to divorce). English Protestantism is really Catholicism without the Pope. As in the case of the Jews, Durkheim is reminding us that the same empirical indicators do not always measure the same theoretical concept.

7. See Ernst Breisach, *Historiography: Ancient, Medieval, and Modern* (Chicago: University of Chicago Press, 1983).

8. See William Julius Wilson, *The Declining Significance of Race: Blacks and Changing American Institutions* (Chicago: University of Chicago Press, 1978; 2nd ed., 1980, with an epilogue).

9. Note that if big income differences exist between men and women in the same occupation, then apparently "racial" differences in income may really be due to gender discrimination.

10. Wilson presents an explicitly Weberian view of the society, in which the "economy" and the "polity" are separate institutions that interact. The Weberian perspective is also shown in the key terms "power," "resources," "control," and "elite" (all used several times on p. 13).

11. This definition contains the assumption that income is highly correlated with contribution to an employer in the labor market, a view of economic inequality as rationally justified.

12. Note that this statement involves a series of theoretical assumptions necessary to make the simplifying empirical statements. For example, how is income defined, by family or by the individual? Is "black" something we observe (i.e., skin color) or a self-report? Is class something we measure from objective information (income, occupation, education), is it a subjective report (answers to the question "What is your social class?"), or is it inferred from life style, residential neighborhood, friendships, and family status? The empirical categories flow from his theory about both class and race.

13. Affirmative action programs are directed to higher-paying, higher-skilled sectors of the economy. Because these sectors are the expanding ones, such programs have up to now created relatively little racial conflict (p.16). Such programs have primarily benefitted the growing black middle class, not the underclass, and thus have furthered class divisions within the black community.

14. Some of these studies include Stanley Elkins, *Slavery* (New York: Grosset and Dunlap, 1963); Eugene Genovese, *The Political Economy of Slavery* (New York: Random House, 1965); and Herbert Gutman, *The Black Family in Slavery and Freedom* (New York: Pantheon, 1976). A recent overview of the issues is contained in Michael B. Katz, ed., *The "Underclass" Debate: Views from History* (Princeton: Princeton University Press, 1993).

15. Douglas Massey and Nancy Denton, *American Apartheid* (Cambridge: Harvard University Press, 1993).

16. Time series measures of variables are part of the repertoire of techniques normally used by the quantitative faction among the scientific community committed to a multivariate paradigm.

17. Another multivariate argument is the following: "Quantitative research shows that growing up in a ghetto neighborhood increases the likelihood of dropping out of high school, reduces the probability of attending college, lowers the likelihood of employment, reduces income earned as an adult, and increases the risk of teenage childbearing and unwed pregnancy" (p. 13). This careful statement about observed

empirical correlations does not entail any causal inferences about the effects of segregation.

18. This theoretical position complicates their empirical analysis, because they do attempt to, for example, "consider the socioeconomic character of neighborhoods that poor, middle-income, and affluent blacks and whites can be expected to inhabit, holding education and occupational status constant" (p. 151). They present data for Philadelphia that allegedly demonstrate that "high incomes do not buy entree to residential circumstances that can serve as springboards for further socioeconomic mobility . . . because of segregation, the same income buys black and white families educational environments that are of vastly different quality" (p. 153).

19. Earl Babbie, of Chapman College, author of one of the best-selling textbooks on research methodology, describes the process that turns students from researchers with the ability to do "primitive research" (both quantitative and qualitative) simply from ordinary experience and reading to researchers proficient in some specialized methodological techniques. Babbie has observed that "while it is fairly easy to shift students from being primitive qualitative researchers to being primitive quantitative researchers and often possible to lead them on to proficiency and even mastery in quantitative methods, this process seems to take them farther and farther away from proficiency in qualitative research. More to the point, that proficiency in quantitative methods is often accompanied by a *disdain* for qualitative methods in general" (newsletter of the ASA Section on Methodology, Spring 1995).

CHAPTER 5

1. See endnote 6, Chapter 1, for the full reference to the *Protestant Ethic*. See also Reinhard Bendix, *Max Weber: An Intellectual Portrait op. cit.*, p. 49.

2. See Hans Gerth and C. Wright Mills, *From Max Weber: Essays in Sociology* (New York: Oxford University Press, 1946), p. 11.

3. Weber may have been able to background history more easily here because it plays such an important role in the rest of his work.

4. See the critique of Weber's data by Richard Hamilton, *The Social Misconstruction of Reality* (New Haven: Yale University Press, 1996). One interesting point that underscores the lack of concern for the accuracy of "hard" data (by either Weber or his readers) is Hamilton's point that a numerical error has been transcribed from edition to edition without being corrected.

5. See Gianfranco Poggi, "Historical Viability, Sociological Significance, and Personal Judgment," in Hartmut Lehmann and Guenther Roth, eds., *Weber's Protestant Ethic: Origins, Evidence, Contexts* (Cambridge: Cambridge University Press, 1993), p. 298. Poggi's claim that Weber postulates a causal influence between four different sets of ideas "at the level of meaning" uses the concept of cause in a different sense than I do.

6. (New York: Doubleday Anchor Books, 1961).

7. Goffman got his Ph.D. at the University of Chicago, and his work is full of references to Chicago dissertations and publications.

8. Concrete references to places include German concentration camps, the U.S. navy, Chinese "thought reform" camps, British prisons, a Mexican jail, a U.S. internment camp, British spinning factories, U.S. schools, and Latin American work organizations. Categories of societies or states describe historical locations, but the references have no theoretical significance. He is not trying to explain any differences between Chinese and German institutions. Instead, he is concerned with showing the similarities.

9. Arlie Hochschild, with Anne Machung, *The Second Shift* (New York: Avon Books, 1990). (First published in 1989).

CHAPTER 6

1. Karl Marx and Friedrich Engels, *Collected Works*, vol. 38 (New York: International Publishers, 1982), p. 507.

2. See note 7, Chapter 1, for the reference.

3. The First Republic was established in the French Revolution of 1789. The monarchy was restored in 1815 and lasted until 1848.

4. Much of the criticism of Marx's theoretical concepts and method has missed this crucial point. Just as general bourgeois class interests do not explain how a certain group of small businessmen will behave in any given political situation, so the "social conditions of existence" do not explain what ideas or conceptions of interest will lead to any specific action by any specific individuals at any given moment.

5. Barrington Moore Jr., *Social Origins of Dictatorship and Democracy: Lord and Peasant in the Making of the Modern World* (Boston: Beacon Press, 1966).

6. See William H. Sewell Jr., *Work and Revolution in France: The Language of Labor from the Old Regime to 1848* (New York: Cambridge University Press, 1980). The work won the 1981 Herbert Baxter Adams Prize and was in its ninth printing in 1995.

7. William H. Sewell Jr., "The Structure of the Working Class of Marseille in the Middle of the Nineteenth Century" (Ph.D. dissertation, University of California, Berkeley, 1971).

8. One could argue that even when authored texts are available, they can be used to show how particular ideological discourses are constructed. Sociological texts are an example. One may ask the question "How are ideologies or discourses about sources of social order and change displayed in scholarly monographs?" Such a question is a perfectly legitimate one and does not call into question the empirical validity of other aspects of the monographs.

CHAPTER 7

1. The action commitment behind this topic might be a concern to expand the coverage and the services provided by the welfare state. The action implications of the

research question "How can the welfare state be expanded to serve the needs of the poor?" are quite different from such action questions as "How can the political participation of the poor be rendered less effective than it is now?" or "Will increasing income inequality by cutting welfare programs further economic growth?"

2. Such an attempt to specify an empirical measure makes it crystal clear, if it isn't already, that this is a theoretical exercise. You are not yet confronting the issue of whether you can actually get these data. Organizational elites may or may not be willing to confess how independently they are able to act on their policy preferences.

CHAPTER 8

1. Why has regression analysis become standard? A recent book by a UCLA historian, Theodore Porter, *Trust in Numbers: The Pursuit of Objectivity in Science and Public Life* (Princeton: Princeton University Press, 1995), clarifies that issue. His basic point is that quantification is undertaken in fields that are only weakly insulated from external pressures. Physics, which is highly insulated, is less obsessed with quantitative data than is sociology. Weakly insulated fields must find some way of demonstrating their scientific, impersonal, neutral character; hence the drive to quantify. See also Porter, *The Rise of Statistical Thinking 1820–1900* (Princeton: Princeton University Press, 1986).

2. See the works by Robert S. Lynd and C. Wright Mills cited in the Introduction, notes 6 and 7, as well as Alvin Gouldner, *The Coming Crisis of Western Sociology* (New York: Basic Books, 1970), and his *Against Fragmentation: The Origins of Marxism and the Sociology of Intellectuals* (New York: Oxford University Press, 1985).

3. Seymour Martin Lipset, "The State of American Sociology," *Sociological Forum*, Vol. 9, No. 2, June, 1994, pp. 199–220.

4. Foucault's argument about the way in which power is connected to knowledge appears in his *The Archaeology of Knowledge* (London: Tavistock Publications, 1972), as well as in selected interviews and writings gathered in *Power/Knowledge* (New York: Pantheon, 1980). Marx's and Foucault's approaches to power and knowledge are contrasted in Mark Poster, *Foucault, Marxism, and History: Mode of Production versus Mode of Information* (Cambridge: Polity Press, 1984).

5. For examples, primarily from biology, see David Hull, *Science as a Process: An Evolutionary Account of the Social and Conceptual Development of Science* (Chicago: University of Chicago Press, 1988).

6. See, for an exemplary example of the impact of sociological findings on moral commitments, the preface to Kristin Luker, *Abortion and the Politics of Motherhood* (Berkeley: University of California Press, 1984). I am indebted to Alan Wolfe for this point.

7. The current drive to create a field called "cultural studies" is an example of an incipient paradigm of inquiry that at the moment is liberating because it cuts across established disciplines but, once "established" (literally and figuratively), will have

exactly the same problems as existing ones—maintaining boundaries, defining the internal subject matter, and establishing a curriculum, standards, examinations, and criteria for assessing "good work."

8. See Robert K. Merton and Alan Wolfe, "The Cultural and Social Incorporation of Sociological Knowledge," *American Sociologist* 26, no. 3, (Fall 1995), pp. 15–39, on the usage of sociological concepts in the media.

9. Page ix. For citation, see n. 2, Introduction.

Selected Readings

The following bibliography contains a personal and unsystematic selection of classic and recent books on the themes relevant to *The Craft of Inquiry*. Recent books are favored, as well as those that contain relatively full bibliographies on their topics. The emphasis is on both theory (broadly defined to include philosophy of social science as well as different sociological traditions) and methodology, broadly defined to include a variety of texts that deal with strategies of integrating theories, methods, and evidence. Works are included that attempt to bridge different paradigms of inquiry, as well as those securely contained within one. My brief comments only indicate how the book is relevant to this one. Needless to say, I do not agree with all of the arguments: Many of these works are not only broad and diverse but combative.

The classifications into topics may help readers locate relevant works but are somewhat arbitrary. I include participant observation studies and field work under the category of ethnography, for example. Following are the topic headings for the bibliography, in a sequence roughly from the most general (i.e., philosophical and epistemological issues) to the most concrete (i.e., techniques of gathering evidence and writing papers: philosophy of social science; the classical canon (Durkheimian, Weberian, Marxian); paradigms; sociological theory; sociology of science; scientific method; postmodernism; feminist theory and methodology; action research; research methods; case studies as analytic strategy; multivariate theorizing; survey research; interpretive theorizing; qualitative methods; ethnomethodology; ethnography; historical theorizing; historical sociology; historical methods; professionals, scholars, and the academy; the craft of inquiry; writing as cultural and scientific activity; sociologists writing about their work; and finally, help with getting the argument right.

PHILOSOPHY OF SOCIAL SCIENCE

Philosophers concerned with epistemology normally deal not with theories of evidence from the standpoint of research *practices* but rather with the logic of the assumptions that underlie such practices.

An old but still important book is Abraham Kaplan's *The Conduct of Inquiry: Methodology for Behavioral Science* (San Francisco: Chandler Publishing Company, 1964).

Other valuable works include:

Harold Kincaid, *Philosophical Foundations of the Social Sciences.* (New York: Cambridge University Press, 1996). A realist approach.

Peter T. Manicas, *A History and Philosophy of the Social Sciences* (Oxford: Basil Blackwell, 1987). A comprehensive overview of philosophical issues, from a historical perspective.

Mary Tiles and Jim Tiles, *An Introduction to Historical Epistemology: The Authority of Knowledge* (Oxford: Basil Blackwell, 1993). Uses Francis Bacon's Idols of the Tribe, Theater, Marketplace, and Cave as the analytic framework.

Scott Gordon, *The History and Philosophy of Social Science* (London: Routledge, 1991). Encyclopedic review.

Michael Root, *Philosophy of Social Science* (London: Blackwell, 1993). Emphasizes the relationship between "facts" and "values."

Donald T. Campbell, *Methodology and Epistemology for Social Science: Selected Papers*, edited by E. Samuel Overman (Chicago: University of Chicago Press, 1988). Eclectic essays by a leading scholar of strategies of integrating theories, methods, and evidence.

Andrew Sayer, *Method in Social Science: A Realist Approach*, 2d ed. (London: Routledge, 1992). Methods and evidence in practice and in theory.

Allan Megill, ed., *Rethinking Objectivity* (Durham, N.C.: Duke University Press, 1994). Thirteen essays on objectivity within different fields.

THE CLASSICAL CANON

The classical trio—Marx, Weber, and Durkheim—each deserve separate treatment, because a literature has developed that debates each of their approaches to the relationship among theories, methods, and evidence.

A: The Durkheimian Heritage

Durkheim's famous *The Rules of Sociological Method* (written in 1895) is concerned with developing the concept of "social fact"—rules or norms that exert external constraints on individual behavior—not with analyzing research techniques. See Emile Durkheim, *The Rules of Sociological Method*, translated by W. D. Halls (New York: Free Press, 1982). This edition also includes a selection of other works by Durkheim on sociological methodology and a useful Introduction by Steven Lukes.

Other works on Durkheim include:

Steven Lukes, *Emile Durkheim: His Life and Work, a Historical and Critical Study* (New York: Harper and Row, 1973). A magisterial biography.

Frank Pearce, *The Radical Durkheim* (London: Unwin Hyman, 1989). A critical review of Durkheim's epistemology and a reformulation of the argument of *Suicide*.

B. The Weberian Heritage

Weber's essays on method, written between 1903 and 1917, are collected in Max Weber, *The Methodology of the Social Sciences*, translated and edited by Edward A. Shils and Henry A. Finch (Glencoe, Ill.: Free Press, 1949).

Other valuable works:

Max Weber, *Economy and Society: An Outline of Interpretive Sociology* (New York: Bedminster Press, 1968). The introduction, by Guenther Roth, is an extensive essay, with one sentence worth quoting here: "Sociologists live, and suffer, from their dual task: to develop generalizations and to explain particular cases" (p. xxxi).

Reinhard Bendix, *Max Weber: An Intellectual Portrait* (Garden City, N.Y.: Doubleday, 1960). Not a biography, but an overview of Weber's work.

Stephen Kalberg, *Max Weber's Comparative Historical Sociology* (Chicago: University of Chicago Press, 1994). Focuses on ideal types and causal analysis.

Kurt Samuelsson, *Religion and Economic Action: A Critique of Max Weber* (New York: Harper and Row, 1964; originally published 1957). A detailed critique of the evidence and argument of *The Protestant Ethic and the Spirit of Capitalism.*

Thomas Burger, *Max Weber's Theory of Concept Formation: History, Laws, and Ideal Types* (Durham, N.C.: Duke University Press, 1976). On the active role of the human mind in constructing both scientific and cultural significance.

C: The Marxian Heritage

Although Karl Marx regarded himself as developing a science of social change, his dialectical and historical materialism was very different from Durkheim's, and not only because of his revolutionary commitments. Marx's own reflections on methodology are contained in his preliminary notes or drafts of *Capital*, arbitrarily labeled the *Grundrisse* ("Notebooks" or "Outlines") by subsequent editors and translators. His various texts on methodology are collected in Terrell Carver, ed., *Karl Marx: Texts on Method* (Oxford: Basil Blackwell, 1975). A fascinating work on the actual way that Marx read, took notes on, and wrote critical comments on other works as part of his preparatory work for his own writing is Thomas M. Kemple, *Reading Marx Writing: Melodrama, the Market, and the 'Grundrisse'* (Stanford: Stanford University Press, 1995). See also David McLellan, *Karl Marx: His Life and Thought* (New York: Harper and Row, 1973), a biography and summary of the work of Marx (and Engels).

Two books that analyze the relationship between Marx's methodology and Hegel's work are Tony Smith, *The Logic of Marx's Capital: Replies to Hegelian Criticisms* (Albany: State University of New York Press, 1990), and Fred Moseley, ed., *Marx's Method in Capital: A Reexamination* (New Jersey: Humanities Press, 1993).

The relationship of Marx to scientific method is dealt with in Patrick Murray, *Marx's Theory of Scientific Knowledge* (New Jersey: Humanities Press, 1988), and Daniel Little, *The Scientific Marx* (Minneapolis: University of Minnesota Press, 1986).

Marx's method is analyzed in an active literature. See Bertell Ollman, 1993). *Dialectical Investigations* (New York: Routledge, 1993). There is a four-page bibliography on dialectical method, which includes fourteen books published in the 1970s, twenty from the 1980s, and three from the 1990s, not including his own. See also Rob Beamish, *Marx, Method, and the Division of Labor* (Urbana: University of Illinois Press, 1992), a review of Marx's study notebooks to see how he developed concepts.

Also useful are:

Richard F. Hamilton, *The Bourgeois Epoch: Marx and Engels on Britain, France and Germany* (Chapel Hill: University of North Carolina Press, 1991). A detailed reexamination of the evidence supporting Marxist arguments.

Pauline Marie Vaillancourt, *When Marxists do Research* (New York: Greenwood Press, 1986). A review and critique of the different research traditions within a "Marxian" perspective.

PARADIGMS

Among the works on paradigms are:

Thomas S. Kuhn, *The Structure of Scientific Revolutions*, 2d ed., enlarged (Chicago: University of Chicago Press, 1970; first edition: 1962). The classic statement of the importance of paradigmatic communities in the organization of inquiry.

Imre Lakatos and Alan Musgrave, eds., *Criticism and the Growth of Knowledge* (Cambridge: Cambridge University Press, 1970). The first collection of works to evaluate critically Kuhn's argument about paradigms; includes a reply from Kuhn. See also Gary Gutting, ed., *Paradigms and Revolutions: Applications and Appraisals of Thomas Kuhn's Philosophy of Science* (Notre Dame: University of Notre Dame Press, 1987), for still more commentary and critique.

Paul Hoyningen-Huene, *Reconstructing Scientific Revolutions: Thomas S. Kuhn's Philosophy of Science* (Chicago: University of Chicago Press, 1993). An exhaustive review of Kuhn and his critics, with an extensive bibliography.

Arthur Donovan, Larry Laudan, and Rachel Laudan, eds., *Scrutinizing Science: Empirical Studies of Scientific Change* (Baltimore: Johns Hopkins University Press, 1992). Fifteen chapters on historical innovations in the physical sciences, testing explicit hypotheses about the fate of theoretical claims and empirical generalizations about paradigms.

SOCIOLOGICAL THEORY

For an excellent overview (that does not deal with the implications of theory for methods or evidence), see Randall Collins, *Four Sociological Traditions* (New York: Oxford University Press, 1994). Collins here emphasizes Weber's similarity to Marx as "conflict theorists" rather than the differences between them, which I emphasize in this book. He also deals with the Durkheimian tradition, the microinteractionist tradition (in which he includes Goffman), and the utilitarian tradition (also called exchange theory or rational choice).

See also:

James B. Rule, *Theory and Progress in Social Science* (Cambridge: Cambridge University Press, 1997). An important evaluation of the success and failure of several research programs: rational choice, ethnomethodology, interaction process, networks, feminism, functionalist theory, and theory as a means to explanation, as an end in itself, and as a strategy of "coping."

Anthony Giddens and Jonathan Turner, eds., *Social Theory Today* (Stanford: Stanford University Press, 1987. Summaries of major theoretical traditions, by advocates and critics.

Charles Lemert, ed., *Social Theory: The Multicultural and Classic Readings* (Boulder: Westview Press, 1993). From Marx to Judith Butler and Vaclav Havel.

Bryan S. Turner, ed., *The Blackwell Companion to Social Theory* (Oxford: Blackwell, 1996) Fifteen chapters on all major contemporary theoretical programs.

Llewellyn Gross, ed., *Symposium on Sociological Theory* (Evanston, Ill.: Row Peterson, 1959). An old but still classic collection of essays.

SOCIOLOGY OF SCIENCE

Volumes on this subject include:

Robert K. Merton, *On Social Structure and Science,* edited and with an introduction by Piotr Sztompka (Chicago: University of Chicago Press, 1996). A collection of major essays by a founder of the sociology of science.

Jon Clark, Celia Modgil, and Sohan Modgil, *Robert K. Merton: Consensus and Controversy* (London: Falmer Press, 1990). Includes rare and important dialogues among scholars about theoretical and empirical issues.

Andrew Pickering, ed., *Science as Practice and Culture* (Chicago: University of Chicago Press, 1992). Fifteen chapters on scientific knowledge as a social product.

Stephen Cole, *Making Science: Between Nature and Society* (Cambridge, Mass.: Harvard University Press, 1992). Core knowledge and the research frontier.

Joshua Lederberg, ed., *The Excitement and Fascination of Science: Reflections by Eminent Scientists,* vol. 3, parts 1 and 2 (Palo Alto, Calif.: Annual Reviews, 1990). Autobiographical reflections by more than one hundred scientists in eighteen different fields, ranging from biology and chemistry to anthropology (six) and sociology (two), on how they do their work.

SCIENTIFIC METHOD

Useful works include:

Barry Gower, *Scientific Method: A Historical and Philosophical Introduction* (London: Routledge, 1997). The ideas of classic figures in the philosophy of science, including Bacon, Mill, Whewell, Poincaré, Duhem, Peirce, Reichenbach, Popper, and Carnap.

Peter Galison and David J. Stump, eds., *The Disunity of Science: Boundaries, Contexts and Power* (Stanford: Stanford University Press, 1996). A collection of essays by historians and philosophers of science, with an extensive bibliography.

POSTMODERNISM

Among the works in this area are:

Steven Seidman and David G. Wagner, eds., *Postmodernism and Social Theory* (Cambridge: Blackwell, 1992). Twelve essays both defending and challenging the usefulness of postmodern theory.

Robert Hollinger, *Postmodernism and the Social Sciences: A Thematic Approach* (Thousand Oaks, Calif.: Sage Publications, 1994). A summary of the debates between modernity and postmodernity.

Pauline Marie Rosenau, *Post-Modernism and the Social Sciences: Insights, Inroads, and Intrusions* (Princeton: Princeton University Press, 1992). A clear exposition and critique of the core concepts of postmodern social science.

FEMINIST THEORY AND METHODOLOGY

A comprehensive and eclectic overview is given by Shulamith Reinharz, *Feminist Methods in Social Research* (New York: Oxford University Press, 1992). An older and diverse collection of readings is Helen Roberts, ed., *Doing Feminist Research* (London: Routledge and Kegan Paul, 1981)

A collection of articles by leading figures is Linda Alcoff and Elizabeth Potter, *Feminist Epistemologies* (New York: Routledge, 1993), which contains a comprehensive bibliography. Another collection of articles that focuses on the "research act" is Mary Margaret Fonow and Judith A. Cook, *Beyond Methodology: Feminist Scholarship as Lived Research* (Bloomington: Indiana University Press, 1991).

Two important works by Dorothy Smith include *The Everyday World as Problematic: A Feminist Sociology* (Toronto: University of Toronto Press, 1987) and *The Conceptual Practices of Power: A Feminist Sociology of Knowledge* (Boston: Northeastern University Press, 1990).

ACTION RESEARCH

Contributions in this area include:

Charles E. Lindblom, *Inquiry and Change: The Troubled Attempt to Understand and Shape Society* (New Haven: Yale University Press, 1990). How social knowledge can help (or prevent!) problem solving.

Irving Louis Horowitz, *The Decomposition of Sociology* (New York: Oxford University Press, 1993). An attack on much of contemporary sociology for becoming committed to politicized and ideological critiques of modern society.

Paulo Freire, *Pedagogy of the Oppressed* (New York: Continuum Books, 1993; first published 1970). Teaching as an ideal dialogue of freedom, rather than as domination. See also Peter McLaren and Peter Leonard, eds., *Paulo Freire: A Critical Encounter* (London: Routledge, 1993), for analyses of "critical pedagogy."

Charles Lemert, *Sociology After the Crisis* (Boulder: Westview Press, 1995). Reflections on the current role of sociology in the world, as scientific, moral, and cultural agent.

Bernard Barber, *Effective Social Science: Eight Cases in Economics, Political Science, and Sociology* (New York: Russell Sage Foundation, 1987). The book is based on detailed narratives of their action research by eight social scientists interviewed by Barber, on subjects including income taxes, privacy, transport regulation, the ethics of human subjects research, and the volunteer army.

RESEARCH METHODS

An excellent overview of a wide variety of "methods" (in the narrow sense of techniques for gathering and analyzing different kinds of evidence) is Russell Bernard, *Research Methods in Anthropology: Qualitative and Quantitative Approaches*, 2d ed. (Thousand Oaks, Calif.: Sage Publications, 1994). Bernard stresses how important it is not to identify quantification with science; he goes through basic quantitative procedures, with many illuminating examples.

Other resources are:

Matthew B. Miles and A. Michael Huberman, *Qualitative Data Analysis: An Expanded Sourcebook*, 2d ed. (Thousand Oaks, Calif.: Sage Publications, 1994). Comprehensive review of different analytic procedures.

Joel H. Levine, *Exceptions Are the Rule: An Inquiry into Methods in the Social Sciences* (Boulder: Westview Press, 1993). How to use numbers sensibly.

Earl Babbie, *The Practice of Social Research*, 7th ed. (Belmont, Calif.: Wadsworth, 1995). A standard textbook that covers most methods, with an emphasis on multivariate analysis.

David Freedman, Robert Pisani, Roger Purves, and Ani Adhikari, *Statistics*, 2d ed. (New York: W.W. Norton, 1991). Statistics as the "art of making numerical conjectures about puzzling questions" (from the Preface to the first edition).

W. Lawrence Neuman, *Social Research Methods: Qualitative and Quantitative Approaches*, 2d ed. (Boston: Allyn and Bacon, 1994). Positivist, interpretive, and critical social science.

Morton Hunt, *Profiles of Social Research: The Scientific Study of Human Interactions* (New York: Russell Sage Foundation, 1985). Fascinating case studies of the theories and practices of research.

Peter Frost and Ralph Stablein, eds., *Doing Exemplary Research* (Newbury Park, Calif.: Sage Publications, 1992). Case studies of seven research "journeys," including excerpts from seven published articles, retrospective views by the authors, and commentaries by other scholars on the research process exemplified by the article. Most of the studies deal with some aspect of organizational theory and behavior.

Harris Cooper and Larry V. Hedges, eds., *The Handbook of Research Synthesis* (New York: Russell Sage Foundation, 1994). A collection of essays on strategies of synthesizing multivariate research on a problem by people drawn primarily from information science, statistics, psychology, education, and social policy analysis. How to formulate research questions is not dealt with, nor are any forms of interpretive or historical arguments. "Theory" is defined as "estimates of magnitudes of effects for theorized relations" between variables (p. 21). The assumption is that quantitative analysis is almost synonymous with "science." (There is almost no overlap in the references in this book and the *Handbook of Qualitative Research).*

CASE STUDIES AS ANALYTIC STRATEGY

Valuable sources in this area include:

Charles C. Ragin and Howard S. Becker, eds., *What Is a Case? Exploring the Foundations of Social Inquiry* (Cambridge: Cambridge University Press, 1992). Ten important chapters by practitioners on how cases build arguments.

Robert E. Stake, *The Art of Case Study Research* (Thousand Oaks, Calif.: Sage Publi-
    cations, 1995). Applications to teaching and school reform by a professor of ed-
    ucation.
Joe R. Feagin, Anthony M. Orum, and Gideon Sjoberg, eds., *A Case for the Case
    Study* (Chapel Hill: University of North Carolina Press, 1991). Ten chapters on
    methodological issues.

MULTIVARIATE THEORIZING

For a classic statement of how to theorize using chains of causal variables, see Arthur
    Stinchcombe, *Constructing Social Theories* (Chicago: University of Chicago Press,
    1968). A thoughtful critique of the assumptions entailed in making multivariate ar-
    guments is Stanley Lieberson, *Making It Count* (Berkeley: University of California
    Press, 1985).

SURVEY RESEARCH

Useful volumes in this area are:
Stanley L. Payne, *The Art of Asking Questions* (Princeton: Princeton University Press,
    1951). A classic guide to the construction of a survey.
Charles L. Briggs, *Learning How to Ask: A Sociolinguistic Appraisal of the Role of the In-
    terview in Social Science Research* (Cambridge: Cambridge University Press, 1986).
Judith M. Tanur, ed., *Questions About Questions: Inquiries into the Cognitive Bases of
    Surveys* (New York: Russell Sage Foundation, 1992). Thirteen chapters on cogni-
    tive and social processes which affect survey responses.
William Foddy, *Constructing Questions for Interviews and Questionnaires: Theory and
    Practice in Social Research* (Cambridge: Cambridge University Press, 1993). A
    symbolic interactionist approach.

INTERPRETIVE THEORIZING

A valuable collection of articles is Paul Rabinow and William M. Sullivan, *Interpretive
    Social Science: A Second Look* (Berkeley: University of California Press, 1987),
    which contains classic articles by Charles Taylor, Gadamer, Habermas, Foucault,
    Hirschman, Geertz, Jameson, and others.
Several conferences in the past decade or so have resulted in volumes of essays that
    assess the role of "rhetoric," sometimes called the "interpretive turn" in the hu-
    man sciences. Chapters by scholars from many fields maintain that the way argu-
    ments are constructed affects one's predisposition to accept them. See John S.
    Nelson, Allan Megill, and Donald N. McCloskey, *The Rhetoric of the Human Sci-
    ences: Language and Argument in Scholarship and Public Affairs* (Madison: Uni-
    versity of Wisconsin Press, 1987); David R. Hiley, James F. Bohman, and
    Richard Shusterman, eds., *The Interpretive Turn: Philosophy, Science, Culture*
    (Ithaca: Cornell University Press, 1991), and Herbert W. Simons, ed., *The
    Rhetorical Turn: Invention and Persuasion in the Conduct of Inquiry* (Chicago:
    University of Chicago Press, 1990).

Bryan D. Palmer's book, *Descent into Discourse: The Reification of Language and the Writing of Social History* (Philadelphia: Temple University Press, 1990), is a critique of the "linguistic" or "rhetorical turn" in social history.

See also:

Clifford Geertz, *The Interpretation of Cultures* (New York: Basic Books, 1973). Classic essays on "thick descriptions" of symbolic meanings.

On symbolic interactionism, see:

Herbert Blumer, *Symbolic Interactionism: Perspective and Method* (Berkeley: University of California Press, 1969). A collection of articles, including his critique of multivariate arguments, "Sociological Analysis and the 'Variable,' " by one of the founders of this paradigm

Robert Prus, *Symbolic Interaction and Ethnographic Research: Intersubjectivity and the Study of Human Lived Experience* (Albany: State University of New York Press, 1996). A broad survey of the practices of the interpretive paradigm, paying attention to theories, methods, and evidence. Extensive bibliography.

Howard S. Becker and Michal M. McCall, *Symbolic Interaction and Cultural Studies* (Chicago: University of Chicago Press, 1990). Includes chapters relating symbolic interaction to history, religion, philosophy, art, science, the body, and language.

QUALITATIVE METHODS

Norman K. Denzin and Yvonna S. Lincoln, eds., *Handbook of Qualitative Research* (Thousand Oaks, Calif.: Sage Publications, 1994), presents thirty-six comprehensive chapters on every aspect of "qualitative" research, but the emphasis is on constructing interpretive arguments. There is one chapter on historical methods, by Gaye Tuchman. The editors, in a brief history of qualitative research, say that "all histories [are] somewhat arbitrary." No chapters deal with the relationship of interpretive arguments to multivariate ones, and there is almost no overlap with the references in the *Handbook of Research Synthesis*.

ETHNOMETHODOLOGY

Harold Garfinkel, *Studies in Ethnomethodology* (Cambridge, Mass.: Polity Press, 1967), has written the seminal work on how ordinary people construct a relatively stable social world through everyday actions. Garfinkel's work is assessed in John Heritage, *Garfinkel and Ethnomethodology* (Cambridge: Polity Press, 1984). A more general overview (with an extensive bibliography) is Graham Button, ed., *Ethnomethodology and the Human Sciences* (Cambridge: Cambridge University Press, 1991).

ETHNOGRAPHY

Paul Atkinson, *The Ethnographic Imagination: Textual Constructions of Reality* (London: Routledge, 1990), is an examination of how selected ethnographic arguments are constructed.

Other valuable books in this area are:

Michael Burawoy et al., *Ethnography Unbound: Power and Resistance in the Modern Metropolis* (Berkeley: University of California Press, 1991). A report of field work in progress by ten Berkeley graduate students, with their reflections on how ethnographic research can help answer action questions, as well as reflections on the "extended case method" by their instructor.

Annette Lareau and Jeffrey Shultz, eds., *Journeys Through Ethnography: Realistic Accounts of Fieldwork* (Boulder: Westview Press, 1996). Reflections by several field workers on their projects.

John Camaroff and Jean Camaroff, *Ethnography and the Historical Imagination* (Boulder: Westview, 1992). An attempt to synthesize interpretive and historical arguments, using a variety of case studies by the authors, by two anthropologists who specialize in African cultures. Contains extensive bibliography of anthropological classics.

Robert M. Emerson, Rachel I. Fretz, and Linda L. Shaw, *Writing Ethnographic Fieldnotes* (Chicago: University of Chicago Press, 1995). A concrete handbook on how to cope with extensive field notes. See also a slightly older volume, Robert M. Emerson, *Contemporary Field Research: A Collection of Readings* (Boston: Little Brown, 1983).

John van Maanen, *Tales of the Field: On Writing Ethnography* (Chicago: University of Chicago Press, 1988). A contrast of realist, confessional, and impressionist "tales."

Roger Sanjek, ed., *Fieldnotes: The Makings of Anthropology* (Ithaca: Cornell University Press, 1990). Thirteen anthropologists analyze the tradition and uses of field notes in the construction of arguments.

George W. Stocking Jr., *The Ethnographer's Magic and Other Essays in the History of Anthropology* (Madison: University of Wisconsion Press, 1992). Emphasizes the contributions of Franz Boas and Bronislaw Malinowski to the dominance of fieldwork in anthropology. An autobiographical introduction.

Martyn Hammersley, *What's Wrong with Ethnography?: Methodological Explorations* (London: Routledge, 1992. Reject both a "naive realism" and also postmodern relativism, advocating that ethnography should be integrated into "mainstream" methodology.

HISTORICAL THEORIZING

Hayden White, *Metahistory: The Historical Imagination in Nineteenth-Century Europe* (Baltimore: Johns Hopkins University Press, 1973), distinguishes four "modes of historical consciousness" on the basis of their tropes: metaphor, synecdoche, metonymy, and irony, which constitute "traditions of inquiry" in history. Includes detailed analyses of the work of Hegel, Michelet, Ranke, Tocqueville, Burckhardt, Marx, Nietzsche, and Croce.

See also:

Christopher Lloyd, *The Structures of History* (Oxford: Blackwell, 1993). As the title suggests, the work emphasizes the structural causes and consequences of events, not the construction of narratives. Extensive bibliography.

Eric H. Monkkonen, ed., *Engaging the Past: The Uses of History Across the Social Sciences* (Durham, N.C.: Duke University Press, 1994). Essays on historical approaches in anthropology, economics, sociology, and geography.

Alex Callinicos, *Theories and Narratives: Reflections on the Philosophy of History* (Durham, N.C.: Duke University Press, 1995). A reconstruction of a Marxist view of historical arguments.

Frank Ankersmit and Hans Kellner, *A New Philosophy of History* (Chicago: University of Chicago Press, 1995). An important collection of essays defending the intrinsic interdisciplinary character of historical arguments.

Ralph Cohen and Michael S. Roth, *History And . . . Histories Within the Human Sciences* (Charlottesville: University Press of Virginia, 1995). Essays, critiques, and responses on the relationship of history to literature, music, medicine, music, anthropology, philosophy, feminism, and culture.

HISTORICAL SOCIOLOGY

Valuable sources include:

Dennis Smith, *The Rise of Historical Sociology* (Philadelphia: Temple University Press, 1991). A summary of the resurgence of historical sociology, focusing on Marshall, Bendix, Bloch, Moore, Skocpol, Tilly, Anderson, Wallerstein, Braudel, Mann, Runciman, and Giddens.

Theda Skocpol, ed., *Vision and Method in Historical Sociology* (Cambridge: Cambridge University Press, 1984). Critical syntheses of the work of Bloch, Polanyi, Eisenstadt, Bendix, Anderson, Thompson, Tilly, Wallerstein, and Moore.

HISTORICAL METHODS

See:

David Hackett Fischer, *Historians' Fallacies: Toward a Logic of Historical Thought* (New York: Harper and Row, 1970). A classic review of mistakes in the construction of historical arguments, starting with a chapter "Fallacies of Question-Framing."

Carlo Ginzburg, *Clues, Myths, and the Historical Method* (Baltimore: Johns Hopkins University Press, 1989). A collection of reflective essays by a historian on issues of evidence.

PROFESSIONALS, SCHOLARS, AND THE ACADEMY

Among the books in this field are:

David Damrosch, *We Scholars: Changing the Culture of the University* (Cambridge, Mass.: Harvard University Press, 1995). Reflections by a scholar of comparative literature on general and specialized education and the politics of academic specialization.

Theodore S. Hamerow, *Reflections on History and Historians* (Madison: University of Wisconsin Press, 1987). Reflections by a historian on "history as a way of life."

Burton R. Clark, *Places of Inquiry: Research and Advanced Education in Modern Universities* (Berkeley: University of California Press, 1995). Comparative studies of the institutional relations between teaching and research in Germany, Britain, France, the United States, and Japan.

Terence C. Halliday and Morris Janowitz, *Sociology and Its Publics: The Forms and Fates of Disciplinary Organization* (Chicago: University of Chicago Press, 1992). Eleven essays by sociologists on external influences on the structure of the discipline.

THE CRAFT OF INQUIRY

Two books that have almost the same title and deal with some of the same issues but in quite different ways are Pierre Bourdieu, Jean-Claude Chamboredon, and Jean-Claude Passeron, *The Craft of Sociology: Epistemological Preliminaries* (Berlin: Walter de Gruyter, 1991; originally published 1968), and Wayne C. Booth, Gregory G. Colomb, and Joseph M. Williams, *The Craft of Research* (Chicago: University of Chicago Press, 1995). The Bourdieu book is true to its subtitle and in a real sense formulates the epistemological foundations of this book. The Booth volume deals with how to ask questions and frame arguments, but more than half of it deals with how to use sources and actually draft and revise the written presentation of the argument, in keeping with the background of the authors as professors of English. Very little is said about theoretical versus empirical questions.

An older classic is Aaron Cicourel, *Method and Measurement in Sociology* (New York: Free Press, 1964), which deals explicitly with the relationship of theoretical assumptions and methodological procedures.

WRITING AS CULTURAL AND SCIENTIFIC ACTIVITY

Useful works include:

Jack Seltzer, ed., *Understanding Scientific Prose* (Madison: University of Wisconsin Press, 1993). Critical essays on an article in evolutionary theory.

Charles Bazerman, *Shaping Written Knowledge: The Genre and Activity of the Experimental Article in Science* (Madison: University of Wisconsin Press, 1988). Scientific writing as a social practice.

Richard Harvey Brown, ed., *Writing the Social Text: Poetics and Politics in Social Science Discourse* (New York: Aldine de Gruyter, 1992). Thirteen chapters on different aspects of the construction of texts.

SOCIOLOGISTS WRITING ABOUT THEIR WORK

Two collections of essays edited by Bennett Berger and Philip E. Hammond contain examples of sociologists' reporting—no doubt with varying degrees of honesty—on the dilemmas they faced in deciding on their research questions. See Phillip E. Hammond, ed., *Sociologists at Work* (New York: Basic Books, 1964), and Bennett Berger, ed., *Authors of Their Own Lives: Intellectual Autobiographies by Twenty American Sociologists* (Berkeley: University of California Press, 1990).

HELP WITH GETTING THE ARGUMENT RIGHT

Useful guidance on writing is contained in:

Mary-Claire van Leunen, *A Handbook for Scholars*, rev. ed. (New York: Knopf, 1992). Advice on how to cite, quote, footnote, use references, and prepare manuscripts.

William Strunk Jr. and E. B. White, *The Elements of Style* (New York: Macmillan, 1959; originally published 1935). The classic "little book" on how to omit needless words.

Howard S. Becker (with a chapter by Pamela Richards), *Writing for Social Scientists: How to Start and Finish Your Thesis, Book, or Article* (Chicago: University of Chicago Press, 1986). Tips on editing, voice, authority, "getting it out the door."

Richard Marius, *A Writer's Companion* (New York: Knopf, 1985). Helpful guidance on sentences, paragraphs, drafts, metaphors, diction, wordiness.

Susan Krieger, *Social Science and the Self: Personal Essays on an Art Form* (New Brunswick, N.J.: Rutgers University Press, 1991). Self in context, as expressed in different forms of writing.

Sharon Friedman and Stephen Steinberg, *Writing and Thinking in the Social Sciences* (Englewood Cliffs, N.J.: Prentice Hall, 1989). Experiments, observations, interviews, documents, and how to write them up.

Index

Abortion and the Politics of Motherhood (Luker), 145n.6
Abstract categories, 38
Abstract empiricism, 50
Action agendas, 25, 26, 27
    in *American Apartheid*, 67–70
Action commitments, 128
Actors, 43, 44, 45, 113
Acts of Meaning (Bruner), 136n.9
Adhikari, Ani, 153
Affirmative action, 37, 60, 61, 142n.13
After the Fact (Geertz), 136n.9
Against Fragmentation (Gouldner), 145n.2
Agrarian Socialism, 136n.6
Alcoff, Linda, 152
Alexander, Jeffrey C., 140n.12, 141n.15
Altruistic suicide, 55
American Apartheid (Massey & Denton), 9, 58, 63–70, 142n.15
    action agendas in, 67–70
    dialectical explanations in, 67
American Autobiography: Retrospect and Prospect (Eakin), 136n.9
Anderson, Elijah, 140n.8
Anderson, Perry, 141n.14, 157
Ankersmit, Frank, 157
Anomic suicide, 55
Anthropology, 44
Anxiety, cognitive and emotional sources of, 22–24
Applied research, 127
Archaeology of Knowledge, The (Foucault), 145n.4
Argument construction, 8–9, 21, 32–53; *see also* Foreground historical arguments; Foreground interpretive arguments; Foreground multivariate arguments
    divorce of theory and evidence in, 49–50
    evidence and theory in, 34–37
    human agency in, 37–38
Arguments, 6, 8, 25; *see also* Argument construction
Aristotle, 123
Art of Asking Questions, The (Payne), 154
Art of Case Study Research, The (Stake), 154
Asylums (Goffman), 7, 9, 72, 76–82, 136n.8
    evidence and theory in, 80–81
Atkinson, Paul, 155
Authors of Their Own Lives (Berger), 158

Babbie, Earl, 143n.19, 153
Background, 8, 32
Background interpretive arguments, 67
Bacon, Francis, 148, 151
Ballard, Hoyt B., 136n.7
Bannister, Robert C., 141n.1
Barber, Bernard, 152
Bazerman, Charles, 158
Beamish, Rob, 149
Becker, Howard S., 138n.2, 153, 155, 159
Bendix, Reinhard, 5, 6, 73, 135n.3, 137n.8, 141n.14, 149, 157

Benedict, Ruth, 44, 140n.9
Berger, Bennett, 158
Berk, Richard, 139n.2
Bernard, Russell, 153
Best and the Brightest, The (Halberstam), 45, 140n.11
Beyond Methodology: Feminist Scholarship as Lived Research (Fonow & Cook), 152
Black Family in Slavery and Freedom, The (Gutman), 142n.14
Black migration, 65
Blacks; *see also American Apartheid; Declining Significance of Race, The*
    segregation and, 63–70
    significance of race vs. class for, 58–63
Blackwell Companion to Social Theory, The (Turner), 151
Blalock, Hubert M., Jr., 139n.2
Bloch, Marc, 141n.14, 157
Block-busting, 65–66
Blue Collar Community (Kornblum), 42, 140n.6
Blumer, Herbert, 5, 6, 7, 155
Boas, Franz, 156
Bohman, James F., 154
Boll weevil infestation, 65
Bonaparte, Louis, 28, 87–93; *see also Eighteenth Brumaire of Louis Bonaparte, The*
BonJour, Lawrence, 138n.8
Booth, Wayne C., 158
Bottomore, Tom, 137n.1, 141n.3
Boudon, Raymond, 12, 135n.5
Bourdieu: Critical Perspectives (Craig, LiPuma & Postone), 140n.7
Bourdieu, Pierre, 44, 140n.7, 158
Bourgeois, 9, 87, 88, 90, 91, 93, 144n.4
Bourgeois Epoch, The: Marx and Engels on Britain, France and Germany (Hamilton), 150
Branch, Taylor, 45, 140n.11
Braudel, Fernand, 157
Breisach, Ernst, 58, 142n.7
Briggs, Charles L., 154
Britain; *see* England
Brown, Richard Harvey, 158
Bruner, Jerome, 136n.9
Bulmer, Martin, 140n.5
Burawoy, Michael, 156
Burckhardt, Jacob, 156
Bureaucracy and Participation: Political Cultures in Four Wisconsin Cities (Alford & Scoble), 135n.1
Bureaucratization of knowledge, 129
Bureau of Applied Social Research, 5, 6
Burger, Thomas, 149
Burns, Tom, 136n.8
Button, Graham, 155

C. Wright Mills: An American Utopian (Horowitz), 136n.7
C. Wright Mills and the Power Elite (Domhoff & Ballard), 136n.7
Calhoun, Craig, 140n.7

Callinicos, Alex, 157
Calvinism, 9, 14, 73
Camaroff, Jean, 156
Camaroff, John, 156
Campbell, Donald T., 148
Capital (Marx), 149
Capitalism, 60, 62, 73–76; *see also Protestant Ethic and the Spirit of Capitalism, The*
Carnap, Rudolf, 151
Caro, Robert A., 45, 140n.11
Carver, Terrell, 149
Case for the Case Study, A (Feagin, Orum & Sjoberg), 154
Categories, 38
Catholics, 55, 56, 57, 74–75, 141n.5, 141n.6
Causality, 44, 50
  in *Eighteenth Brumaire*, 92
  multivariate paradigms distinguished from, 33–34
  in *Social Origins*, 95
  in welfare state study, 113
Causal variables; *see* Independent variables
Central Hospital, 82
Chamboredon, Jean-Claude, 158
Changarnier, General, 88
Chicago school, 7, 42, 140n.5, 143n.7
Chicago School of Sociology, The (Bulmer), 140n.5
China, Communism in, 93–98; *see also Social Origins of Dictatorship and Democracy, The*
Choices, 27
Cicourel, Aaron, 158
City University of New York, 4
Civil rights movement, 63
Civil Wars in France, The (Marx), 86
Clark, Burton R., 157
Clark, Jon, 151
Clark, Kenneth B., 63
Class, 58–63, 64, 67; *see also Declining Significance of Race, The*
Classic canon, 13–15
Clifford, James, 44, 140n.10
Clues, Myths, and the Historical Method (Ginzburg), 157
Cognitive interpretations, 74
Cognitive shortcuts, 44
Cognitive sources of anxiety, 22–24
Cohen, Ralph, 157
Cold War, 5
Cole, Stephen, 151
Collected Works (Marx & Engels), 137n.7, 144n.1
Collins, Randall, 150
Colomb, Gregory G., 158
Columbia University, 4, 5, 6
Coming Crisis of Western Sociology, The (Gouldner), 145n.2
Communism, 9, 93–98; *see also Social Origins of Dictatorship and Democracy, The*
Comparative context, 40
Comparative-historical sociology, 14
Comparative studies, 105
Comte, August, 49, 131
Concepts, 33, 41, 44
Conceptual Practices of Power, The: A Feminist Sociology of Knowledge (Smith), 152
Concrete categories, 38
Condorcet, Marquis de, 48
Conduct of Inquiry Methodology for Behavioral Science, The (Kaplan), 147
Conflict and the Web of Group Affiliations, 137n.8
Conjunctures, 45
Consensus, 36
  elite, 110–111, 113, 115
Constructed evidence, 35
Constructing Questions for Interviews and Questionnaires (Foddy), 154
Constructing Social Theories (Stinchcombe), 154
Construction of arguments; *see* Argument construction

Contemporary Field Research (Emerson), 139n.9
Contextual variables, 112
Continuous variables, 107–108
Control variables, 38
  defined, 39
  in revolution study, 117
  in welfare state study, 105, 112
Cook, Judith A., 152
Cooper, Harris, 153
Corporate language, 98–99
Corporatism, 108–109, 113
Correlation, 112, 116, 117
Coser, Lewis, 137n.8
Craft of Research, The (Booth, Colomb & Williams), 158
Craft of Sociology, The: Epistemological Preliminaries (Bourdieu, Chambordon & Passeron), 158
Created evidence, 35
Crisis of production, 15, 17–18
Crisis of rationality, 15, 16–17
Crisis in sociology, 125
Crisis of solidarity, 15–16
Criticism and the Growth of Knowledge (Lakatos & Musgrave), 150
Croce, Benedetto, 156
Culture, 8
  oppositional, 66
Culture of poverty, 63, 64–65, 66, 69
Culture of segregation, 65, 66, 69
Currie, Gregory, 138n.1

Damrosch, David, 157
Darwinian theories, 49
Data, 12, 26, 39, 139n.1; *see also* Empirical indicators; Measures
Declining Significance of Race, The (Wilson), 9, 58–63, 142n.8
Decomposition of Sociology, The (Horowitz), 152
Deconstruction, 50
Deductive theory, 29, 30
Democracy, 9, 52, 93–98; *see also Social Origins of Dictatorship and Democracy, The*
Democracy in America (Tocqueville), 37, 139n.3
Demographers, 129
Denton, Nancy, 9, 58, 64–70, 142n.15
Denzin, Norman, 155
Department of Housing and Urban Development (HUD), 69
Dependent variables, 40
  in *Declining Significance of Race*, 59
  defined, 38
  in multiple paradigms, 122
  in revolution study, 117
  in *Social Origins*, 94
  in welfare state study, 105–108, 112
Descent into Discourse: The Reification of Language and the Writing of Social History (Palmer), 155
Description, 29
Designing a research project; *see* Research project design
Dialectical explanations, 10, 14, 28, 49, 70, 120, 123–125
  in *American Apartheid*, 67
  defined, 123
  in *Eighteenth Brumaire*, 93
  in *Work and Revolution*, 100
Dialectical Investigations (Ollman), 149
Dichotomous variables, 107–108
Dictionary of Twentieth-Century Social Thought (Outhwaite & Bottomore), 12, 137n.1
DiMaggio, Paul, 135n.1
Discipline, 24
Discourse analysis, 50
Discovery of Grounded Theory, The (Glaser & Strauss), 138n.7, 139n.10
Disorder of Things, The: Metaphysical Foundations of the Disunity of Science (Dupre), 139n.8

Disunity of Science, The: Boundaries, Contexts and Power (Galison & Stump), 151
Documents, 35, 45
Doing Exemplary Research (Frost & Stablein), 153
Doing Feminist Research (Roberts), 152
Domhoff, G. William, 136n.7
Donovan, Arthur, 150
Duhem, Pierre, 137n.2, 151
Dupre, John, 139n.8
Durkheim, Emile, 8, 9, 13–16, 18, 28, 29, 40, 51, 54–58, 120, 129, 131, 137n.5, 141n.2, 141n.5, 141n.15, 148

Eakin, Paul John, 136n.9
Economy and Society: An Outline of Interpretive Sociology (Weber), 149
Effective Social Science: Eight Cases in Economics, Political Science, and Sociology (Barber), 152
Egoistic suicide, 55
Eighteenth Brumaire of Louis Bonaparte, The (Marx), 9, 14, 86, 87–93, 137n.7
Eisenstadt, S. N., 141n.14, 157
Elements of Style, The (Strunk & White), 159
Elias, Norbert, 136n.9
Elite consensus, 110–111, 113, 115
Elkins, Stanley, 63, 142n.14
Emerson, Robert M., 139n.9, 156
Emile Durkheim: His Life and Work, a Historical and Critical Study (Lukes), 137n.5, 148
Emotional sources of anxiety, 22–24
Empirical entry points, 8, 26, 27, 31
  in *Social Origins*, 94
  in *Suicide*, 55
Empirical generalizations, 8, 15, 38, 50, 70, 102
  in *Declining Significance of Race*, 61
  in *Second Shift*, 84
  in social knowledge, 128
Empirical indicators, 39, 52; *see also* Measures
Empirical Knowledge (Goldman), 138n.8
Empirical questions, 8, 15, 18, 19, 25, 27, 30–31
  in *American Apartheid*, 64
  defined, 26
  in *Eighteenth Brumaire*, 87
  in foreground historical arguments, 48
  in foreground interpretive arguments, 44–45
  in foreground multivariate arguments, 41
  purpose of, 29
  in social knowledge, 128
  in welfare state study, 106
Empirical tracks of analysis, 23, 28–30
  in revolution study, 116–119
  in welfare state study, 106, 107
Engaging the Past: The Uses of History Across the Social Sciences (Monkkonen), 156
Engels, Friedrich, 87, 137n.7, 144n.1
England; *see also Social Origins of Dictatorship and Democracy, The*
  democracy in, 93–98
  suicide in, 56
  Enlightenment and Despair: A History of Sociology (Hawthorn), 141n.1
Entry points, 8, 25–28, 29; *see also* Empirical entry points; Theoretical entry points
Epistemology, 3, 48
Erving Goffman (Burns), 136n.8
Erving Goffman and Modern Sociology (Manning), 136n.8
Essays in Sociological Theory, 141n.15
Ethnic studies, 127, 128
Ethnographer's Magic and Other Essays in the History of Anthopology, The (Stocking), 156
Ethnographic Imagination, The: Textual Constructions of Reality (Atkinson), 155
Ethnography, 9, 12, 72
  in *Asylums*, 76
  Chicago school of; *see* Chicago school
  in *Second Shift*, 82

Ethnography and the Historical Imagination (Camaroff), 156
Ethnography Unbound: Power and Resistance in the Modern Metropolis (Burawoy), 156
Ethnomethodology, 12
Ethnomethodology and the Human Sciences (Button), 155
Evaluating Chicago Sociology (Kurtz), 140n.5
Everyday World as Problematic, The: A Feminist Sociology (Smith), 152
Evidence, 1, 12, 19, 26, 30, 32, 33–37, 139n.1, 139n.11
  in *Asylums*, 80–81
  in classic canon, 13–15
  constructed, 35
  created, 35
  in foreground historical arguments, 48
  found, 35
  human agency and, 37–38
  natural, 35
  primary, 35, 36–37, 39
  secondary, 35, 39
  theory distinguished from, 34
  theory divorced from, 49–50
Exceptions Are the Rule: An Inquiry into Methods in the Social Sciences (Levine), 153
Excitement and Fascination of Science, The: Reflections by Eminent Scientists (Lederberg), 151
Exorcism, 8, 27
Experience, 24
Explanation, 29, 32
  dialectical, 123
Explanatory variables; *see* Independent variables

Facts, 35–36
Farmers Alliance, 62
Fascism, 9, 93–98; *see also Social Origins of Dictatorship and Democracy, The*
Feagin, Joe R., 154
Feminist Epistemologies (Alcoff & Potter), 152
Feminist Methods in Social Research (Reinharz), 152
Feminist theories, 129
Field notes, 35, 37
Fieldnotes: The Makings of Anthropology (Sanjek), 156
Field work, 8–9, 28
Finch, Henry A., 148
First-level panic, 3, 8, 23
Fischer, David Hackett, 157
Focused Interview, The (136n.9
Foddy, William, 154
Fonow, Mary Margaret, 152
Foreground, 8, 32
Foreground historical arguments, 9, 45–49, 52, 86–102
  in *Eighteenth Brumaire*, 87–93
  in *Social Origins*, 93–98
  in *Work and Revolution*, 98–102
Foreground interpretive arguments, 9, 42–45, 52, 72–85
  in *American Apartheid*, 66
  in *Asylums*, 76–82
  in *Protestant Ethic*, 73–76
  in *Second Shift*, 82–84
Foreground multivariate arguments, 9, 38–41, 51–52, 54–71
  in *American Apartheid*, 63–70
  in *Declining Significance of Race*, 58–63
  in *Suicide*, 55–58
Foucault, Marxism, and History* (Poster), 145n.4
Foucault, Michel, 29, 72, 127, 145n.4, 154
Found evidence, 35
Four Sociological Traditions (Collins), 150
Frame Analysis: An Essay on the Organization of Experience (Goffman), 42, 43, 136n.8, 138n.3
France, 98–102; *see also Eighteenth Brumaire of*

Louis Bonaparte, The; Work and Revolution in France
Bonaparte coup d'état in, 87–93
suicide in, 58
Freedman, David, 139n.2, 153
Freeman, Richard, 59
Freire, Paulo, 152
French Revolution, 46, 95, 98–102; *see also Work and Revolution in France*
Fretz, Rachel I., 156
Friedland, Roger, 135n.1
Friedman, Sharon, 159
Frisby, David, 137n.8
From Max Weber: Essays in Sociology (Gerth & Mills), 143n.2
Frost, Peter, 153
Fulghum, Robert, 21
Functions of Social Conflict, The (Coser), 137n.8

Gadamer, H.G., 154
Galison, Peter, 151
Garfinkel, Harold, 155
Garfinkel and Ethnomethodology (Heritage), 155
Gay and lesbian studies, 128
Geertz, Clifford, 101, 136n.9, 154, 155
Gender strategies, 83
Genovese, Eugene, 63, 142n.14
Germany, suicide in, 58
Gerth, Hans, 73, 143n.2
Ghetto, The, 42
Ghettos, 65–66, 67–68
Giddens, Anthony, 29, 150, 157
Giesen, Bernhard, 140n.12
Ginzburg, Carlo, 157
Glaser, Barney, 138n.7, 139n.10
Glassner, Barry, 138n.2
Glock, Charles, 5, 7
Goffman, Erving, 5, 6–7, 9, 30, 42–43, 72, 76–82, 85, 102, 131, 136n.8, 138n.3, 143n.7
Gold Coast and the Slum, The, 42
Goldman, Alan, 138n.8
Gordon, Scott, 148
Gossez, Remi, 99
Gouldner, Alvin, 125, 145n.2
Gower, Barry, 151
Green, Donald P., 140n.12
Gross, Llewellyn, 151
Grounded theory, 12, 139n.10
Grundrisse (Marx), 149
Gutting, Gary, 150
Gutman, Herbert, 63, 142n.14

Habermas, Jurgen, 29, 131, 154
Habitus, 44
Halberstam, David, 45, 140n.11
Halliday, Terence, 158
Halls, W. D., 148
Hamerow, Theodore, 157
Hamilton, Richard F., 137n.3, 143n.4, 150
Hammersley, Martyn, 156
Hammond, Philip E., 158
Handbook for Scholars, A (van Leunen), 159
Handbook of Qualitative Research (Denzin & Lincoln), 155
Handbook of Research Synthesis, The (Cooper & Hedges), 153
Harvard University, 5
Hawthorn, Geoffrey, 141n.1
Health Care Politics: Ideological and Interest Group Barriers to Reform (Alford), 135n.1
Hechter, Michael, 140n.12
Hedges, Larry V., 153
Hegel, Georg Wilhelm Friedrich, 14, 48, 49, 156
Herder, Johann Gottfried von, 48
Heritage, John, 155
Hidden power, 72
Hiley, David R., 154

Hirschman, Albert O., 154
Historians' Fallacies: Toward a Logic of Historical Thought (Fischer), 157
Historical methodology, 12
Historical paradigms, 2, 8, 35, 40–41, 43, 50, 139n.1; *see also* Foreground historical arguments
in *American Apartheid,* 65–66
in *Asylums,* 81–82
in *Declining Significance of Race,* 61–63
in *Eighteenth Brumaire,* 88–89
evidence in, 36, 37
multivariate and interpretive paradigms compared with, 48, 49
in *Protestant Ethic,* 74
in revolution study, 119–120
in *Second Shift,* 83–84
in *Social Origins,* 94, 95–96
in *Suicide,* 57–58
in welfare state study, 113–115
in *Work and Revolution,* 98–99
working vocabulary of, 51(table)
Historical sociology, 46, 47–49, 140–141n.14
Historiography, 48, 50, 58
Historiography: Ancient, Medieval, and Modern (Breisach), 142n.7
History And...Histories Within the Human Sciences (Cohen & Roth), 157
History and Philosophy of Social Science, The (Gordon), 148
History and Philosophy of the Social Sciences, A (Manicas), 148
History of Sociological Analysis, A (Bottomore & Nisbet), 141n.3
History of Sociological Research Methods in America, A: 1920–1960 (Platt), 140n.5
Hobo, The, 42
Hochschild, Arlie, 9, 26, 42, 72, 82–84, 85, 144n.9
Hollinger, Robert, 152
Hollywood Ten, 5
Horowitz, Irving Louis, 136n.7, 152
Housework, 26, 82–84; *see also Second Shift, The*
Housing discrimination, 65–66, 69–70, 124
Hoyningen-Huene, Paul, 150
Huber, Joan, 140n.12
Huberman, A. Michael, 153
Hull, David, 145n.5
Human agency, 37–38, 122
Hunt, Morton, 153

I, 72, 78
Ideal type, 14
Incommensurability, 32–33
Independent variables, 40
defined, 38–39
in multiple paradigms, 122
in revolution study, 117
in *Social Origins,* 94, 95, 96, 97
in welfare state study, 107, 108–111, 112, 114–115
Individual identities, 76–82; *see also* Asylums
Inductive theory, 30
Industrial period, 62
Inquiry and Change: The Troubled Attempts to Understand and Shape Society (Lindblom), 152
Institutional constraints, 125–128
Institutional levels of abstraction, 93
Intellectual capital, 129, 130, 131
Interaction effects, 61, 96
defined, 39
Interpretations of Cultures, The (Geertz), 155
Interpretive paradigms, 2, 8, 139n.1; *see also* Foreground interpretive arguments
divorce of theory and evidence in, 50
evidence in, 37
historical paradigms compared with, 48, 49

Interpretive paradigms (*continued*)
  in welfare state study, 106
  working vocabulary of, 51t
Interpretive Social Science: A Second Look (Rabinow
  & Sullivan), 154
Interpretive Turn: Philosophy, Science, Culture
  (Hiley, Bohman & Shusterman), 154
Intervening variables, 38, 117
  defined, 39
Introduction to Historical Epistemology, An: The
  Authority of Knowledge (Tiles), 148
Introduction to the Study of History, An (Langlois
  & Seignobos), 58
Invitation to Reflexive Sociology, An (Wacquant),
  140n.7
IQ, 41

Jameson, Fredric, 154
Janowitz, Morris, 158
Japan, fascism in, 93–98; *see also Social Origins of*
  Dictatorship and Democracy, The
Jews, 56, 57
Jim Crow policies, 60
Johnson, Lyndon, 45
Journeys Through Ethnography: Realistic Accounts of
  Fieldwork (Lareau & Shultz), 156

Kalberg, Stephen, 149
Kant, Immanuel, 48
Kaplan, Abraham, 147
Karl Marx: His Life and Thought (McLellan), 149
Karl Marx: Texts on Method (Carver), 149
Katz, Jack, 139n.9
Katz, Michael, 142n.14
Kellner, Hans, 157
Kemple, Thomas M., 149
Kendall, Patricia L., 135n.5
Kennedy, John F., 45
Kincaid, Harold, 148
King, Martin Luther, 45
King, Rodney, 36
Kings or People: Power and the Mandate to Rule
  (Bendix), 5, 135n.3
Kinsey, Alfred, 35
Knowledge, 3, 129, 145n.4
  bureaucratization of, 129
  social; *see* Social knowledge
Knowledge and Evidence (Moser), 138n.8
Knowledge for What? (Lynd), 6, 135n.6
Kornblum, William, 42, 140n.6
Krieger, Susan, 159
Kuhn, Thomas S., 150
Kurtz, Lester R., 140n.5

Labor, 98–102; *see also Work and Revolution in*
  France; Working class
  organized, 109
Lakatos, Imre, 54, 138n.1, 150
Langlois, Charles, 58
Language, 2–3, 43–44
  in *Work and Revolution*, 98–102
Language, Symbolism and Politics: Essays in Honor
  of Murray Edelman (Merelman), 135n.1
Language of Social Research: A Reader in the
  Methodolology of Social Research (Lazarsfeld &
  Rosenberg), 135n.5
Lareau, Annette, 156
Laudan, Larry, 150
Laudan, Rachel, 150
Lazarsfeld, Paul F., 5, 6, 7, 11, 135n.5
Leadership Council for Metropolitan Open
  Communities, 68
Learning How to Ask (Briggs), 154
Lederberg, Joshua, 151
Left party, power of, 109–110, 112–114
Lehmann, Hartmut, 143n.5
Leisure gap, 84
Lejeune, Phillippe, 136n.9

Lemert, Charles, 151, 152
Leonard, Peter, 152
Levine, Joel H., 153
Lieberson, Stanley, 138n.6, 154
Liebow, Elliot, 44, 140n.8
Lincoln, Yvonna s., 155
Lindblom, Charles E., 152
Linear correlation models, 33
Lipset, Seymour Martin, 5, 7, 125, 131, 136n.6,
  145n.3
LiPuma, Edward, 140n.7
Little, Daniel, 138n.8, 149
Lloyd, Christopher, 156
Logic of Marx's Capital, The: Replies to Hegelian
  Criticisms (Smith), 149
Logic of Practice, The (Bourdieu), 140n.7
Louis Philippe, King, 87
Loyalty oaths, 5
Luker, Kristin, 145n.6
Lukes, Steven, 137n.5, 148
Lynd, Helen Merrell, 6, 135n.6
Lynd, Robert S., 5, 6, 125, 135–136n.6, 145n.2

McCall, Michael M., 138n.2, 155
McCarthy, Joseph, 5
McCloskey, Donald N., 154
Machung, Anne, 144n.9
McLaren, Peter, 152
McLellan, David, 149
Macro levels of analysis, 1, 48, 72, 85, 102, 103,
  140n.12
Macro-Micro Linkages in Sociology (Huber),
  140n.12
Making It Count (Lieberson), 138n.6, 154
Making Science: Between Nature and Society
  (Cole), 151
Male and Female: A Study of the Sexes in a
  Changing World (Mead), 140n.9
Malinowski, Bronislaw, 44, 140n.9, 156
Manicas, Peter T., 148
Mann, Michael, 157
Manning, Philip, 136n.8
Mapping, 8, 27–28, 104, 122
Marcus, George E., 44, 140n.10
Marius, Richard, 159
Marshall, T. H., 157
Marx, Karl, 8, 9, 13–15, 17–18, 28, 29, 36, 49,
  68, 86, 87–93, 102, 130, 131, 137n.7,
  141n.15, 144n.1, 144n.4, 145n.4, 149, 156
Marx, Method, and the Division of Labor
  (Beamish), 149
Marxism, 129
  Declining Significance of Race and, 59, 60, 62
  Social Origins and, 94
Marx's Method in Capital: A Reexamination
  (Mosley), 149
Marx's Theory of Scientific Knowledge (Murray),
  149
Mason, William M., 139n.2
Massey, Douglas, 9, 58, 64–70, 142n.15
Max Weber: An Intellectual Portrait (Bendix), 5,
  135n.3, 149
Max Weber's Comparative Historical Sociology
  (Kalberg), 149
Max Weber's Theory of Concept Formation: History,
  Laws, and Ideal Types (Burger), 149
Me, 72, 78
Mead, George Herbert, 6, 50, 72, 78, 81
Mead, Margaret, 44, 140n.9
Measures, 39, 40, 41, 106, 125; *see also* Empirical
  indicators
Megill, Allan, 148, 154
Mental hospitals, 7, 76–82; *see also Asylums*
Merleau-Ponty, Maurice, 50
Merton, Robert K., 5, 6, 7, 11, 131, 135n.4,
  136n.9, 137n.2, 146n.8, 151
Metahistory: The Historical Imagination in
  Nineteenth-Century Europe (White), 156

Method, 1, 123, 125–126
  in classic canon, 13–15
  social knowledge and, 128
  vs. theory and research, 11–13
Method and Measurement in Sociology (Cicourel),
  158
Method in Social Science: A Realist Approach 2d ed.
  (Sayer), 148
*Methodology and Epistemology for Social Science:
  Selected Papers* (Overman), 148
Methodology of the Social Sciences, The (Weber), 148
Michelet, Jules, 156
Microfoundations of Macrosociology, The (Hechter),
  140n.12
Micro levels of analysis, 1, 72, 85, 93, 102, 103,
  140n.12
Micro-Macro Link, The (Alexander, Giesen &
  Smelser), 140n.12
Middle-range theory, 5, 11
Middletown (Lynd), 6, 135n.6
Middletown in Transition (Lynd), 6, 135n.6
Miles, Matthew B., 153
Mill, John Stuart, 151
Mills, C. Wright, 5, 6, 11, 20, 38, 50, 73, 125,
  129, 136n.7, 143n.2, 145n.2
Modernist Impulses in the Human Sciences (Ross),
  141n.1
Modgil, Celia, 151
Modgil, Sohan, 151
Monkkonen, Eric H., 156
Moore, Barrington, Jr., 9, 86, 93–98, 102,
  141n.14, 144n.5, 157
Moseley, Fred, 149
Moser, Paul K., 138n.8
Moses, Robert, 45
Multiple conceptions of the self, 79
Multiple paradigms of inquiry, 10, 24, 103–120,
  121–123, 129
  about revolutions, 115–120
  about the welfare state, 103–115, 120
  in *Work and Revolution*, 101
Multivariate methodology, 6
Multivariate paradigms, 2, 4, 7, 8, 41, 43, 46,
  139n.1; *see also* Foreground multivariate
  arguments
  in *American Apartheid*, 64–65
  in *Asylums*, 80
  causality distinguished from, 33–34
  in *Declining Significance of Race*, 59–61
  divorce of theory and evidence in, 49–50
  in *Eighteenth Brumaire*, 90–93
  evidence in, 36–37
  historical paradigm compared with, 48, 49
  in *Protestant Ethic*, 74–76
  in *Second Shift*, 84
  in *Social Origins*, 94, 96–97
  in *Suicide*, 55–56
  in welfare state study, 115
  in *Work and Revolution*, 99–100
  working vocabulary of, 51(table)
Murray, Patrick, 149
Musgrave, Alan, 150

Narrative history, 37, 45, 47, 51, 114
Natural evidence, 35
Nelson, John S., 154
Neuman, W. Lawrence, 153
*New Institutionalism in Organizational Analysis,
  The* (Powell & DiMaggio), 135n.1
New Philosophy of History, A (Ankersmit &
  Kellner), 157
New York University, 4
Nietzsche, Friedrich Wilhelm, 156
Nisbet, Robert, 4–5, 7, 133, 135n.2, 141n.3
Noise, 40

Objectivity, 124, 125
Observation, 9, 72, 139n.1

Occupational prestige socres, 41
Ollman, Bertell, 149
On Autobiography (Lejune), 136n.9
On Social Research and Its Language (Boudon),
  135n.5
On Social Structure and Science (Merton), 151
Ontology, 3
Oppositional culture, 66
Organic solidarity, 15, 16
Organizational levels of abstraction, 93
Organized labor, strength of, 109
Origins of American Social Science, The (Ross),
  141n.1
Orum, Anthony M., 154
Outcome variables; *see* Dependent variables
Outhwaite, William, 137n.1
Overman, E. Samuel, 148

Palmer, Bryan D., 155
Paradigms and Revolutions (Gutting), 150
Paradigms of inquiry, 2–6, 8, 32–33, 50; *see also*
  Historical paradigms; Interpretive paradigms;
  Multiple paradigms of inquiry; Multivariate
  paradigms
  defined, 2
Parsons, Talcott, 11, 29, 49–50, 131, 141n.15
Participant observation; *see* Observation
Participant Observer: An Autobiography (Whyte),
  136n.9
Parting the Waters: America in the King Years
  (Branch), 45, 140n.11
Party and Society: The Anglo-American Democracies
  (Alford), 135n.1
Passeron, Jean-Claude, 158
Paternalism, 61, 63
Path analysis, 33
Pathologies of Rational Choice Theory (Green &
  Shapiro), 140n.12
Patriarchy, 83–84
Patterns of Culture (Benedict), 140n.9
Paulo Freire: A Critical Encounter (McLaren &
  Leonard), 152
Payne, Stanley L., 154
Pearce, Frank, 148
Peasantry, 9, 88–89, 91–92
Pedagogy of the Oppressed (Freire), 152
Peirce, C. S., 151
Pennsylvania Hospital, 81
*Personal Knowledge: Towards a Post-Critical
  Philosophy* (Polanyi), 138n.4
Phenomenological philosophy, 50
Philosophical Foundations of the Social Sciences
  (Kincaid), 148
Philosophical Papers (Worrall & Currie), 138n.1
Philosophy of Social Science (Root), 148
Pickering, Andrew, 151
Pisani, Robert, 153
Place on the Corner, A (Anderson), 140n.8
*Places of Inquiry: Research and Advanced
  Education in Modern Universities* (Clark), 157
Platt, Jennifer, 140n.5
Poggi, Gianfranco, 76, 143n.5
Poincare, Henri, 151
Polanyi, Karl, 141n.14, 157
Polanyi, Michael, 138n.4
Political Economy of Slavery, The (Genovese),
  142n.14
Political sociology, 12
Popper, Karl, 151
Popular legitimacy of the welfare state, 110
Porter, Theodore, 145n.1
Positivism, 2, 3, 29, 34, 49, 64
Poster, Mark, 145n.4
Postmodernism, 2, 3
Postmodernism and Social Theory (Seidman &
  Wagner), 151
*Postmodernism and the Social Sciences: A Thematic
  Approach* (Hollinger), 152

Post-Modernism and the Social Sciences: Insights,
  Inroads, and Intrusions (Rosenau), 152
Postone, Moishe, 140n.7
Potter, Elizabeth, 152
Powell, Walter W., 135n.1
Power, 130, 145n.4
  hidden, 72
Power Broker, The: Robert Moses and the Fall of
  New York (Caro), 45, 140n.11
Power Elite, The (Mills), 6, 136n.7
Power/Knowledge (Foucault), 145n.4
Powers of Theory: Capitalism, the State and
  Democracy (Alford & Friedland), 135n.1
Practice of Social Research, The 7th ed (Babbie), 153
Preindustrial period, 61
Presentation of Self in Everyday Life, The
  (Goffman), 6, 42, 77, 136n.8
Primary evidence, 35, 36–37, 39
Problems, 8, 26, 28
  research questions distinguished from, 25
  selection of, 24–25
Proctor, Robert, 138n.5
Production, crisis of, 15, 17–18
Professions, 127
Profiles of Social Research: The Scientific Study of
  Human Interactions (Hunt), 153
Protestant Ethic and the Spirit of Capitalism, The
  (Weber), 9, 14, 72, 73–76, 137n.3, 137n.6,
  143n.1
Protestants, 55, 56, 57, 141n.5, 141n.6; *see also*
  Protestant Ethic and the Spirit of Capitalism,
  The
Prus, Robert, 155
Public policy programs, 127
Purves, Roger, 153

Qualitative Data Analysis (Miles & Huberman),
  153
Qualitative techniques, 1, 12, 39, 122, 143n.19
Quantitative techniques, 1, 12, 33–34, 39, 70,
  122, 142n.17, 143n.19
  in *American Apartheid,* 64
  in *Social Origins,* 96
Questions About Questions: Inquiries into the
  Cognitive Bases of Surveys (Tanur), 154

Rabinow, Paul, 154
Race; *see also American Apartheid; Declining*
  Significance of Race, The
  class vs., 58–63
  segregation and, 63–70
Radical Durkheim, The (Pearce), 148
Ragin, Charles C., 153
Ranke, Otto, 156
Rational choice theory, 129, 132
Rationality, crisis of, 15, 16–17
Reading Marx Writing: Melodrama, the Market,
  and the 'Gundrisse' (Kemple), 149
Reconstructing Scientific Revolutions: Thomas S.
  Kuhn's Philosophy of Science (Hoyningen-
  Huene), 150
Redlining, 66
Reflections on a Life (Elias), 136n.9
Reflections on History and Historians (Hamerow),
  157
Regression analysis, 33, 112–113, 122, 145n.1
Reichenbach, Hans, 151
Reinharz, Shulamith, 152
Religion and Economic Action: A Critique of Max
  Weber (Samuelsson), 149
Research, 11–13, 123; *see also* Research project
  design; Research questions
Research Method in Anthropology: Qualitative and
  Quantitative Approaches 2d ed. (Bernard),
  153
Research project design, 8, 21–31
  cognitive and emotional sources of anxiety in,
  22–24

problem selection in, 24–25
research questions as entry points in, 25–28
Research questions, 1, 17, 18–19, 30–31, 46, 50,
  139n.9; *see also* Empirical questions;
  Theoretical questions
  in *American Apartheid,* 68
  bad, 28
  as entry points, 25–28
  evidence and, 34
  foreground and background, 8, 32, 137n.4
  problems distinguished from, 25
  in social knowledge, 128
  about the welfare state, 104
Response variables; *see* Dependent variables
Rethinking Objectivity (Megill), 148
Revolutions, 10, 115–120
Rhetorical Turn: Invention and Persuasion in the
  Conduct of Inquiry (Simons), 154
Rhetoric of the Human Sciences, The (Nelson,
  Megill & McClosky), 154
Richards, Pamela, 159
Rise of Historical Sociology, The (Smith), 157
Rise of Statistical Thinking, The (Porter), 145n.1
Robert K. Merton: Consensus and Controversy
  (Clark & Modgil), 151
Roberts, Helen, 152
Rolling reformulations, 8, 27, 108
Root, Michael, 148
Rosenau, Pauline Marie, 152
Rosenberg, Ethel, 5
Rosenberg, Julius, 5
Rosenberg, Morris, 135n.5
Ross, Dorothy, 141n.1
Roth, Guenther, 143n.5, 149
Roth, Michael S., 157
Rule, James B., 150
Rules of Sociological Method, The (Durkheim), 148
Runciman, W. G. R., 157

St. Elizabeth's Hospital, 77, 81
Samuelsson, Kurt, 149
Sanjek, Roger, 156
SAS, 34
Sayer, Andrew, 148
Schneider, David M., 136n.9
Schneider on Schneider (Schneider), 136n.9
Schutz, Alfred, 50
Science as a Process (Hull), 145n.5
Science as Practice and Culture (Pickering), 151
Scientific Marx, The (Little), 149
Scientific method, 3
Scientific Method: A Historical and Philosophical
  Introduction (Gower), 151
Scientific research programs, 54
Scoble, Harry M., 135n.1
Scrutinizing Science: Empirical Studies of Scientific
  Change (Donovan & Laudan), 150
Secondary evidence, 35, 39
Second-level panic, 3, 8, 23
Second-order texts, 36
Second Shift, The (Hochschild), 9, 26, 42, 72,
  82–84, 144n.9
Segregation, 63–70; see also *American Apartheid*
Segregation indexes, 41
Seidman, Steven, 151
Seignobos, Charles, 58
Self-fulfilling prophecy, 69
Seltzer, Jack, 158
Selvin, Hanan, 5, 7
Selznick, Philip, 5
Semiprofessions, 127
Sewell, William H., Jr., 9–10, 86, 98–102, 144n.6,
  144n.7
Sex and Repression in Savage Society (Malinowski),
  140n.9
Shaping Written Knowledge (Bazerman), 158
Shapiro, Ian, 140n.12
Shaw, Linda L., 156

Shibutani, Tamotsu, 6
Shils, Edward A., 148
Shultz, Jeffrey, 156
Shusterman, Richard, 154
Sica, Alan, 138n.5
Simmel, Georg, 137n.8
*Simmel and Since: Essays on Georg Simmel's Social
   Theory* (Frisby), 137n.8
Simons, Herbert W., 154
Simpson, George, 137n.5
Simpson, O. J., 45
Situational levels of abstraction, 93
Sjoberg, Gideon, 154
Skocpol, Theda, 48, 94, 140n.14, 157
Slavery, 61, 63
Slavery (Elkins), 142n.14
Slippage, 27
Smelser, Neil J., 5, 140n.12
Smith, Dennis, 157
Smith, Dorothy, 152
Smith, Tony, 149
Social construction, 42
Social evolution, 49
Social facts, 13–14, 28, 40, 51, 54
Social history, 46, 48, 140–141n.14
Social inquiry, 25
Social knowledge, 14, 130, 131
   institutional constraints on, 125–128
Social Misconstruction of Reality, The (Hamilton),
   137n.3, 143n.4
Social movements, 128
Social needs, 111
Social Origins of Dictatorship and Democracy, The
   (Moore), 86, 93–98, 144n.5
Social Origins of Dictatorship and Democracy
   (Moore), 9
*Social Research Methods: Qualitative and
   Quantitative Approaches* 2d ed. (Neuman),
   153
Social roles, 78
*Social Science and the Self: Personal Essays on an Art
   Form* (Krieger), 159
Social selves, 78
Social stratification, 12
Social Theories of Talcott Parsons, The, 141n.15
*Social Theory: The Multicultural and Classic
   Readings* (Lemert), 151
Social Theory and Social Structure (Merton), 5,
   135n.4, 137n.2
Social Theory Today (Turner), 150
Societal integration, 54, 55–58; *see also Suicide: A
   Study in Sociology*
Society, 24
Socioeconomic status (SES), 41
Sociological imagination, 129–131
Sociological Imagination, The (Mills), 6, 11, 38,
   136n.7
Sociological Methodology, 139n.2
Sociological Tradition, The (Nisbet), 4, 133, 135n.2
Sociologists at Work (Hammond), 158
Sociology After the Crisis (Lemert), 152
*Sociology and Its Publics: The Forms and Fates of
   Disciplinary Organizations* (Halliday &
   Janowitz), 158
*Sociology and Scientism: The American Quest for
   Objectivity* (Bannister), 141n.1
Sociology as an Art Form (Nisbet), 4–5, 135n.2
Sociology of Georg Simmel, The (Wolff), 137n.8
Sociology of organizations, 12
Solidarity, crisis of, 15–16
Soviet Union, 46
Spaulding, John A., 137n.5
Specialization, 126
Split labor-market theory, 60
SPSS, 34
Stablein, Ralph, 153
Stake, Robert E., 154
States and Social Revolutions (Skocpol), 94

Statistical analysis, 12, 28, 34
Statistics 2d ed. (Freedman et al), 153
Steinberg, Stephen, 159
*Stigma: Notes on the Management of Spoiled
   Identity* (Goffman), 136n.8
Stinchcombe, Arthur, 154
Stocking, George W., Jr., 156
Strategic Interactions (Goffman), 43, 136n.8
Strauss, Anselm, 138n.7, 139n.10
Street Corner Society (Whyte), 42, 44, 140n.8
Structural functionalism, 49
Structuralism, 50
Structure of Empirical Knowledge, The (BonJour),
   138–139n.8
Structure of Scientific Revelations, The (Kuhn), 150
Structure of Social Action, The (Parsons), 141n.15
"Structure of the Working Class of Marseille"
   (Sewell), 144n.7
Structures of History, The (Lloyd), 156
Strunk, William, Jr., 159
Studies in Ethnomethodology (Garfinkel), 155
Stump, David J., 151
Subcultures, 8
Subfields, 128
Subjective meanings, 40, 50
Substantive rationality, 17
Suburbanization, 66
Suicide, 28, 55–58, 120, 141n.5
   altruistic, 55
   anomic, 55
   egoistic, 55
Suicide: A Study in Sociology (Durkheim), 9, 14,
   55–58, 137n.5
Sullivan, William M., 154
Survey analysis, 7
Symbolic Interaction and Cultural Studies (Becker
   & McCall), 138n.2, 155
Symbolic Interaction and Ethnographic Research
   (Prust), 155
Symbolic interactionism, 6, 12, 42, 72, 129
Symbolic Interactionism: Perspective and Method
   (Blumer), 155
Symbolic meanings, 32, 40, 44, 71
   in *American Apartheid,* 66–67
   in *Asylums,* 78–79
   in *Declining Significance of Race,* 63
   in *Eighteenth Brumaire,* 89–90
   in *Protestant Ethic,* 73–74
   in *Second Shift,* 82–83
   in *Social Origins,* 97–98
   in *Suicide,* 56–57
   in *Work and Revolution,* 100–102
Symposium on Sociological Theory (Gross), 151
Systems theory, 49
Szántó, Andras, 135n.1
Sztompka, Piotr, 151

Tales of the Field: On Writing Ethnography (van
   Maanen), 156
Tally's Corner (Liebow), 44, 140n.8
Tanur, Judith M., 154
Tautology, 52
Taxi Dance Girl, The, 42
Taylor, Charles, 154
Texts, 37, 74
   second-order, 36
Theoretical claims, 8, 15, 33, 36, 38, 50
   in *Asylums,* 78–79
   in *Eighteenth Brumaire,* 92
   in foreground historical arguments, 47, 102
   in foreground interpretive arguments, 44
   in foreground multivariate arguments, 70
   in social knowledge, 128
Theoretical entry points, 8, 26, 27, 31, 55
Theoretical Logic in Sociology (Alexander), 141n.15
Theoretical questions, 8, 15, 18, 19, 25, 27, 30
   in *Asylums,* 77
   defined, 26

Theoretical questions (*continued*)
  in *Eighteenth Brumaire*, 87
  in foreground historical arguments, 48
  in foreground interpretive arguments, 44–45
  purpose of, 29
  in social knowledge, 128
  in welfare state study, 106
Theoretical tracks of analysis, 8, 23, 28–30
  in revolution study, 116–119
  in welfare state study, 106, 107
Theories and Narratives: Reflections on the
  Philosophy of History (Callinicos), 157
Theory, 1, 19, 32, 33–34, 123, 125–126, 139n.11
  in *Asylums,* 80–81
  in classic canon, 13–15
  evidence distinguished from, 34
  evidence divorced from, 49–50
  method and research vs., 11–13
  social knowledge and, 127
Theory and Progress in Social Science (Rule), 150
Theory and Society (Szántó), 135n.1
Thompson, E. P., 141n.14, 157
Three-variable hypotheses, 39
Tiles, Jim, 148
Tiles, Mary, 148
Tilly, Charles, 141n.14, 157
Time series analysis, 40, 142n.16
Tiryakian, Edward A., 141n.3
Tocqueville, Alexis de, 37, 139n.3, 156
Total institutions, 30, 76–82; *see also Asylums*
Totality, 45
Tracks of analysis, 8; *see also* Empirical tracks of
  analysis; Theoretical tracks of analysis
  in revolution study, 116–119
  in welfare state study, 105
  in *Work and Revolution,* 101
Trust in Numbers (Porter), 145n.1
Truth, 124
Tuchman, Gaye, 155
Turner, Bryan S., 151
Turner, Jonathan, 150
Typology, 107–108

Underclass culture, 63
"Underclass" Debate, The: Views from History
  (Katz), 142n.14
Understanding Scientific Prose (Seltzer), 158
United Autoworkers, 5
Units of analysis, 38
  in *American Apartheid,* 65
  for the welfare state, 105
University of California at Berkeley, 4, 5, 6
University of California at San Francisco, 4
University of California at Santa Barbara, 4
University of California at Santa Cruz, 4
University of Chicago, 5
University of Essex, 4
University of Wisconsin at Madison, 4
Urban renewal, 66

Vaillancourt, Pauline Marie, 150
Value-Free Science: Purity and Power in Modern
  Knowledge (Proctor), 138n.5
Value-neutrality, 138n.5
van Leunen, Mary-Claire, 159
van Maanen, John, 156
Variables, 36–37, 38–39, 45, 46, 51
  contextual, 112
  continuous, 107–108
  control; *see* Control variables
  defined, 38
  dependent; *see* Dependent variables
  dichotomous, 107–108
  independent; *see* Independent variables
  intervening, 38, 39, 117
  as measures certifying reality, 125
Varied Sociology of Paul F. Lazarsfeld, The
  (Kendall), 135n.5

Varieties of Social Explanation (Little), 138n.8
Verstechen, 14, 28
Vico, Giambattista, 48
Vision and Method in Historical Sociology
  (Skocpol), 140n.14, 157

Wacquant, Loic J. D., 140n.7
Wagner, David G., 151
Wallerstein, Immanuel, 141n.14, 157
Warranting community, 36
Weber, Irrationality, and Social Order (Sica),
  138n.5
Weber, Karl David, 73
Weber, Marianne, 73
Weber, Max, 5, 8, 9, 13–15, 16–17, 18, 28, 29,
  36, 42, 49, 59, 72, 73–76, 85, 86, 94, 120,
  129, 130, 131, 137n.6, 141n.15, 143n.3,
  143n.4, 148, 149
Weber's Protestant Ethic: Origins, Evidence,
  Contexts (Lehmann & Roth), 143n.5
Welfare state, 10, 103–115, 120
  dependent variables in study of, 105–108,
    112
  independent variables in study of, 107,
    108–111, 112, 114–115
  popular legitimacy of, 110
  units of analysis for, 105
We Scholars: Changing the Culture of the University
  (Damrosch), 157
Weydemeyer, Joseph, 87
What Is a Case? Exploring the Foundations of Social
  Inquiry (Ragin & Becker), 153
What's Wrong with Ethnography? (Hammersley),
  156
When Marxists do Research (Vaillancourt), 150
Whewell, William, 151
White, E. B., 159
White, Hayden, 156
Whyte, William Foote, 42, 44, 136n.9, 140n.8
Williams, Joseph M., 158
Wilson, William Julius, 9, 58–63, 67, 142n.8,
  142n.10
Wolfe, Alan, 146n.8
Wolff, Kurt H., 137n.8
Women's studies, 127, 128
Woodward, C. Vann, 62
Work and Authority in Industry (Bendix), 5,
  135n.3
Work and Revolution in France (Sewell), 9–10, 86,
  98–102, 144n.7
Working class, 60, 62; *see also* Labor
Working vocabulary, 1, 19, 33, 519(table); *see also*
  Arguments; Background; Empirical entry
  points; Empirical generalizations; Empirical
  research questions; Entry points; Exorcism;
  First-level panic; Foreground; Historical
  paradigms; Interpretive paradigms; Mapping;
  Multivariate paradigms; Paradigms of inquiry;
  Problems; Rolling reformulations; Second-
  level panic; Theoretical claims; Theoretical
  entry points; Theoretical questions; Tracks of
  inquiry
  research project design and, 23–24
  works illustrating, 7–10
World system theories, 129
World War I, 65
World War II, 66
Worrall, John, 138n.1
Writer's Companion, A (Marius), 159
Writing and Thinking in the Social Sciences
  (Friedman & Steinberg), 159
Writing Culture (Clifford & Marcus), 44, 140n.10
Writing Ethnographic Fieldnotes (Emerson, Fretz &
  Shaw), 156
Writing for Social Scientists (Becker), 159
Writing the Social Text: Poetics and Politics in
  Social Science Discourse (Brown), 158